STAR PAPERS.

STAR PAPERS;

OR,

Experiences of Art and Nature.

BY

HENRY WARD BEECHER.

New York:
J. C. DERBY, 119 NASSAU STREET.
BOSTON:—PHILLIPS, SAMPSON & CO.
CINCINNATI:—H. W. DERBY.
1855.

Printed and Stereotyped by Billin and Brother, 20 North William St., N. Y.

PREFACE.

The author has been saved the trouble of searching for a title to his book from the simple circumstance that the articles of which the work is made up appeared in the columns of the *New York Independent* with the signature of a STAR, and, having been familiarly called the Star Articles, by way of designation, tney now become, in a book form, STAR PAPERS.

Only such papers as related to Art and to rural affairs, have been published in this volume. It was thought best to put all controversial articles in another, and subsequent, volume.

The Letters from Europe were written to home-friends, during a visit of only four weeks; a period too short to allow the subsidence of that enthusiasm which every person must needs experience who, for the first time, stands in the historic places of the Old World. An attempt to exclude from these letters any excess of personal feeling, to reduce them to a more moderate tone, to correct their judgments, or to extract from them the fiery particles of enthusiasm, would have taken away their very life.

The other papers in this volume, for the most part, were written from the solitudes of the country, during the vacations of three summers. I can express no kinder wish for those who may read them, than that they may be one half as happy in the reading as I have been in the scenes which gave them birth.

CONTENTS.

LETTERS FROM EUROPE.

EXPERIENCES OF NATURE.

LETTERS FROM EUROPE.

I.

RUINS OF KENILWORTH.—WARWICK CASTLE.

THE sun is shining through haze of smoke and vapor: and every body says, what a splendid day! at least, every body whose ideas of a fine day are English. It is a fine day in England when it does not actually ɪain. To-day, then, blessed with a sun that shines visibly, but with a tender brightness, I will go to Kenilworth; and to Warwick castle; and to Stratford-on-Avon, more interesting to me than either. "Waiter, will you bring my bill? I leave in the 10½ o'clock train to Coventry." "Yez-zur." Ah, very reasonable. I have been here a day and a-half, and it is but five dollars and a-quarter, servants' fees and all; which, by the way, I will always have included in the bill. I do not like to settle with four landlords at every inn;—the chambermaid landlady, the boots landlord, the waiter landlord, the porter landlord, and *the* landlord —five instead of four. To the railway station is but a step; the waiter bids me a very polite good-bye—we don't shake hands—and the porter with my baggage follows me to the cars. A trim little engine, with a smoke-pipe not larger than our stove-pipes, is amusing itself with every antic possible to a thing of its nature. It runs out with a fierce whistle, for no other reason, apparently, than to run back again with another whistle. It reminds one of a rheumatic old gentleman pacing about to limber his joints. After a little sport he sobers down to business and falls to work making up a train. I am booked for the second-class cars, which are about one-third cheaper than the first class, and a good deal more than that uncomfortable, as I will by and by explain. My shining patent-leather valise and my rival shining carpet-bag, (for one is American and the other is English, and so I call them my John and Jonathan,) are put into the compartment and piled up on the seat before me; my overcoat, neatly folded, is put upon the uncushioned oak seat for me by the obliging porter. In spite of my determination to fee none of the railway servants, I did slip a sixpence into his hands, and he did shut his fingers upon it without apparent pain.

And now, the bustle over—for, true to American habits, I became quite eager, and stepped about much more lively than there was any need for—I will watch other people. I am struck with the ease manifested. These plump people will not sweat themselves. Nice old gentlemen walk as quietly along as if passing out to tea in their own houses. The railway servants in uniform, with their number worked in white upon their coat-collars, are diligent, but very measured in their functions. One is stowing this man's luggage on the top of the car—for large baggage goes upon the top, and small stuff goes into the car with you; another trundles a wheeled basket with packages, careful to knock no one down; another stops respectfully to answer a gentleman's questions. I hear no shouting, see no racing about, hear no oaths or contentions; there is no higgling for fares, but every thing is very easy and orderly. Now steps out a man with the largest of hand-bells, with which he gives three or four strokes, saying as plainly as words could say it, "Get into the cars, all who mean to." In a moment more he strikes again, and *chunk* comes the engine into connection with the train. Without further signal you move away slowly out of the station-house and thread your way through a perfect maze of tracks.

We are rushing through the open fields. The lots are small, seldom of more than one or two acres, divided by hedges, which, for the most part, are uncombed, ragged, and full of gaps; yet, even thus, more agreeable to the eye than rigid fences. Trees, in groups of two or three, but more often in rows along the hedges, have that unvarying dark, almost black, green, which, thus far, has characterized the foliage which I have seen about Liverpool, Manchester, and Birmingham. The shades of green which we see in America, and the liveliness and airiness of foliage seem wanting. But the eye is never weary with the landscape. As we drive through the cuts, the bank on either hand is carved evenly with a perfect slope to the top, and is there ruffled with a close-cut hedge, while the sides are grassed down to the road, and the edges of the grass cut as regularly along the whole way as a border of turf in a gentleman's garden. When the road rises above the surrounding country, the sides of it are planted; so that the eye is cheered with a beautiful *arboretum,* in which are elms, maples, mountain ash, poplars, and, among others, a beautiful drooping tamarack or larch, as it appears to my eye. The stations are little gems of places. The way-stations, out of towns, are frequently decorated with flowers and miniature pleasure-grounds. If there be a bit of ground but ten feet square, it is a turf-plat, with a raised bed cut out of it, or cut into it, on which are displayed fine, thrifty tufts of flowers. They are not, either, dumped down just as it may happen; but are arranged with uniform good taste. Thus a *fuchsia*, two or three feet high, covered with brilliant crimson blossoms, has growing behind it a tuft of tall grass, upon whose vivid green the plant is admirably contrasted. Neat little spots of pansies, of different varieties, foxglove, marigolds, geraniums, roses, and, always, profusely, the fragrant minionette, fill up the bed.

I had read enough of English agriculture to know very well that there was much waste soil—fens, sand-wastes, etc. But I had read and heard also that England was a *garden.* This expression, as more poetical, had clung to my imagination; and I found myself a little disappointed when I came upon poor and neglected lands and waste spots, most ungardenlike. But this is only one of a hundred things which teaches me how much better it is to *see* a thing, than to read about it or imagine it. The fields of grain were rapidly changing from green to a golden russet. The sickle, in a few days, will grow bright in its work. Fields of turnips, planted in long rows, straight as a rule could draw them, are being hoed and thinned out by men, women and children. They do not even look up as we shoot past them.

Ride to Kenilworth Castle.

Calling for a cab, I started from Coventry upon a five-miles ride to Kenilworth. The road was smooth as a floor, rising and falling over gentle swells of ground, bordered the whole way with oaks and elms. The sky above was perfectly clear, but, all around the horizon, banks of cloud were piled up in huge cliffs, rounded masses, but at the edge fleecy and melting off to a mist. Beautiful, most beautiful are the fields, some close cut—for haying is over—some with grain, and a few just plowed. The hedges are full of flowers which I do not recognize. And now, I am riding to a famous old castle. I shall but look on it and pass on. Others would enjoy this more than I shall. It requires a store of historical associations; and much of the sentiment of veneration; or else a lively relish for antiquarian lore; none of which have I. My thoughts were broken by the driver—honest soul!—asking to what inn he should go. Yankee like, I replied by asking where it was best to go. "To King's Head, sir." "Very well, King's Head let it be." We turn the corner. Here is a Lord's carriage, I suppose, just before us. Well, he has as much right to go to Kenilworth as I. Paying the driver—not so honest a soul after all—two shillings more than he should have had, because he declined giving change, under a plea of begging for a gratuity—I sallied forth toward the ruins. As the road wound among trees, I was close upon them before I saw them. When they rose up before me I found myself trembling, I knew not why. I could not help tears from coming. I had never in my life seen an *old* building. I had never seen a ruin. Here, for the first time in my life, I felt the presence of a venerable ruined castle! At first I did not wish to go within the walls which enclosed the grounds, and so strolled a little way along the outside. I can not tell what a strange mingling of imagination, and thoughts, and emotions, took possession of me. At length I entered. With a little plan of the building I traced the rooms from point to point—the great banqueting Hall, the scene of wondrous festivities which shall never again disturb its silence, being the most perfectly preserved of any apartment. I was surprised to find how much I knew of Kenilworth Castle. Had one asked me as I rode hither, I should have replied that I knew only that it was old and famous, that it was by Scott wrought into one of his most successful novels. But as I sat in a room, upon a fallen stone, one incident after another from the novel, and from history, came to me, one name after another, until I seemed to be visiting an old and familiar place. And now I am sitting in what was, in its days of glory, the Inner Court, and leaning against Leicester's buildings. Before me is Cesar's Tower—the oldest, the most massive, and the best preserved of any part. It was old a thousand years ago. Masses of ivy cover its recessed angles and its corners. Through its arched windows, where the walls are more than ten feet thick,—yea, sixteen feet, as my book says,—I see trees and a tangled mass of growing vines, rooted upon the ruins that have fallen and enclosed by the walls of its former halls. Through the square windows above I see fleecy clouds sailing lazily in the air. In what was the "three Kitchens" are growing old butternut trees and haws. The banqueting hall, whose side presented four beautiful windows, has but two of them in a tolerable state of preservation; and projecting fragments show in outline where the others were. I stood in the windows opposite these, where Elizabeth, and hundreds of fairer and better women than she, looked out upon the lake and orchard. But how different were my thoughts and theirs; the scene which they admired and that which I beheld! From beneath these crumbled ruins too, utterly forgotten now, except of God, shall arise many forms to stand with me in judgment. Those who reveled here, squire, knight, and lady, those who rebelled and plotted, they who built and those who destroyed, how do they seem to me now, as I bring them back in imagination!—and how strangely contemptible seems, for the most part, that greatness which was then so great! I have never felt such solemnity in the presence of physical creations. But these stones, these old gateways, these mounds, what power have they to send the soul back through ages of time, and stir it up from its very bottom! I could not bear the approach of men. The children of a party, visiting like myself, came frolicking round the place where I sat; but, for the first time, children and their sports pained me. I would, if I could, come and sit in this court at evening—after sunset, or by moonlight. Then should I not see flitting shadows and forms, and hear low airy voices? As it was, a spirit almost spoke to me; for, going into one of the tower halls of Leicester's building, I heard a clear ringing sound, and a tiny echo like a bird, in the deserted room. Sure enough it was a bird, sitting far up upon a window-sill, and trying his voice in the solitude. Fly away, little friend, this is no place for you; the trees and hedges are yours, but not this old solitude! At last I awoke. Three hours had passed like a dream. I hastened back to my inn, with a strange sadness of spirit, which I did not shake off all day. Perhaps I have some veneration after all, if it were rightly come at.

Warwick Castle.

Taking a cab, I started for Warwick. The same smooth road, the same trees, the same beautifully diversified fields, and the same blue sky over them, only the clouds are all islands now, floating about just above the horizon; but I have not the same light-hearted, singing spirit which I had in the morning; there is a deep, yet a pleasant sadness, which I do not wish to shake off. I was glad that I had visited the place *alone;* no one should go except ALONE. While at Kenilworth, had those I love most been with me, we would have separated, and each should have wandered alone up and down and around the solemn old place. The landscape is full of soft beauty, yet my thoughts are running back to the olden time. But here we come to Warwick! What bands of steel-clad knights have tramped these streets before us! Here is, doubtless, the old gate of the town renewed with modern stone. Ordering dinner at six o'clock, I start for the castle, without the remotest idea of what I shall see. Walking along a high park wall which forms one part of the town, or rather which stops the town from extending further in that direction—the top covered with ivy, that *garment* of English walls and buildings—I come to the gateway of the *approach.* A porter opens its huge leaf. Cut through a solid rock, the road, some twenty feet wide, winds for a long way in the most solemn beauty. The sides, in solid rock, vary from five to twenty feet in height—at least so it seemed to my imagination—the only faculty that I allowed to conduct me. It was covered on both hands with ivy, growing *down* from above, and hanging in beautiful reaches. Solemn trees on the bank, on either side, met overhead, and cast a delicious twilight down upon my way, and made it yet softer by a murmuring of their leaves; while multitudes of little birds flew about and sang merrily. Winding in graceful curves, it at last brings you to the first view of the Castle, at a distance of some hundred rods before you. It opens on the sight with grandeur! On either corner is a huge tower, apparently one hundred and fifty feet high; in the center is a square tower, called properly a gateway; and a huge wall connects this central access with the two corner towers. I stood for a little, and let the vision pierce me through. Who can *tell* what he feels in such a place! How, especially, can I tell *you*—who have never seen, or felt, such a view any more than I had before this time! Primeval forests, the ocean, prairies, Niagara, I had seen and felt. But never had I seen any pile around which were historic associations, blended not only with heroic men and deeds, but savoring of my own childhood. And now, too, am I to see, and understand by inspection, the things which Scott has made so familiar to all as mere words—moats, portcullises, battlements, keeps or mounds, arrow-slit windows, watch-towers. They had a strange effect upon me; they were perfectly new, and yet familiar old friends. I had never seen them, yet the moment I did behold, all was instantly plain; I knew name and use, and seemed in a moment to have known them always. My mind was so highly excited as to be perfectly calm, and apparently it perceived by an intuition. I seemed to spread myself over all that was around or before me, while in the court and on the walls, or rather to draw every thing within me. I fear that I seem crazy to you. It was, however, the calmness of intense excitement.

I came up to the moat, now dry, and lined with beautiful shrubs and trees, crossed the bridge, and entered the outer gateway or arched door, through a solid square tower. The portcullis was drawn up, but I could see the projecting end. Another similar gateway, a few steps further on, showed the care with which the defense was managed. This passed, a large court opened, surrounded on every side with towers, walls, and vast ranges of buildings. Here I beheld the pictures which I had seen on paper, magnified into gigantic realities. Drawings of many-faced, irregular, Gothic mansions, measuring an inch or two, with which my childhood was familiar, here stood before me measuring hundreds and hundreds of feet. It was the first sight of a real baronial castle! It was a historic dream breaking forth into a waking reality.

It is of very little use to tell you how large the court is, by feet and rods; or that Guy's Tower is 128 feet high, and Cesar's Tower 147. But it may touch your imagination, and wheel it suddenly backward with long flight and wide vision, to say that Cesar's Tower has stood for 800 years, being coeval with the Norman Conquest! I stood upon its mute stones and imagined the ring of the hammer upon them when the mason was laying them to their bed of ages. What were the thoughts, the fancies, the conversations of these rude fellows, at that age of the world! I was wafted backward, and backward, until I stood on the foundations upon which old England herself was builded, when as yet there was none of her. There, far back of all literature, before the English tongue itself was formed, earlier than her jurisprudence, and than all modern civilization, I stood, in imagination, and, reversing my vision, looked down into a far future to search for the men and deeds which had been, as if they were yet to be; thus making a prophesy of history; and changing memory into a dreamy foresight.

When these stones were placed, it was yet to be two hundred years before Gower and Chaucer should be born. Indeed, since this mortar was wetted and cemented these stones, the original people, the Normans, the Danes, the Saxons, have been mixed together into one people. When this stone, on which I lean, took its place, there was not then a printed book in England. Printing was invented hundreds of years after these foundations went down. When the rude workmen put their shoulders to these stones, the very English language lay unborn in the loins of its parent tongues. The men that laughed and jested as they wrought, and had their pride of skill; the architect, and the lord for whose praise he fashioned these stones; the villagers that wondered as they looked upon the growing pile; why, they are now no more to men's memories than the grass they trod on, or the leaves which they cast down in felling the oak!

Against these stones on which I lay my hand, have rung the sounds of battle. Yonder, on these very grounds, there raged, in sight of men that stand where

I do, fiercest and deadliest conflicts. All this ground has fed on blood.

I walked across to Guy's Tower, up its long stone stairway, into some of its old soldiers' rooms. The pavements were worn, though of stone, with the heavy grinding feet of men-at-arms. I heard them laugh between their cups, I saw them devouring their gross food, I heard them recite their feats, or tell the last news of some knightly outrage, or cruel oppression of the despised laborer. I stood by the window out of which the archer sent his whistling arrows. I stood by the openings through which scalding water or molten lead were poured upon the heads of assailants, and heard the hoarse shriek of the wretched fellows from below as they got the shocking baptism. I ascended to the roof of the tower, and looked over the wide glory of the scene, still haunted with the same imaginations of the olden time. How many thoughts had flown hence beside mine!—here where warriors looked out, or ladies watched for their knight's return. How did I long to stand for one hour, really, in their position and in their consciousness, who lived in those days; and then to come back, with the new experience, to my modern self!

I walked, in a dream, along the line of the westward wall, surveyed the towers begun, but, for some reason, left unfinished; climbed up the moat and keep, steep enough, and densely covered with trees and underbrush, to the very top.

Grand and glorious were the trees that waved in the

grounds about the castle; but, though some of them had seen centuries, they were juvenile sprouts in comparison of these old walls and towers, on which William the Conqueror had walked, without thinking a word about me, I'll warrant—in which matter I have the advantage of him—following in his footsteps along the top of the broad walls, ten times more lofty in my transcendent excitement than ever was he in his royal excursion.

Already the sun was drooping far down the west, and sending its golden glow sideways through the trees; and the glades in the park were gathering twilight as I turned to give a last look at these strange scenes. I walked slowly through the gateway, crossed the bridge over the moat, turned and looked back upon the old towers, whose tops reddened yet in the sun, though I was in deep shadow. Then, walking backward, looking still, till I came to the woods, I took my farewell of Warwick Castle.

It was half-past six when I left the hotel for Stratford-on-Avon. Can you imagine a more wonderful transition than from the baronial castles to the peaceful village of Stratford? Can there possibly be a more utter contrast than between the feelings which exercise one in the presence of the memorials of princely estates—knightly fortresses, scenes full of associations of physical prowess—jousts and tournaments, knights and nobles, kings and courtiers, war and sieges, sallies, defeats or victories, dungeons and palaces now all alike in confused ruins, and the peaceful, silver Avon, with its little village of Stratford snugged down between smoothly rounded hills; all of whose interest centers upon one man—gentle Shakspeare? And what do you think must be the condition of a man's mind who in one day, keenly excited, is entirely possessed and almost demented by these three scenes? The sun had not long set as I drove across the bridge of Avon, and stopped at the Red Horse Inn. As soon as I could put my things away, the first question asked was for *Henley Street.* It was near. In another moment I was there, looking, upon either side, for Shakspeare's house,—which was easily found without inquiry. I examined the kitchen where he used to frolic, and the chamber in which he was born, with an interest which surprised me. That *I* should be a *hero-worshiper*—a relic-monger, was a revelation indeed.

Now guess where I am writing? You have the place in the picture before you.* It is the room where Shakspeare was born! Two hundred and eighty-six years ago, in this room, a mother clasped her new-born babe to her bosom; perhaps on the very spot where I am writing! Do you see the table on the right side of the picture? It is there I am sitting. The room is represented as it was before it passed into the hands of the Shakspearian society. There are now no curtains to the window which you see, and which looks out from the front of the house into the street; nor are there any pictures; but the room, with the exception of the two side

---

* This letter was written upon pictorial note-paper containing views in and about Stratford.

tables and a few old chairs, is bare, as it should be; leaving you to the consciousness that you are surrounded only by that which the eyes of the child saw when he began to see at all. The room is about fifteen feet wide by eighteen in length. The hight is not great. I can easily touch the ceiling with my hand. An uneven floor of broad oaken plank rudely nailed, untouched, probably, in his day, by mat or carpet. The beams in this room, as also throughout the house, are coarsely shapen, and project beyond the plaster. The original building, owned by Shakspeare's father, has been so changed in its exterior, that but for the preservation of a view taken in 1769, we should have lost all idea of it. It was, for that day, an excellent dwelling-house for a substantial citizen, such as his father is known to have been. It was afterwards divided into three tenements, the center one remaining in possession of Shakspeare's kindred, who resided there until 1646. And it is this portion that is set apart for exhibition;—the sections on either side of it having been intolerably "improved" with a new brick front, by the enterprising landlord of the "Swan and Maidenhead Inn," about 1820! Its exterior has grown rude since Shakspeare's time, for the old print represents a front not unpleasing to the eye, with a gable and a bay window beneath, two dormer windows, and three-light latticed windows upon the ground story. The orchard and garden which were in its rear when purchased by Shakspeare's father, are gone, and their place is occupied by dwellings and stables. There is not a spot for even a shrub to grow in!

I shall spend a portion of three days at Stratford-on-Avon; and I have made a treaty with the worthy woman who keeps the premises, by which I can have free use of the room where I now write. Never have I had such a three days' experience! Kenilworth, Warwick, and Stratford-on-Avon, all in one day! Then I am to spend a Sabbath here! I can neither eat nor sleep for excitement. If my journey shall all prove like this, it will be a severer taxation to *recruit* than to stay at home and labor.

This room, its walls, the ceiling, the chimney front and sides, the glass of the window, are every inch covered and crossed and re-crossed with the names of those who have visited this spot.

I notice names of distinction noble and common, of all nations, mingled with thousands of others known only to the inscribers. In some portions of the room the signatures overlay each other two or three deep. I felt no desire to add my name, and must be content to die without having written any thing on the walls of the room where Shakspeare was born. I must confess, however, to a little vanity—if vanity it be. A book is open for names and contributions to enable the Committee for the preservation of Shakspeare's house to complete the payment of the purchase money. I did feel a quiet satisfaction to know that I had helped to purchase and preserve this place. Strange gift of genius, that now, after nearly three hundred years, makes one proud to contribute a mite to perpetuate in its integrity the very room where the noble babe was born!

But I am exhausted and must sleep, if sleep I can. To-morrow will be my first Sabbath in England—and that Sunday at Stratford-on-Avon!

II.

A SABBATH AT STRATFORD-ON-AVON.

August 4th, 1850.

MY DEAR———: If you have read, or will read, my letter to ———, you will see what a wonderful day was Saturday. Coventry, famous for the legend of Godiva, of which Tennyson has a pretty version; the ruins of Kenilworth Castle, the stately castle of Warwick and its park, and Stratford-on-Avon, all in one day! Do you wonder that my brain was hot and my sleep fitful that night? I tossed from side to side, and dreamed dreams. It was long after midnight before I began to rest, free from dreams; but the sleep was thin, and I broke through it into waking, every half hour.

It was broad daylight when I arose; the sun shone out in spots; masses of soft, fleecy clouds rolled about in the heaven, making the day even finer than if it had been all blue. I purposed attending the village church, in the morning, where Shakspeare was buried; in the afternoon at Shottery, a mile across the fields, where the cottage in which lived Anne Hathaway, his wife, still stands; and in the evening, at the church of the Holy Cross, adjoining the Grammar School; in which, as the school about that time was open, and for a period kept, it is probable that Shakspeare studied.

Never, in all the labors of a life not wont to be idle upon the Sabbath, have I known such excitement or such exhaustion. The scenes of Saturday had fired me; every visit to various points in Stratford-on-Avon added to the inspiration, until, as I sallied forth to church, I seemed not to have a body. I could hardly feel my feet striking against the ground; it was as if I were numb. But my soul was clear, penetrating, and exquisitely susceptible.

You may suppose that every thing would so breathe of the matchless poet, that I should be insensible to religious influences. But I was at a stage beyond that. The first effect, last night, of being here, was to bring up suggestions of Shakspeare from every thing. I said to myself, this is the street he lived in, this the door he passed through, here he leaned, he wandered on these banks, he looked on those slopes and rounded hills. But I had become full of these suggestions, and acting as a stimulus, they had wrought such an ecstatic state, that my soul became exquisitely alive to every influence, whether of things seen, or heard, or thought of. The children going to church, how beautiful they appeared! How good it seemed to walk among so many decorous people to the house of God. How full of music the trees were; music, not only of birds, but of winds waving the leaves; and the bells, as they were ringing, rolled through the air a deep diapason to all other sounds.

As I approached the church, I perceived that we were to pass through the churchyard for some little distance; and an avenue of lime trees meeting overhead formed a beautiful way, through which my soul exulted to go up to the house of God. The interior was stately and beauti ful—it was *to me*, and I am not describing any thing to you as *it* was, but am describing myself while in the presence of scenes with which through books you are familiar. As I sat down in a pew close by the reading-desk and pulpit, I looked along to the chancel, which stretched some fifty or sixty feet back of the pulpit and desk, and saw, upon the wall, the well-known bust of Shakspeare; and I knew that beneath the pavement under that, his dust reposed.

In a few minutes, a little fat man with a red collar and red cuffs, advanced from a side room behind the pulpit and led the way for the rector, a man of about fifty years—bald, except on the sides of his head, which were covered with white hair. I had been anxious lest some Cowper's ministerial fop should officiate, and the sight of this aged man was good. The form of his face and head indicated firmness, but his features were suffused with an expression of benevolence. He ascended the reading-desk, and the services began. You know my mother was, until her marriage, in the communion of the Episcopal Church. This thought hardly left me while I sat, grateful for the privilege of worshiping God through a service that had expressed so often her devotions. I can not tell you how much I was affected. I had never had such a trance of worship, and I shall never have such another view until I gain The Gate.

I am so ignorant of the church service that I can not call the various parts by their right names; but the portions which most affected me were the prayers and responses which the choir sang. I had never heard any part of a supplication—a direct prayer, *chanted* by a choir; and it seemed as though I heard not with my ear, but with my soul. I was dissolved—my whole being seemed to me like an incense wafted gratefully toward God. The Divine presence rose before me in wondrous majesty, but of ineffable gentleness and goodness, and I could not stay away from more familiar approach, but seemed irresistibly, yet gently, drawn toward God. My soul, then thou did'st magnify the Lord, and rejoice in the God of thy salvation! And then came to my mind the many exultations of the Psalms of David, and never before were the expressions and figures so noble and so necessary to express what I felt. I had risen, it seemed to me, so high as to be where David was when his soul conceived the things which he wrote. Throughout the service, and it was an hour and a quarter long, whenever an "Amen" occurred, it was given by the choir, accompanied by the organ and the congregation. O, that swell and solemn cadence rings in my ear yet! Not once, not a single time did it occur in that service from beginning to end, without bringing tears from my eyes. I stood like a shrub in a spring morning—every leaf covered with dew, and every breeze shook down some drops. I trembled so much at times, that I was obliged to sit down. O, when in the prayers breathed forth in strains of sweet, simple, solemn music, the love of Christ was recognized, how I longed then to give utterance to what that love seemed to me. There was a moment in which the heavens seemed opened to me, and I saw the glory of God! All the earth seemed to me a storehouse of images, made to set forth the Redeemer, and I could scarcely be still from crying out. I never knew, I never dreamed before, of what heart there was in that word *amen*. Every time it swelled forth and died away solemnly, not my lips, not my mind, but my whole being said—Saviour, so let it be.

The sermon was preparatory to the Communion, which I then first learned was to be celebrated. It was plain and good; and although the rector had done many things in a way that led me to suppose that he sympathized with over much ceremony, yet in his sermon he seemed evangelical, and gave a right view of the Lord's Supper. For the first time in my life I went forward to commune in an Episcopal Church. Without any intent of my own, but because from my seat it was nearest, I knelt down at the altar with the dust of Shakspeare beneath my feet. I thought of it, as I thought of ten thousand things, without the least disturbance of devotion. It seemed as if I stood upon a place so high, that, like one looking over a wide valley, all objects conspired to make but one view. I thought of the General Assembly and Church of the First Born, of my mother and brother and children in heaven, of my living family on earth, of you, of the whole church intrusted to my hands;—they afar off—I upon the banks of the Avon.

In the afternoon I walked over to Shottery, to attend worship there, but found that I had been misinformed, and that there was no church or service there. I soon found the cottage where Shakspeare's wife, Anne Hathaway, was born, but stayed only for a little time, meaning to visit it more at my leisure on Monday. I hastened back, hoping to reach the village church in Stratford in season for part of the service, but arrived just in time to meet the congregation coming out. I turned aside to the churchyard which surrounds the church on every side. As I stood behind the church on the brink of the Avon, which is here walled up to the hight of some eight feet, looking now at the broad green meadows beyond, and now at a clump of "forget-me-nots" growing wild down at the water's edge, and wondering how I should get them to carry back to my friends, I was accosted by a venerable old man, whose name I found afterwards to be T——. He was not indisposed to talk, and I learned that he was eighty-one years of age; had lost his father in America during our revolutionary war, where he had been a soldier; he remembered the sad tidings, being then eleven years old; he had resided at Stratford for thirty years; he was a turner and carver by trade; he had lately buried his wife, and had come after service to visit her grave. We walked together along the banks of the Avon, he repeating some familiar lines of poetry. He gave me various local information of interest. Among other things, that the vicar was but recently come among them; that he seemed to him very "whimsical," for, said he, "he has got a new brass thing to hold his Bible, down in front of the reading-desk; and he stands sometimes with his back to the people when reading parts of the service, and has a good many scholarly tricks about him, as it seems to me." I forbore making any remarks, not wishing to disturb the associations of the morning. We crossed the stream by a bridge, walked up through the broad, smooth, turfy meadows upon the other side, and on reaching my inn, I pressed him to come in and take tea with me. I did so, in part from interest in him, and in part because he had mentioned, when I apologized for using his time in so long a walk, that his only remaining daughter was gone out to tea, and he did not care to go home and be alone. So we took tea together; after which he proposed waiting upon me to the Church of the Holy Cross, where evening services were then commencing. The interior of the church was plain; and its age and its connection with Shakspeare constituted its only interest to me. I feel greatly obliged to the venerable old man, whose heart seemed guileless and whose mind was simple. This only acquaintance that I have made in Stratford takes nothing away from the romantic interest of my experience here.

MONDAY, *August* 5, 1850.—As I was sitting this morning after breakfast writing busily, my venerable friend T—— came in to bid me good-morning, and to bring me a relic, a piece of the mulberry tree which stood in Shakspeare's garden, but which was cut down by its after owner, he being much annoyed by relic-hunters. He finally destroyed the house itself. The old man also gave me a snuff-box which had been made years and years ago, either from the wood of this same tree, or from a tree sprung from the original. He avers that it was from the original tree; that he obtained it from the former turner, as a model by which to turn boxes, and that he was assured that it was of the real, orthodox, primitive mulberry tree! I do not doubt it. I will not doubt. What is the use of destroying an innocent belief so full of pleasure? If it is not a genuine relic, my faith shall make it so.

ONE OR TWO HOURS LATER.—Alas! I've been out, and among other inquiries, have asked after my old friend T——. I find him to be living in the poorhouse! At first, I confess to a little shame at intimacy with a pauper; but in a moment I felt twice as much ashamed that for a moment I had felt the slightest repugnance toward the old man on this account. I rather believe his story of the tree and the box to be true; at any rate, I have a mulberry snuff-box which I procured in Stratford-on-Avon!

Among the many things which I determined to see and hear in England were the *classic birds,* and especially the *thrush,* the *nightingale* and the *lark;* after these I desired to see cuckoos, starlings and rooks. While in Birmingham, going about one of the manufactories, I was inquiring where I might see some of the first-named. The young man who escorted me pointed across the way to a cage hanging from a second-story window and said, "There's a lark!" Sure enough, in a little cage and standing upon a handful of green grass, stood the little fellow, apparently with russet brown wings and lighter colored breast, ash color, singing away to his own great comfort and mine. The song reminded me, in many of its notes, of the canary bird. In my boyhood, I had innocently supposed that the lark of which I read when first beginning to read in English books, was our meadow lark; and I often watched in vain to see them rise singing into the air! As for singing just beneath "heaven's gate" or near the sun, after diligent observation, with great simplicity, I set that down for a pure fancy of the poets. But I had before this learned that the English sky-lark was not our meadow-lark.

A bird in a cage is not half a bird; and I determined to hear a lark at Stratford-on-Avon, if one could be scared up. And so, early this morning I awoke, according to a predetermination, and sallied out through the fields to a beautiful range of grounds called "Welcombe." I watched for birds and saw birds, but no larks. The reapers were already in the wheat fields, and brought to mind the fable of the lark who had reared her young there. Far over, toward the Avon, I could see black specks of crows walking about, and picking up a morsel here and there in the grass. I listened to one very sweet song from a tree near a farm-house, but it was unfamiliar to my ear; and no one was near from whom I might inquire. Besides, the plain laboring people know little about ornithology, and would have told me that "it is some sort of a singing bird," as if *I* thought it were a goose; and so I said to myself, I've had my labor for my pains! Well, I will enjoy the clouds and the ribbon strips of blue that interlace them. I must revoke my judgment of the English trees; for as I stood looking over upon the masses of foliage, and the single trees dotted in here and there, I could see every shade of green, and all of them most beautiful, and as refreshing to me as old friends. After standing awhile to take a last view of Stratford-on-Avon, from this high ground, and the beautiful slopes around it, and of the meadows of the Avon, I began to walk homeward, when I heard such an outbreak behind me, as wheeled me about quick enough; there he flew, singing as he rose, and rising gradually, not directly up, but with gentle slope—there was the free singing lark, not half so happy to sing as I was to hear! In a moment more, he had reached the summit of his ambition, and suddenly fell back to the grass again. And now, if you laugh at my enthusiasm, I will pity you for the want of it. I have heard *one* poet's lark, if I never hear another, and am much happier for it.

If you will wait a moment or two, till I can breakfast, you shall have the benefit of a stroll over to Shottery—a real old English village. I walked over there yesterday afternoon, to church, as I told you, and so can show you the way without inquiring it three times, as I did then. Emerging from the village, we take this level road, lined on either side with hedges and trees; trees not with naked stems, but ruffled from the hedge to their limbs with short side brush, which gives them a very beautiful appearance. The white clover-turf under foot is soft as velvet; men are reaping in the fields, or going past us with their sickles. We have walked about a mile, and here is a lane turning to the left, and a guide-board pointing to "Shottery." I see the village. A moment's walk brings us to a very neat little brick, gothic cottage, quite pretty in style, and painted cream color; it is covered with roses and fragrant flowering vines, which make the air delicious. By the gate is a Champney rose—the largest I ever saw—its shoots reaching, I should think, more than twelve feet, and terminated with clusters of buds and open roses, each cluster having from fifty to a hundred buds. Yesterday afternoon, as I passed this same cottage, I stopped to admire this rose, and to feed upon the delicious perfume which exhaled from the grounds. A lady, apparently about forty-five, and two young women about eighteen and twenty years of age respectively, seeing a stranger, approached the gate. I bowed and asked,

"Is this a Champney rose?"

"It is a Noisette, sir!"

"I thought so; a Champney of the Noisette family! Will you tell me what flower it is that fills the air with such odor?"

"I don't know; it must be something in the garden."

"Will you be kind enough to tell me the way to Anne Hathaway's cottage?"

"Take the first lane to the left," said the eldest young woman, pointing to the right.

"The lane on the *right,* you mean."

"Oh yes, on the *right,* but I do not know where the cottage is exactly!" and yet it lay hardly two good stone-casts from where they stood. You can see its smoke from the windows. *Did* they not know, or were they ashamed to seem too familiar with a stranger? But William Shakspeare, eighteen years old as he was, had no need of asking his way, as he came by here of a Sabbath evening! What were the thoughts of such a mind drawing near to the place which now peeps out from the trees across the field on the right? What were the feelings of a soul which created such forms of love in after days? I look upon the clouds every moment changing forms, upon the hedges or trees, along which, or such like, Shakspeare wandered, with his sweet Anne, and marvel what were the imaginations the strifes of heart, the gushes of tenderness, the sanguine hopes and fore-paintings of this young poet's soul. For, even so early, he had begun to give form to that which God created in him. One cannot help thinking of Olivia, Juliet, Desdemona, Beatrice, Ophelia, Imogen, Isabella, Miranda; and wondering whether any of his first dreams were afterward borrowed to form these. It is not possible but that strokes of his pencil, in these and other women of Shakspeare, reproduced some features of his own experience. Well, I imagine that Anne was a little below the medium hight, delicately formed and shaped, but not slender, with a clear smooth forehead, not high, but wide and evenly filled out; an eye that chose to look down mostly, but filled with sweet confusion every time she looked up, and that was used more than her tongue; a face that smiled oftener than it laughed, but so smiled that one saw a world of brightness within, as of a lamp hidden behind an alabaster shade; a carriage that was deliberate but graceful and elastic. This is *my* Anne Hathaway. Whether it was Shakspeare's I find nothing in this cottage and these trees and verdant hedges to tell me. The birds are singing something about it—descendants doubtless of the very birds that the lovers heard, strolling together; but I doubt their traditionary lore. I did not care to go in. There are two or three tenements in the long cottage as it now stands; but the middle one is that to which pilgrims from all the world do come; and though it was but a common yeoman's home, and his daughter has left not a single record of herself, she and her home are immortal, because hither came the lad Shakspeare, and she became his wife. I leaned upon this hedge yesterday afternoon, it being the Sabbath, and looked long at the place, and with more feelings than thoughts, or rather with thoughts that dissolved at once into feelings. Here are the rudest cottages; scenery, beautiful indeed, but not more so than thousands of other places; but men of all nations and of every condition, the mingled multitude of refined men are thronging hither, and dwell on every spot with enthusiasm unfeigned. Whatever Shakspeare saw, we long to see; what he thought of, we wish to think of; where he walked, thither we turn our steps. The Avon, the church, the meadows lying over beyond both; the street and the room where he was born;—all have a soul imbreathed upon them, all of them are sacred to us, and we pass as in a dream amid these things. The sun, the clouds, the trees, the birds, the morning and evening, moonlight or twilight or darkness, none of them here have a nature of their own; all of them are to us but memorials or suggestions of Shakspeare.

God gave to man this power to breathe himself upon the world; and God gave us that nature by which we feel the inspiration. Is this divine arrangement exhausted in man's earthly history? Are we not to see and to know a sublime development of it when we come to a knowledge of God himself, face to face? Then, not a hamlet alone, a few cottages, a stream or spire will be suggestive; but throughout the universe, every creature and every object will breathe of God. Not of his *genius*, as Stratford-on-Avon speaks of Shakspeare; but of every trait of character, every shade of feeling, every attribute of power; of goodness, love, mercy and gentleness, magnanimity, exquisite purity, taste, imagination, truth and justice. May we know this revelation; walk amid those scenes of glory, and know the rapture of feeling God effulge upon us from everything which his heart has conceived, or his hand fashioned! But chiefly may we see that noontide glory when we shall gaze unabashed upon his unobstructed face.

III.

OXFORD.

DEAR ———. Did I ever dream of writing you from this renowned seat of learning, memorable in history, the residence of good King Alfred, the birthplace of Richard *Cœur de Lion,* the burning place of Latimer, Ridley, and Cranmer, and the place where many among the greatest historical men were educated? But I must go back a little, for I believe I have said nothing in either of my letters to others, of my route hither.

I send you a forget-me-not which was gathered from the edge of the river Avon, just beneath the wall which divides the face of the churchyard from the water. These little beauties awakened me from a dream by their meek looks, and I determined to send this one to you. To climb down the wall was easy enough, too easy for a man who did not love wetting. I cast about for expedients. For, you must know that the river washes the very wall, and that a little bit of soil, scarcely a foot across, had formed in one spot and proclaimed its triumph by wearing these tufts of flowers for its feather. I studied the wall, speculated upon my relative position to the water and flowers, should I reach such and such a chink. I partly climbed down, and wholly clambered back again, satisfied that it was easier to get myself in, than to get the flowers out. My courage rose with the difficulty. Have them now I would, if I was obliged to swim for them. I walked down to the mill, a little below, and, crossing over, returned up the other bank, opposite to them. They seemed to my wistful looks further off than ever. Happily, before attempting the Hellespont, Hero-like, I espied someway up the Avon, a boat in charge of two young men, and easily engaged them to put me across to the coveted treasure. Though very rough in their exterior, the fellows had some heart; and when they saw what I would be at, they took great pains not to crush the gems with the bow of the boat, and quite eagerly helped me to gather every stalk. You know the story of this flower and its name? A knight, walking in his armor, with his lady-love, attempted, at her wish, just such a feat as I had declined,—for the want of his motive. While reaching down for the flowers he slipped, and was plunged into the deep stream, hopelessly weighed down by his armor. As he sank he threw the flowers toward the bank, crying, "Forget me not."

The morning on which I mounted the coach-top for Oxford was bright. The heavens were beautiful, and the earth was beautiful. The past was grateful to recollection; the future was hopeful. Indeed, I was in harmony with everything—with the driver, the passengers, the horses, the fields with their herds, the trees and hedges. To be sure, I maintained a grave and reserved exterior, all the way; but my heart laughed and sung at every step. We rode through Woodstock, and passed by Blenheim, the seat of the Duke of Marlborough. I could not gratify my wish to go over the grounds and house, as it chanced not to be one of the days on which visitors are allowed.

In drawing near to Oxford, I felt the zeal going up in the thermometer; and dusky shadows of olden histories began to arise. I had a distinct picture of the place in my mind, at least of the University. I imagined it to be a group of buildings, say eight or ten in number, opening upon a common court, not unlike the cotton-factory style of architecture which prevails in New-England Colleges. I had no very distinct idea of their number or extent, but a clear impression, that, more or fewer, they were grouped together upon some one spot.

Accordingly, I inquired with innocent simplicity of a gentleman next to me, in what part of the town the University buildings were, and was answered promptly, "In every part; they are scattered all over the city."

Imagine, then, a city of 25,000 inhabitants, not with narrow streets, and continuous stone houses and shops, like commercial cities; nor yet, like a rural city, full of yards and gardens; but something distinct from either, and peculiar—a city of castles and palaces!

The University comprises twenty distinct Colleges, and five Halls. The Colleges are incorporated; possessing their own rights, buildings, grounds, revenues, laws, and officers. The Halls are not incorporated, or endowed with estates; but, in other respects, are not materially different from the Colleges. Here, then, are twenty-five suites of buildings distributed throughout the city. You must not for a moment imagine a strait-sided, bald, rectangular, five-story building. Exorcise all such brick parallelograms from your thoughts; and call up instead images of castles, palaces, ornate galleries, and atheneums; and that too of the most imposing dimensions. The buildings of Magdalen College cover eleven acres; and of gardens and decorated grounds, there are one hundred acres more! Christ Church College is much more extensive than this. You would suppose yourself under the battlements of an old warlike castle. The front line of wall is four hundred feet, with turrets, bastions, and a huge octagonal tower for a gateway. The College buildings are arranged in systems of quadrangles, called familiarly *quads.*

Thus a central plat of ground is inclosed on every side by the magnificent and continuous College structures, running four hundred by about two hundred and sixty feet; and this forms the Great Quadrangle. A huge gateway opens out of this into another such quadrangle, named the Peckwater, but of less dimensions; and the Canterbury Quadrangle, again, opens out of this. The buildings are of different styles of architecture. Indeed, Christ Church College represents almost the history of architecture, from the times of the Saxons to Sir Christopher Wren. And the diversities and contrasts of architecture increase the impression of vastness and endless extent.

Now, although Christ Church College and Magdalen College are the most extensive, yet, to an eye not accustomed to measurement, and whose lenses are somewhat inclined to magnify through the bewildering excitement of novelty and surprise, the smallest seem scarcely less than the largest. And you may conceive what impression would be made upon my mind in my first walk, alone, at sunset and twilight, through a strange city, composed so largely of such magnificent palatial structures, in which had once dwelt and studied so many names most honorable and prominent in English history. I left my inn almost at once after my arrival, and was glad to be alone: to be unquestioned: to go wherever chance took me; to gaze on the different piles, as they came one after another, until the strangeness grew almost into enchantment! The twilight as it gently settled down made tower and spire seem gigantic; the dusky stones of the ancient structures receded into illusory distances; and the somber pediments, which yet retained a slight silvery glow from the West, seemed lifted up to an incredible hight. By and by the buildings sunk into darkness and disappeared, except where the now multiplying lights in some principal streets, threw another and scarcely less bewitching glare upon them. The same causes which invoked the imagination in respect to single buildings, in like manner produced an impression in respect to the extent of the city, which daylight could not have borne out.

Bright and early the next day, I took an ante-prandial stroll. Every thing was changed. The same buildings were different; there was the soft, somber evening effect in my memory, and the clear lines of accurate daylight in my eye; and the old and new impressions disputed with each other. I had gained a pretty correct topographical knowledge of the city, and had, by my guide-book, identified several of the most noticeable Colleges before returning to breakfast.*

It was my good fortune to be put in the charge of a young lawyer, by the good offices of the same stranger that had ridden with me upon the coach from Woodstock, and at whose suggestion I had lodged at the Miter Inn. He was not only a fine-hearted, generous, and intelligent man, but had the advantage of knowing from boyhood all the under officers, janitors, stewards, butlers, etc., of the various Colleges. It was vacation, and the buildings were for the most part vacant. The frank and gay face of my guide seemed a charm to open doors seldom open to visitors. Had I come to Oxford to take an honorary degree, I should have failed to see much that was shown to me now. An inspec-

* The following are the names, and dates of the founding, of the Colleges in the University of Oxford. The number of officers, members on foundations, and students, at the time we were there, was said to be more than *five thousand.* Merton College, founded 1264. University College, about 1249. Baliol College, about 1263. Exeter College, 1314. Oriel College, about 1326. Queen's College, 1340. New College, 1378. Lincoln College, about 1479. All Souls' College, 1437. Magdalen College, 1457. Brazen Nose College, 1509, named from the circumstance of a brazen nose with a ring in it, swinging as a knocker on the Hall, whose site it occupies, and whose name it also inherited. Corpus Christi College, 1516. Christ Church College, founded by Wolsey, 1524. Trinity College, 1564. St. John's College, 1557. Jesus' College, 1546. Wadham College, 1613 Pembroke College, ——. Worcester College, 1714.

tion of the kitchens, the butteries, the dining-halls, and a rehearsal of the habits of both students and professors, satisfied me that there was most excellent drill of the animal man, whatever befell the moral and intellectual development. The plump, jovial, rubicund professors of *cuisine* were obligingly communicative, giving savory explanations of every thing that seemed strange to me. They courteously proffered me a complimentary mutton chop; and gave me a knowing laugh when I declined beer and wine, as articles that I never employed. A thing more utterly inconceivable than a deliberate rejection of good wine and beer could not be told to an Oxford butler.

At Christ Church College kitchen, I was shown an enormous gridiron, nearly five feet square; formerly used before the introduction of ranges. I could not but imagine a fancy heretic, broiling upon it, like a shrunk robin. They seemed hurt at the suggestion, assured me that it had never served such uses, and swung it aside by its chain which suspended it, as if the associations of such a relic had been ungenerously offended.

When we speak of Dining Halls, pray dismiss all modern halls or hotel saloons from your mind. Summon up rather the noblest, cathedral-like apartment, of the highest architectural embellishments; impressive by its very space, and hung, often profusely, with portraits and pictures. You would suppose upon entering that you saw tables stretched in a gothic church, or in some vast library, or in some picture gallery. The Hall of Jesus College is thirty by sixty feet in dimensions, with an arched ceiling, designed by Sir Christopher Wren. That of New College is seventy-eight by thirty-five feet. Wadham College Hall is eighty-two by thirty-five, and thirty-seven feet high. The Hall of Christ Church College is one hundred and fifty feet in length, forty feet wide, and fifty feet high, having about one hundred and twenty pictures upon its walls.

These quite put to shame my ignoble ideas of College dining-halls;—as the larders and butteries did the fare of College commons. These Colleges resemble American institutions in the fact that they are resorts of students, that they have corps of tutors and professors, rooms and dormitories, libraries and halls; but, a visitor wandering through them in vacation, would think them literary hotels, as in many respects they really are.

One who has only seen the plain stone of American buildings, uncarved, and scarcely chiseled, will be struck with the carving and decorations in stone. The cornices were not wood painted *like* stone, but stone curled, and carved—as if in olden times cutting stones had been the easiest of all occupations. We are accustomed to decorations in paste, in wax, in plaster, in wood. We do not think it strange to see picture-frames wreathed with vines, or furniture sculptured into flowers and fruits; but the time and expense required for working stone has forbid such ornaments in America, with the exception of execrable carving on lamentable grave-stones, that can not but keep alive a sense of pain, in the spectator, as long as they last.

In Oxford, in all the Colleges and other public buildings, uncarved stone would seem to be accounted as almost unseemly. The doorways, the window-sills and caps, the cornices, the capitals, the pediments, are profusely decorated. Grotesque heads, lion's faces, satyrs, distorted human faces, birds, flowers, leaves, rosettes, seize upon every projection of the Gothic buildings. Where the buildings represented Greek architecture, they were decorated more severely, but with scarcely less profusion of carving.

I was even more delighted with the grounds and walks, than with the twilight seclusion of the cloistered rooms. I sat down in the recess of a window, in one of the student's rooms, and looked out into an exquisite nook, with a large mound, not unlike some of our conical hills in the rolling lands of the West, planted with shrubs and trees to the very top. Is there any thing more bewitching than to look up, beneath the branches of trees, upon the ascent of a hill? The grass was like the pile of velvet, thick, even, deeply green, and with a crisp, succulent look, that made you feel that Nebuchadnezzar had not so bad a diet after all. The grounds were laid out with parterres of flowers, clumps of trees, graveled walks artfully traced to produce the utmost illusion, vines, and upon every unsightly object, and along the stone fence, that glorious sheet of ivy that, everywhere in England, incases walls and towers in vegetable emerald. In these delicious coverts, birds hopped about in literary seclusion, or chatted with each other in musical notes, such as Jenny Lind might be supposed to sing to her sleeping cradle, or to a frolicking child. It is a very paradise of seclusion. Noise seemed like an antediluvian legend as I sat and dreamed in the slumberous stillness.

Nor was I flattered by the painful contrast which my memory supplied of American Colleges, with frigid rooms, without gardens or secluded walks, with grounds undecorated except by chips, ashes, and the dank and molded droppings of paper, rags, and various fragments of nocturnal feasts, which may often be found beneath the windows, among rank and watery weeds, on the neglected side of College buildings, where every side is neglected. But, if all the stories told me be true, or the half of them, cloistered rooms are not necessarily productive of profound study, any more than cloistered cells of profound piety. The Fellows of the Colleges are unmarried men, who have suites of rooms, ample gustatory provision for the earthly man, and revenues for gentlemanly support, that they may give themselves utterly to study. And in many cases, study, that makes other men lean, is blessed to these fellows, even as was the simple pulse to the companions of Daniel.

One can scarcely realize the treasures of literature and of art which are gathered into this city. Beside the libraries of each College, which are large, there is the Bodleian Library with books and manuscripts enough to turn the heads of the whole nation. Each College has in profusion, beside architectural treasure, busts and statues of distinguished men, pictures by all the great masters of art, in great numbers; prints, coins, and literary and archaiological curiosities without number, and cabinets of natural history. I stood in the midst of such treasures as helpless and as hopeless of ever looking at them with a more individual recognition, as I was when I first trod a prairie, journeying from dawn till dark through the dwarf floral groves, and beheld millions of acres of flowers. I passed by rare treasures without a look, which, at another time, would have eagerly occupied hours. The mind was sated with literary riches.

As I stood beneath the arches of Christ Church College, I was impressed with the immortality of earthly influence when rightly embodied. Wolsey's designs for national education have gone through generations performing the noblest services, and perpetuating among men the blessings which his life and personal conduct failed to render to his fellows. His endowments have been noble, undying, undecaying. Nay, Time, that wastes monuments and plucks up the longest lived forests, has but consolidated his gifts to learning, and renewing their strength in every generation. They are stronger, more vigorous, with a surer hope of good for the future, than when in the freshness of their original youth. It were not an unworthy ambition to desire such posthumous influence, having one's name gratefully mentioned through hundreds of years, amidst scenes of learning, by the noblest spirits, who were deriving their very life from your benefaction!

Every one, familiar with his own mind, knows how differently that subtile and mysterious agency works within him, on different days. But I never felt the difference so strikingly as since I have been ranging through these historic places; and I find that the keen, and fine excitement, which inevitably steals upon one in the walks and galleries of these venerable Colleges, is precisely of the kind favorable for the appreciation of pictures. They cease to be pictures. They are realities. The canvas is glass, and you look through it upon the scene represented as if you stood at a window. Nay, you enter into the action. For, once possessed with the spirit of the actors or of the scene, all that the artist thought lives in you. And if you are left, as I was once or twice, for an hour quite alone, in the halls, the illusion becomes memorable. You know the personages. You mingle in the action as an actor. You gaze upon the Apostles of Guido, and it is not the ideal head that you see, but the character, the life, the career, extend in shadowy length before you. At last you are with them! No longer do you look through the eighteen hundred years at misty shadows. The living men have moved down toward you, and here you are face to face! I was much affected by a head of Christ; not that it met my ideal of that sacred front, but because it took me in a mood that clothed it with life and reality. For one blessed moment I was with the Lord. I knew Him. I loved Him. My eyes I could not close for tears. My poor tongue kept silence, but my heart spoke, and I loved and adored. The amazing circuit of one's thoughts in so short a period is wonderful. They circle round through all the past, and up through the whole future, and both the past and future are the present, and are one. For one moment there arose a keen anguish, like a shooting pang, for that which I was, and I thought my heart would break that I could bring but only such a nature to my Lord; but in a moment, as quick as the flash of sunlight which follows the shadow of summer clouds across the fields, there seemed to spring out upon me, from my Master, a certainty of love so great and noble as utterly to consume my unworth, and leave me shining bright; as if it were impossible for Christ to love a heart, without making it pure and beautiful by the resting on it of that illuming affection, just as the sun bathes into beauty the homeliest object when he looks full upon it. But why should I seek to imprison in words the thoughts and feelings that nothing but the heart itself had power to utter? Words belong to the body. But when we are "in the spirit," thoughts and feelings are expressed by the very act of existing, and syllable themselves by their own pulsations.

In the same mood I stood before the busts and portraits of England's most illustrious names. But a volume would not suffice to record the experience of a single hour, even if my memory could compass the blessed illusion with words.

Few places affected me more than the Libraries, and especially the Bodleian Library, reputed to have half a million printed books and manuscripts. I walked solemnly and reverently among the alcoves and through the halls, as if in the pyramid of embalmed souls. It was their life, their heart, their mind, that they treasured in these book-urns. Silent as they are, should all the emotions that went to their creation have utterance, could the world itself contain the various sound? They longed for fame? Here it is—to stand silently for ages, moved only to be dusted and catalogued, valued only as units in the ambitious total, and gazed at, occasionally, by men as ignorant as I am, of their name, their place, their language, and their worth. Indeed, unless a man can link his written thoughts with the everlasting wants of men, so that they shall draw from them as from wells, there is no more immortality to the thoughts and feelings of the soul than to the muscles and the bones. A library is but the soul's burial-ground. It is the land of shadows.

Yet one is impressed with the thought, the labor, and the struggle, represented in this vast catacomb of books. Who could dream, by the placid waters that issue from the level mouths of brooks into the lake, all the plunges, the whirls, the divisions, and foaming rushes that had brought them down to the tranquil exit? And who can guess through what channels of disturbance, and experiences of sorrow, the heart passed that has emptied into this Dead Sea of books?

It seemed to me that I was like one who walked in the forests of the tropics, astounded at the gigantic growths, and at their uselessness. Centuries had nursed them to their present stature; but not one in ten thousand of them will ever be sought for commerce or for use. Where they stand, they will drop, and where they fall they will decay. It is always so—life striking its roots into the dead, and feeding upon decay.

I visited the Taylor and Randolph Gallery in Oxford, in which are casts of all of Chantrey's statues and busts; and many original drawings of Raphael and Michael Angelo! One hundred and ninety sketches and drawings in pencil, ink, and by other means, of Raphael; and eighty-seven by Angelo! They were from their rude school-boy essays to their latest efforts! Here was the sketch from which Angelo drew the Last Judgment; hands, feet, faces, the body in every conceivable attitude, the face expressing mirth, joy, surprise, grief. These were in some respects even more interesting than the *after* works would have been for which these prepared the way. For here I saw the idea as it originally dawned upon the great mind, and was instantly dashed down upon paper. Sometimes you see the very germ and the growth of it—as when at first it was a faint pen-sketch; then, on the same sheet, another and another thought were added, and finally all of them grouped together. I could have cried with regret at being obliged to race through these collections like a hound on a hunt. It seemed almost degrading to me to be anything other than obedient to the high attractions which drew me; yet, many things burned themselves upon my imagination never to grow out or grow over! But I must leave Oxford—though I have scarcely touched the mass of impressions which I there received

IV.

THE LOUVRE—LUXEMBOURG GALLERY.

PARIS, *August*, 1850.

* * * NEXT I visited Faubourg St. Antoine, where the Archbishop of Paris was killed while endeavoring to stop the fighting in the Revolution of 1848, I believe. Thence I went to the *Jardin des Plantes,* which, beside its most admirable collection of plants, has a noble zoological collection, a museum of natural history that well nigh epitomises the living tribes of the earth, together with mineralogical and geological cabinets. I seemed to have God's wide-spread earth presented to me at a sight. I never before had such a conception of what had been done in making our globe. But I resolve a hundred times a day that I will leave Paris, that I may not be so tantalized! For it is a greater pain than enjoyment just to glance at a department long enough to feel deeply, and almost only, what you are losing in not being able calmly to examine and be filled with its treasures. One whole day would not suffice for the most cursory glance at this one ground, and I passed through in an hour! It lies in my memory like a dream.—Thence to the *Pantheon,* a temple of glory; much admired, but to me vast, cold and empty.—Thence to the Palace de Luxembourg. But here there is a gallery of paintings! Ah, what a new world has been

opened to me! And what a new sense within myself. I knew that I had gradually grown fond of pictures from my boyhood. I had felt the power of some few. But nothing had ever come up to a certain ideal that had hovered in my mind; and I supposed that I was not fine enough to appreciate with discrimination the works of masters. To find myself absolutely intoxicated—to find my system so much affected that I could not control my nerves—to find myself trembling and laughing and weeping, and almost hysterical, and that in spite of my shame and resolute endeavor to behave better,—such a power of these galleries over me I had not expected. I have lived for two days in fairy-land,—wakened out of it by some few sights which I have mechanically visited, more for the sake of pleasing dear friends at home, when I return, than for a present pleasure to myself; but relapsing again into the golden vision. The Gallery of the Luxembourg has about three hundred paintings by two hundred and thirty-six artists now living.

I shall give you some account of the effect on my mind of my visits to this gallery yesterday and to the *Louvre* to-day. This last collection is enormous. To examine it in one or two visits is like attempting to read an encyclopedia at one sitting. One can only take the general effect, and record his experiences in the midst of this wilderness of beauty. I had as lief attempt to pluck and examine each special flower growing in France, as to single out and observe carefully each picture. Indeed, your first feeling is that of despair. But an intense hour will do more than dreamy years;

and I gathered much. It contains a vast collection of antique statues, Greek and Roman; cabinets of curiosities, which *are* curiosities; coins; the utensils of various ages and nations; arms and armor; vases, cameos, jewelry; the costly plate of royal families, engraved stones, &c., &c.; Indian and Chinese collections; machinery; and in particular the models of French ships, and the history, in models, of ship-building, not only from the keel to the last rope of rigging, but also of the progress of marine architecture from age to age. But this is only a thing aside. It has a vast collection of *the* great schools of painters ancient and modern. Each school has its saloons; and they follow one after another until the mind reels and staggers under the before unconceived and inconceivable riches! No description will impress you with the multitudinousness of this repository of art. All the streams of pictorial beauty seem, since the world began, to have flowed hither, and this is the ocean. I mean first to give you in some detail the states of my mind, as I now look back upon them; and then I will take you with me into the galleries, and step by step I will soliloquize, or describe, or paint with my pen:—at least I shall fill out this intention unless some new excitement bursting on me quite drives this purpose from the field. You have lost, or perhaps rather escaped, several descriptions and wonderful experiences in this way. For if I do not write almost at once what I have to say, a new crop springs up and grows so rankly as quite to smother down the growth of yesterday.

The first feeling which overwhelmed me was that of surprise—profound wonder. It seemed as if all picture-admiration, before, had been of one sort, but this of another and higher,—the result of instant conversion, if the expression be not irreverent. The number of pictures—the great number of good pictures!—not stuff to fill up,—but noble, enchanting pieces, some of vast size, of wonderful brilliancy, of novel subjects, in positions the most favorable for the finest effect,—all this filled me with exquisite surprise. Can you imagine the feelings which you would have, if, after all the flowers you have seen, you should, in a chance drive, unexpectedly come into some mountain-pass, and find the sides far up perfectly overspread with flowers, the most beautiful and new, of all forms, of every color, of fragrance surpassing any hitherto found, of every size, and so growing that one set off another, and all of them spread abroad on ruby rocks, with diamonds, and every precious stone, gleaming out between the leaves! In some such way did I stand surprised when first in these grand galleries.

This surprise soon changed to a more complex pleasure. It was not the enjoyment of color, alone; nor of form, nor of the composition, nor of the sentiment of the pieces, but a harmony of pleasure from all of these. The walls beam upon you as if each was a summer; and, like one strolling at summer's eve, you can not tell whether it be the clouds, the sky, the light, the shadows, the scenery, or the thousand remembrances which rise over the soul in such an hour, that give the pleasure.

I saw all that the painter painted, and more; I imagined in each scene (for the most were pictures of human forms) what had gone before, and what had followed. I talked with the beautiful or fearful creatures, and they spake to me. As I gradually journeyed down the gallery, the sense of multitudinous beauty increased, and all that I had seen and all that I was seeing seemed to *run together* and form a bewildering sense of tropical luxuriance of conception and execution. There was that same individuality of picture that there is of trees in a forest; and yet, like trees, each picture seemed to extend its branches into others, so that there was a unity—a forest.

The sense of beauty—beauty of every kind—of form, feature, expression, attitude, intent, grouping—beauty of drawing, of coloring, of each thing by itself, and of all together—was inexpressible.

After a time this passed away, and I began to select one and another picture for special examination. They contested with each other for supremacy in my regard. One is sustained for a longer time under a degree of attention and high excitement, than you could have supposed it possible. Hour after hour passes, and no sense of exhaustion warns you of time. Joy, and the higher powers of pleasurable excitement, I think have no such thing as *time.* Poets have sung this of love. But I am conscious now that it is a fact of all intense and pure excitements that have in them a loving spiritual element.

I could not tell whether hours or minutes were passing. It was a blessed exhalation of soul, in which I seemed freed from matter and, as a diffused intelligence, to float in the atmosphere. I could not believe that a dull body was the center from which thought and emotion radiated. I had a sense of expansion, of etherealization, which gave me some faint sense of a spiritual state. Nor was I in a place altogether unfitted for such a state. The subjects of many of the works—suffering, heroic resistance, angels, Arcadian scenes, especially the scenes of Christ's life and death—seemed a not unfitting accompaniment to my mind, and suggested to me, in a glorious vision, the drawing near of a redeemed soul to the precincts of Heaven! O, with what an outburst of soul did I implore Christ to wash me and all whom I loved in His precious blood, that we might not fail of entering the glorious city, whose builder and maker is God! All my sins seemed not only *sins*, but great deformities. They seemed not merely affronts against God, but insults to my own nature. My soul snuffed at them, and trod them down as the mire in the street. Then, holy and loving thoughts toward God or toward man, seemed to me to be as beautiful as those fleecy islets along the west at sunset, crowned with glory; and the gentler aspirations for goodness and nobleness and knowledge seemed to me like silvery mists through which the morning is striking, wafting them gently and in wreaths and films heavenward. Great deeds, heroism for worthy objects, for God or for one's fellows, or for one's own purity, seemed not only natural, but as things without which a soul could not live.

But at length I perceived myself exhausted, not by

any sense of fatigue (I had no sense or body), but by perceiving that my mind would not fix upon material objects, but strove to act by itself. Thus, a new picture was examined only for an instant, and then I exhaled into all kinds of golden dreams and visions.

I left the gallery, and in this mood, as I threaded my way back, how beautiful did every thing and every body seem! The narrow streets were beautiful for being narrow, and the broad ones for being broad; old buildings had their glory, and new structures had theirs; children were all glorified children; I loved the poor workmen that I saw in the confined and narrow shops; the various women, young and old, with huge buck-baskets, or skipping hither and thither on errands, all seemed happy, and my soul blessed them as I passed. My own joy of being, overflowed upon every thing which I met. Sometimes, singing to myself or smiling to others, so as to make men think, doubtless, that I had met some good luck, or was on some prosperous errand of love, I walked on through street after street, turning whichever corner, to the right or left, happened to please the moment, neither knowing nor caring where I went, but always finding something to see, and enjoying all things. Nor do I know yet by what instinct I rounded up my journeyings by finding my proper lodging. That night I slept, as to my body, but felt little difference between dreaming asleep and dreaming awake.

And now I dare say you will all of you criticise such a wild way of examining pictures. You will pronounce it most unphilosophical, rendering one liable to admire without discrimination or justice. But in things that respect the feelings, no man is sane who does not know how to be *insane* on proper occasions! As to a critical judgment, or technical study of pictures upon a first visit, I should as soon think of reading my wife's letter as a grammarian, or of looking at a rose sent me for a token of love, with the eye of a mere botanist. To make my *first* visit to a gallery of paintings a process of studying causes, instead of experiencing effects, would be to throw away an exquisite pleasure, and one which omitted could never be recalled. Only once in a man's life can he be or see what I have been or seen. There is but ONE *first time* to any thing; and he is foolish indeed that squanders it by giving himself to analysis, instead of yielding himself to sympathy and enthusiasm; and the more artless and unashamed his enjoyment, the better. The first merit of pictures is the effect which they can produce upon the mind;—and the first step of a sensible man should be to receive involuntary effects from them. Pleasure and inspiration first, analysis afterward. The more perfectly one can abandon himself, the more true he can be to his real feelings and impressions, the wiser he is. It is a glorious thing to have a freshet in the soul! To have the better feelings overflow their banks and carry out of the channel all the dull obstructions of ordinary life. It reveals us to ourselves. It augments the sense of being. In these higher moods of feeling there is intuitional moral instruction, to the analysis of which the intellect comes afterward with slow steps. Therefore, I said to the pictures, "I am here; I am yours; do what you will with me; I am here to be intoxicated." My feelings opened out to them as flowers upon a southward slope would open to the morning sun, letting its stimulation develop whatever was in them to be developed. They took me at my word, and such another revel—such an ethereal intoxication, drunk from the cup of heavenly beauty, I shall not have again, until I drink that new wine of the Kingdom of Heaven!

Gallery of Paintings at the Luxembourg.

I have come again to spend the day here. If I feel that I can express any of the thoughts which rise and which would interest you, I will do it. But they will be detached. For when any view or thought springs up, I shall stop upon the spot and dash it down as it first lives in me.

Did you ever, after very dear friends, with whom all the sympathies of your heart were affiliated, had left places in which you and they had lived much in a short time, experience a gentle, serene happiness, and stroll about—*sorry and glad* that they were gone—feeling their presence in every thing, and having from every object around you a bright emanation of remembrance of them? Well, then you know, not *how* I feel to-day, in this gallery, but you know the *direction* in which to imagine it. I am calm, happy, full of sympathy—but rational—piercingly appreciative—and yet, there is everywhere a second sense, or bright over-current of remembrance of the golden joys of my first visit. The visit of day before yesterday seems like the guardian angel of to-day's visit—a spirit hovering round its charge!

It is surprising to what an extent one may learn his own mental peculiarities in such a gallery, by remarking the pictures which affect him most, and those, equally good, and better as works of art, from which he turns soon and carelessly. I do not feel attracted by pictures which express *only* veneration, nor by those which express unmingled sorrow, or horror, or fear. There is here a noble painting, by Scheffer, of a distant battle between the Turks and Suliot Greeks, and the near figures composed of the Suliot women witnessing the defeat of their husbands and parents, and resolving to cast themselves down from the high rocks on which they are grouped. I can not look at it for a moment. There are eighteen women, exhibiting very different effects of grief, and three beautiful children in the group;—when is *not* a child beautiful? I linger upon these little fellows more than upon all the rest.

In another picture, by Delorme, Hector reproaches Paris for not going out to the war, but living in effeminate enjoyment with Helen. She is the center figure, the very impersonation of light, simple, confiding love; not the deep, silent love, but the laughing, childlike affection. She is disrobed the one half, with gossamer about one arm, and a delicate cherry-colored robe about her loins and limbs. Hector stands on the left, his back to the light, so that his face and whole front are in the shadow of his own body, enhancing the expression of high honorable reproach conveyed by his face, position, and full apparel of arms. Paris, stung by his words, has risen up hastily from dalliance with Helen, and is striding away, wearing an expression of shame and honorable resolve upon a face which yet retains, in part, the recent sweetness of love. He tears a chaplet of flowers from his head; and a thin filmy scarf, which his forward motion luckily entangles, sweeps upon him judiciously, just in time to save him from being quite naked. A statue of Venus in the dim, but light background, a fan of peacock's feathers in her hand, falling upon her right shoulder, a couch behind with a leopard's skin upon it, sufficiently indicate the auspices under which they hitherto had dwelt.

Romans during the Decline.—This picture alone is larger than the whole side of one of our parlors, measuring about thirty feet by twenty, and contains thirty-five figures larger than life size. It represents a luxurious Roman banquet, in its last stages; flowers, roses, princely and gorgeous garments of Tyrian dye, lie on the marble table in front; a couch and table extend the whole length of the portico, which is open to the air on the far side, from which the light comes. The whole indicates the utmost luxury of dress—which, however, seems to have very little to do with their bodies—and the utmost abandonment to wine and pleasure. The men are in every stage of intoxication—some being carried out by slaves—some asleep on the floor, or dozing at the table—some drinking wine—some kissing their beautiful neighbors, who are profusely scattered through the picture in every conceivable condition, except decent ones. It is full of nakedness, lust, and drunken revelry. There is an air of earnestness about the whole, of an utter abandonment of themselves, soul and body, to revelry, that makes the effect awful. This is hightened by powerful accessories. The vast building, a fruit of old Roman greatness of conception; the statues of the noble Romans of other days standing up in gigantic size against the background, and two noble, virtuous and indignant Romans, on one side, who are looking in, ashamed and heart-faint at the beastliness of their countrymen—these give such an effect to the whole, that one can not help feeling his indignation rising against the luxurious wretches. The utmost breath of sensuous pleasure excites not one sympathy in you for the pleasure, but you mourn for the state which is cankered and destroyed by such citizens.

O, what a noble, melancholy picture is the next, by Delaroche—the Death of Elizabeth, Queen of England. I never before have seen a death-scene *painted* that equaled the occasion. But what can I say more of a picture, in which *Elizabeth* is dying, Cecil trying to comfort her, her nobles and chief women being present, than that it *more* than equals the imagination? It lifts it up

—it gives it to know, as it never did before, what such a scene must have been! I will describe it if I get home —language may indicate the ideas, but never the coloring, the strength of the figures, the depth of the whole thing. It was hardly more real, in life, than on the canvas.

I never before realized the right effect of *size* in pictures. Large canvas conveys something which is more than the mere figures—there is a sense of reality in things of life-size, or even greater than the natural, which does not belong to and can not be conveyed by under-sizes.

I have finished—six hours are gone—from ten to four —the gallery closes, and I look probably for the last time on these treasures of the living French Artists! Well, many of these pictures I shall continue to see as long as I live. By the help of some of them I believe I shall preach better hereafter.

Being all new pictures, that is, not fifty years old, they have a great freshness of color, which is both a help and a hindrance. It gives vividness to them, but then there is lacking that subdued mellowness that age gives to pictures.

I think, of the artists which I have seen thus far, these are the best, and in this order, Vernet, Delaroche, Scheffer, Schnetz, Delorme. It is hard to decide between the first two. I suppose Vernet *is* the better, but I certainly like the two pictures of Delaroche—the Death of Elizabeth, and another without name—far better.

I am heartily tired of French nakedness. Their second-rate painters seem to abhor nothing so much as linen. I think myself not to be fastidious in such things. I am willing always to see the human form sculptured or painted when it seems to subserve a good purpose. If it be natural that it should under such and such circumstances be disrobed, I do not turn away from it, provided the sentiment is noble, and predominates to such a degree as to make the condition of the figure a secondary and scarcely perceived affair. But, so to paint women, that, against the propriety of the thing (to say nothing of morals), you admire *beauty* instead of following the sentiment; or to select subjects which require effeminacy and luxury, and corresponding representatives, is too bad. I am sick of naked harems. The Turk refuses a sight of his women even when dressed. The French are courteous to the other extreme. I could not help feeling, at length, and not alone of this gallery, that a yard of linen would be, of itself, almost an object of beauty; and quite original, too, as an idea of art, among a certain class of French painters.

But enough of this. You are yawning by this time, and wishing my gallery, painters, and writer too, in Jericho—for dullness—and I will stop. Perhaps I may add a chapter to-morrow.

V.

THE LOUVRE.

PARIS.

HERE am I, in the Gallery of Statues. I shall jot down, here and there, notes of my impressions, and if they do not interest you, skip them and save them for *me;* for I can not write in my private note-book many things which I wish to remember.

How strange is the feeling which subdues one in the presence of this vast collection—thousands of statues, brought from Rome and adjacent places, and made in the best days of her greatness. Here is a Jupiter made when men *believed* in his power; here are Cesars carved when that name made the world tremble; here are Bacchus, Venus, Apollo, Minerva, centaurs, cupids, nymphs, vestals, and they are almost to me as if they lived; because I feel that *when they were made,* they were, to the age, realities, and not mythological, as they are to us. Besides, these marbles once represented the mind and heart of the world. What mighty changes have rolled over the globe since the day when not to believe and to worship these, and such as these, was infidelity! Since then, they have fallen from the niches and pedestals—have been buried in ruin. They slept awhile; the world wrought and grew, and at length, secure for centuries, they are dug out and reërected. But how changed—not they, but we; now, only a fool or some poet-mad creature worships. One, in looking at them, feels a dim and misty history of this long period and its changes rising before him, and filling his soul with a strange somber joy and sadness.

Every statue of *Trajan* is alike in representing his head *low* in the moral region, very large perceptives and very small reflectives, full in the sides, back and top.

All the heads of Augustus are good, and the face noble. It is the face of a *man*—genius and frank good-heartedness.

The head of Demosthenes, as here carved, is not remarkable; language small; brow good, but not commanding; equally developed in perceptive and reflective faculties—not such an one as I imagined.

One easily reads the condition of women in the most refined days and nations of antiquity, in the idealization of them in statues. In this respect the French painters are like the ancients;—grace, extreme physical beauty, and an inviting softness of expression, characterize their women. But genius, intelligence, nobleness of purity, and that capacity for loving which wins admiration but awes familiarity—these attributes, in which *we* conceive of woman, do not belong to the statues, as they probably did not belong to the living women that sculptors knew, in antiquity, or to the ideal conceptions of them. Women are a new race, recreated since the world received Christianity. I *feel*, in this gallery, among these memorials, what it would be to go back to the time before Christianity enlightened the world.

All the heads of Venus are finer in profile than in

front. Contrary to my expectation, the greatest number of statues of Venus, as a divinity, are anything but voluptuous. Her freaks, in the fabulous histories, were surely wanton enough; but the ancients evidently had a conception of her which we do not at all take in. As the divinity *of new life;* of *fresh existence;* and so of yet unstained purity. We must separate in our minds the Venus of pleasure from the more purely and poetically conceived Venus. Youth, beauty, hope, and health, characterize her. If this ideal be separated from the grosser associations, it is not wanting in beauty. I am greatly but agreeably disappointed in the statues of Venus.

I have often heard of grand stairs; but with us, stairs are such matters of mere convenience that I had no conception of the architectural effects of which they are susceptible. For, when a space larger than the whole of two such houses as yours is devoted to them, and they are twelve or fifteen feet broad, and broken every twenty steps by a platform, surrounded by columns, decorated with vases and carved sides, and they run to such a length as to form a grand vista, narrowing in the distance, they are among the most striking objects which you will see.

Painted Ceilings.—The fact is that *we* have no ceilings to paint, ours being low, circumscribed, and without grandeur. But when you have domes that swell above your head almost like the heavenly vault, and vast but diversified ranges of ceilings, you feel the propriety of covering them with every device. The richness of the compartments, and the complexity of the borders, the innumerable figures, the inexhaustible fertility of subjects, and the neck-breaking weariness of trying to look straight up long enough to enjoy them—these things one must experience to understand or appreciate. But so much richer in interest are the things around, that I can look at ceilings but in passing. One feels, however, how grand a field it gives to an artist—such an unobstructed space! And when the rooms are, like these, each devoted to a given purpose, the artist by some allegorical painting gives to the ceiling the name and character of the collections. Thus the hall where I write, and the room just left, are called from Herculaneum and Pompeii. In the first room, the ceiling represents the genii of the arts under the form of women, quite beautiful and quite nude, looking with pleasure upon a youth, who represents Charles X., the collector of these treasures. Still more appropriately in this room of the destroyed cities, the artist represents the presiding goddess, or rather represents the cities that were destroyed, under the form of beautiful goddesses, who sit sadly upon the awful sides of the mountain, which already is lurid with eruption, and from whose fiery summit-gulf the dark and angry god of fire is rushing forth to destroy.

In the Egyptian saloon, little winged spirits draw a drapery from before a throne on which sits a beautiful majestic Egyptian princess; at her feet are symbols of Art and Religion, and, receding in the distance, are seen the dim summits of the pyramids; while Art and

Learning are advancing toward her as if surprised by the discovery.

One soon begins to feel, in examining such an endless gallery of representations as this, how little he knows minutely and accurately, even of the most familiar things in nature. The range of subjects covers almost the whole ground of human knowledge. One must be multifariously learned to follow the painter even superficially. But when we reflect that each artist—men of signal genius and intelligence—devoted their lives to the minute study of the topics which they represent, it appears plain that, in details, their pictures *ought to be* beyond the criticism of most men. I can criticise a floral picture; but the dogs and game of Desportes, which nearly fill one room, are perfectly life-like, and every time I look I see some new excellence and it grows to wonder; and the exact knowledge of the painter, the close observation, the minute study of the minutest things, all impress me with a feeling of how much there is in the least thing that God has made. In some respects, God's works are more surprising to us through the imitations of men than in themselves.

We pass to another saloon—filled with the works of Lesuer, Rigaud, Mignard, and Claude Lorraine. The ceiling represents, with exquisite beauty and effect, the popular love of art in their age. A noble statue, a man pounced upon by a lion, has just been opened in the public grounds, and crowds are assembled to inspect it. Doubtless many of the faces are portraits. The variety of expressions of face, indicating the effects of a fine work of art on different dispositions, is admirable. Then as to position and drapery, and intensely rich colors and contrasts, it is wonderful. These ceilings grow on me. But, O, my neck!

Who that has read at all has not read of Claude's sunsets? At length I see them with my own eyes! The whole air is full of ether-gold! There are other artists who put more color into their pictures—into the trees, the forms, the clouds. He puts it into the *atmosphere.* Every thing is then bathed and suffused with *its* glow.

It is two hours since I wrote the above. My mind refused to reproduce in writing its thoughts long before it was too much wearied to enjoy. But now I am only half through the gallery, and am utterly exhausted. I can neither feel, think, nor look. There are Murillos, Titians, Carraccis, and others of equal note; but I see only a vast wilderness of color, and the sense of beauty, jaded and sated, sinks under the burden. If you average these saloons, each one is larger than the gallery of the New York *Art Union* (single saloon). There are forty-four saloons! Five or six only are devoted to cabinets of coins, etc., and the rest to pictures! Yet, nearly a half of the collection is shut up and can not be seen until the improvements are completed in the saloons where the pictures are to hang! Only think of nearly eighty saloons of pictures classified into the French, Italian, Flemish, German, English and Ancient Schools! But this does not include the *basement,* devoted to marble statuary, or the upper story devoted to marine models of ships, engines, etc., etc. Such is the Louvre!

DOVER CLIFFS, *Friday morning,* 7 *o'clock, August* 23, 1850.—I am sitting upon the very edge of these cliffs which Shakspeare has made memorable! Dover lies at the base, and its sounds rise up to me through the long distance. The channel is spotted with sails—the sun shines mistily—the air is mild, and hardly a breath waves the harebells which grow round me. I pluck from the very edge of the cliff, where they have looked below and above, and felt every wind of summer, three delicate flowers for you, for Shakspeare's sake and for my own. Four doves flying far up have just alighted near me on the brink; had I their wings I would soon prove the ocean deeps, not of water but of ether! O, how sweet it is again to hear one's mother tongue, even when spoken by strangers! I blessed even the everlasting waiter dunning me for fees, because he asked in English, and overpaid him. But how could I have contained myself had the greeting been from tried friends! Hastily snatching a morsel of food, needed after an all-night journey from Paris, I determine to stand a moment on the highest cliff—and to leave in my letter a little memorial of it. Imagine me standing up against the clear blue sky and waving my hand, as I do heartily, to you and yours, both a good morning and a farewell from Dover! Good bye—I hasten down lest I lose the train—and with it my very amiable mood!

VI.

LONDON NATIONAL GALLERY.

LONDON.

WE often suppose, in the heat and noise and weariness of the city, that could we find retirement among cool shades, amid flowers and trees, by brooks or airy mountains, we should *rest.* So we should if we could carry with us our friends, or else leave behind and forget our friendships! But even with our friends about us in the city, we are wearied by the noise and endless excitement. In seclusion, without our friends, we are soon wearied by the trouble that rises up *within.* But could friends go with us into the quiet of rural life, that were the highest reach of earthly happiness.

The long discontinuance of regular occupation, produces sadness and depression, by a sense of personal waste and worthlessness, which makes the day long and life almost a burden. I am less able to dispose of my Sabbaths than any other part of my time; partly, because they are days that always bring up the remembrances of childhood to me—the days of stillness and brightness which used to visit me when young, in Litchfield, and possess me with visions and dreams, or reveries and imaginations, which I did not then understand. But, aside from these associations, the Sabbath, for more than fifteen years, has been a day of intense activity, of the highest mental and moral excitement. Now I am idle:

I seem like a broken-stemmed flower that the river has cast up on the bank, and that lies there, seeing the stream go past, but itself lying still. Or rather like a branch wrenched off from its stock, and drifted and drifting without aim or rest. I seem a useless thing. I quite envy men that have capacity to do anything. To be sure, I have a latent pride that would not allow others to treat me as if they thought so too. But when I am by myself, or sauntering about the streets, or in church, I feel as if I were much like a thistle-down in a bright summer's day, that neither lifts up into the air nor settles down, but floats here and there as chance may blow it,—and no one will ask to-morrow (who saw it to-day), Where is it? So that I find a man, out of his associations and life-connections, to be little better than an odd wheel of a machine, good for nothing without its fellows.

Now, too, I am apt, if I do not fall asleep soon enough,—or more frequently when I wake, hours before it is the fashion here to get up,—to lie and think over my way of life hitherto; and my life-work seems to me to have been so little and so poorly done, that I feel discouraged at the thought of resuming it! I have, everywhere, in my travelings,—at the shrine of the martyrs in Oxford, at the graves of Bunyan and Wesley in London, at the vault in which Raleigh was for twelve years confined in the Tower, asked myself whether *I* could have done and endured what they did, and *as* they did! It is enough to make one tremble for himself, to have such a heart-sounding as this gives him.

I cast the lead for the depth of my soul, and it strikes bottom so soon that I have little reason for pride.

Had it not been for paintings, flowers, trees, and landscapes, I do not know what I should have done with myself. Often, when extremely depressed, I have gone to the parks or out of the city to some quiet ground, where I could find a wooded stream, and the wood filled with birds, and found, almost in a moment, a new spirit coming over me. I was rid of *men*—almost of myself. I seemed to find a sacred sweetness and calmness, not coming *over* me but *into* me. I seemed nearer to Heaven. I felt less sadness about life, for God would take care of it; and my own worthlessness, too, became a source of composure; for, on that very account, it made little difference in the world's history whether I lived or died. God worked, it seemed to me, upon a scale so vast and rich in details, that anything and anybody could be spared, and not affect the results of life. There is such a view of the sufficiency of God as to make your own littleness and feebleness a source of very true and grateful pleasure. What if this or that flower perishes, is the summer bereaved? A single leaf plucked from the oak makes no difference. What if I should die abroad? A shock it would be to many,—but in a month's time only a few would *feel it.* In a year, and perhaps half-a-dozen only out of the world's crew would have a thought or a sadness about it. The ship would sail merrily on. Yea, my own children, elastic with youth, would, soonest of any, grow past regret; and the two or three who clung to the broken reed, would themselves soon come on and greet me in Heaven! How wisely is this so. There were no end to grief, and no room for joy, if we carried all the accumulated troubles of life with undiminished sensibility from year to year. First we bury friends, then time buries our grief.

How often and often have I blessed God for the treasures and dear comforts of his *natural world!* Shall I ever be grateful enough for TREES! Yet, without doubt, better trees there might be than even the most noble and beautiful now. I suppose God has, in His thoughts, much better ones than he has ever planted on this globe. They are reserved for the glorious land. Beneath them may we walk!

NATIONAL GALLERY, LONDON.

I have now seen so many pictures, here and on the continent, by the greatest masters, ancient and modern, that my mind begins to inter-compare them. Every painter of note has a holy family—a Madonna, a Christ and John, a Crucifixion, a Descent from the Cross, and a Magdalen. Often, the same artist has several on the same subject: two I have seen this morning, a Magdalen by Guido, in the British Institution, and another is before me here, and a much finer one. In the fact that so many painters engage upon the same subject, I find a secondary pleasure of no small degree, *i. e.* in comparing the pictures of each with the other. If I could only retain in my mind all that I have seen, and have an *interior* gallery of the memory, it seems to me that I should be enriched for life. The finest head of a youthful Christ is one by Guido. He is apparently about fifteen or sixteen years of age. Without at all resembling those countenances which you see of Raphael, he is yet of the same style of face. It is full of youth and love, calm yet vivacious, with a look of dignity THAT IS TO BE. He is looking upon John (Baptist), who, with a swarthier and more rugged face, but suffused with reverence and love commingled, is gazing also upon Christ, and putting one hand upon his shoulder. There is another picture by *Leonardo da Vinci*, representing Christ disputing with the Doctors. It is only half-length, small, Christ's head and bust in the center, and two heads on each side. Christ is speaking apparently to you, and not to them, with his hands before him, the forefinger of his right hand upon the tip of the middle finger of his left, as if making a point of argument. The painting is beautiful, the expression exceedingly serene, soft, yet sagacious. Yet, it is not Christ; but one imagines that Guido's *is*, or might have been.

Indeed, in almost all the heads of Christ which I have seen, there is much to admire but nothing to satisfy. They are more than human, but not divine. They carry you up a certain distance, but then leave you unsatisfied. If they are majestic, they are stern; if severe, they are flat and expressionless; if loving, they are effeminate. Many of them, by old masters, are absolutely *shaggy* and repulsive. There has been but one which I felt to be even an approximation; but I have, in the ocean of pictures, lost trace of it, and can not recall the painter. You may well suppose that in Roman Catholic countries this subject would be universally tried by the pencil. A very large gallery made up only of pictures of Christ might be collected; and, on some accounts, it would not be a thing amiss.

I have before me an admirable piece by *Garcia*—a dead Christ. He lies at full length across the knees of his mother, his lower extremities sustained by an angel, who, gazing at his feet, is evidently full of the *past;* his head is lovingly upheld by another angel, whose bright and almost smiling face is full of the *future;* while his mother wears the perfect expression of deep, inward, maternal anguish; not the grief which outbursts, but the still grief which suffocates and kills. The face of Christ is very noble: it has the severest wisdom, a divine intelligence, a sweet, placid endurance. But it lacks that suffusion of love, from which all these other expressions should seem to spring. It is this that *was* true of Christ, and it is this that all pictures lack. Love was the true nature of Christ. It was love that sent, that animated, that sustained him. Only because of his great loving did he become a man of sorrow. All other qualities must spring from that. That must be the atmosphere, and other expressions must be bathed in it. It is this very element that painters have failed to depict. It was not possible for it to be otherwise. The world's idea of Christ was crude and partial; and the part which was entertained was magisterial.

Veneration—in an age of veneration, when worship was only or mostly reverential, and not through justification by a faith which *works by love*—naturally sought to produce a kingly head of the Saviour—a head that should express purity, wisdom, patience, loftiness. But these should have been the adjuncts of Love. Therefore, it not being so, I feel an aching want in the presence of every representation. The youthful Christ of Guido is the nearest to my wish, and will live in my remembrance.

At times I can not but be deeply moved by these pictures of the Saviour. I seem really to stand in his presence. I feel overwhelmed with unworthiness. It seems as if my inmost soul were known to him, my secret sins were spread before him, and I hardly dared to look up. I know that he will forgive them—but will he deliver me from them? It is not a want of faith in Christ for the past that I lack—but, O, that I might have a Christ who should assure me of rescue and purity in every period of life to come! All my life I have seen what was holy, just and good; and all my life, that which I would be is so far beyond what I am, and seemingly must be, that the struggle seems well nigh useless, and Death is invoked as the only effectual deliverer.

O! what a riches of enjoyment must there be to those that have such galleries to resort to at leisure, and in all their different moods. It is impossible to be *omni-mooded*, and yet without this it is not possible to be in sympathy with all the subjects; and unless you *are* you can not rightly behold them. Could I come when sadness prevails, single out a few and feed upon them,—and come again when love and joy predominated, and select such as that inspiration craved,—and come again when feelings of reverence would make it easy to enter into the conceptions of old masters, and so on through all the variations of the mind's estate,—how rich an addition would such galleries be to the refined enjoyments of life. But now I am always hastening and always haunted with the feeling that I may never see them again; that I must omit nothing which I should regret afterward; and so one picture destroys another, and my mind, like a daguerreotype process, constantly interrupted, is not a gallery of distinct impressions, but for the most part a recess of gorgeous confusion. Yet I have reaped much. I shall be able to think many things and preach many things which otherwise had been impossible.

Correggio.—His *name* was always familiar, but I have learned to love his pictures. Before me is his "*Ecce Homo,*" or Christ crowned with thorns, delivered up by Pilate. The painting, merely, is exquisite. The expression of Christ is that of weariness and drooping under suffering. It is too human. I do not see the God shining through and bearing up under sorrow. The *Satan* of Milton could endure! And if we can not but admire the infernal heroism, how much more do we demand it to meet our conception of a God! His mother, fainting, is falling into the arms of John. I had felt a contempt for this picture from having seen some engravings of it, in which the face of Mary was pleasure-loving, almost voluptuous; but in the *painting* it is that of intense love yet lingering on a mother's face *in a swoon,* and is rarely and exquisitely beautiful.

How different, how violent the contrast between this and the next of his pieces, and one of the finest of his pencil: Cupid instructed by Mercury under the auspices of Venus. Nothing can be rounder, softer, and more beautiful than every figure here. Mercury is full of arch sagacity, as if inwardly laughing at what he is doing; Cupid has the slyest mirth all over his face, as if almost ready to burst into laughter at the mischiefs in prospect, while Venus at full length by his side, holding his bow, entirely nude, seems—I do not know how, neither arch, nor mirthful, nor voluptuous, but all of them!

RUBENS.—There are here not a few specimens of the works of this artist. He was twice married, and his *second* wife he seems to have loved entirely, as she is forced into almost every picture which contains a female face. Thus, in the decision of Paris, when he awarded the apple to the handsomest of all the goddesses, Venus has his wife's face. In the fine allegorical picture of Peace and War, the central figure is his wife. In the abduction of the Sabine women, a fine Roman has had the luck to get *his* wife, the finest woman of the crowd. In that noble picture, the Brazen Serpent, the prominent female figure is his wife again; and in the Holy Family he has painted not only her again, but all his family. This fondness for his wife is amiable enough; but it redounds to the credit of his heart more than to the fertility of his fancy I soon am tired of his women. They are so well fed, and have so amazingly thriven on their food. They are not alone plump, but fat. Therefore you may imagine that one less sensitive than I to the ridiculous would feel how ludicrous is one little thing of his entitled an *Apotheosis,* in which the warrior, about to become divine, is lying all abroad in the air with his armor on, his booted feet sprawling wide apart, and himself sustained by five or six angelic forms, whose solidity makes the idea of *floating* even, still more of *rising*—and that too with such a dumpish jackanapes in tow—supremely laughable.

CUYP.—I have been particularly struck with the landscapes, both here and at Paris, of this artist, and had compared him to *Claude* in the margin of my catalogue; and was pleased, this morning, at finding the same sentence in the descriptive catalogue of the National Gallery. I know so little about painting that when by any perception or sympathy I judge as I ought to, and as masters have done who both *feel* and *know* better than I, it certainly gives me pleasure.

The portraits from the hand of Rembrandt and of Vandyke, are almost as interesting to look long at, as a group of figures or a landscape. I can not tell you, who have not seen them, what it is that arrests the eye, and fixes it upon a simple *head,* perhaps of an imaginary person. But if you were to see one, you would appreciate it.

When I read the criticisms of eminent artists, I perceive how many things there are in painting of which I knew nothing—things which are known only by *education*—as in literature, the graces, the style, the delicate shades of thought, the richest beauties, are those which the untutored do not grasp, and which we appreciate only after long familiarity. Some few of these things I begin to find struggling for a birth in my mind; and I have a feeling that, had I the opportunity, I could soon grow wise. But now, when I have the pictures, I have no leisure to read such works as would greatly assist me; and by and by, when I have the leisure and the books, I shall not have the pictures! Well, one can not be everything! Yet, at times, I rebel at the thoughts of how much in the world lies within the grasp of my industry, and yet that I should live a mere nothing!

I visited the Vernon collection also to-day. I do not by any means enjoy it as I do the National Gallery. Yet it possesses treasures, which at home would be counted precious wonders. I saw the originals of the engravings which have enriched the London Art-Union Journal for several years past.

Nothing can exceed the minute accuracy of the painting, or the very life and spirit of animals, to be found in Landseer's paintings. Fine as the engravings are, they no more express the merit of the canvas, than the canvas expresses the actual vitality of dogs and deer.

I was delighted with Wilkie's pictures; for example, Reading the News, The Piper; and, in the National Gallery, The Penny Wedding, The Blind Fiddler, The Village Festival, etc.

Such of Turner's pictures as I saw were utterly displeasing to me. I rejoiced over Gainsborough, a copy of one of whose little landscapes, you will remember, I have. Ettey's paintings seemed all tinsel to me—skin—skin, without depth or thought, just such things on canvas as we find engraved in ladies' magazines for fashions. Ah, how I wished that I might own, or have within reach, the young female figures of *Greuze*—a French painter. I never saw such sweetness, innocence, and simplicity of character. They are not at all insipid, as innocence usually is, at least on canvas.

Teniers and Ostade are names which are almost words of description with novelists and descriptive writers, and it was pleasant to me to see a few of their works. Such as I saw were very close and smooth imitations of natural objects.

Poussin always seemed cold and stiff to me, and I could not persuade myself to look upon his pictures. They chilled me, or tended to check good spirits.

As this letter is a sort of Charivari, I may as well stop my comment upon pictures, and tell some of my rambles. I visited the graves of Wesley, Watson, and Adam Clarke; and opposite to the yard where they lie, in Bunhill fields, the graves of Wesley's mother, of Dr. Owen, Dr. Watts, and, what was more than all to me, John Bunyan! Think of the difference, in their day, of this poor tinker, and the notable bishops and lords. But now I feel insulted, or rather I feel worried and annoyed, to see the worthless names of men who were in their life great by the outside only or chiefly;—while

I feel inspired and blessed to stand by the spot which bears the names of such men as Bunyan and Wesley! Such as they are the *true* men! Their own day knew them not. The world could not know them until the breadth of their fame was developed by time. On yesterday I visited Cripplegate church—in which Ben Jonson was married—Oliver Cromwell, also—where Fox, the martyrologist, is buried. But it was not for these that I went, but to have the privilege of standing upon the stone beneath which are the ashes of John Milton! I found the street where he lived. The place on which his house stood was afterwards a bear garden, then a brewery, then a theater, then a Methodist chapel, and now is built again into dwelling-houses!

EXPERIENCES OF NATURE.

EXPERIENCES OF NATURE.

I.

A DISCOURSE OF FLOWERS.

HAPPY is the man that loves flowers! Happy, even if it be a love adulterated with vanity and strife. For human passions nestle in flower-lovers too. Some employ their zeal chiefly in horticultural competitions, or in the ambition of floral shows. Others love flowers as curiosities, and search for novelties, for "sports," and vegetable monstrosities. We have been led through costly collections by men whose chief pleasure seemed to be in the effect which their treasures produced on others, not on themselves. Their love of flowers was only the love of being praised for having them. But there is a choice in vanities and ostentations. A contest of roses is better than of horses. We had rather be vain of the best tulip, dahlia, or ranunculus, than of the best shot. Of all fools, a floral fool deserves the eminence.

But these aside, blessed be the man that really loves

flowers!—loves them for their own sakes, for their beauty, their associations, the joy they have given, and always will give; so that he would sit down among them as friends, and companions, if there was not another creature on earth to admire or praise them! But such men need no blessing of mine. They are blessed of God! Did He not make the world for such men? Are they not clearly the owners of the world, and the richest of all men?

It is the end of art to inoculate men with the love of nature. But those who have a passion for nature in the natural way, need no pictures nor galleries. Spring is their designer, and the whole year their artist.

He who only does not appreciate floral beauty is to be pitied like any other man who is born imperfect. It is a misfortune not unlike blindness. But men who contemptuously reject flowers as effeminate and unworthy of manhood, reveal a certain coarseness. Were flowers fit to eat or drink, were they stimulative of passions, or could they be gambled with like stocks and public consciences, they would take them up just where finer minds would drop them, who love them as revelations of God's sense of beauty, as addressed to the taste, and to something finer and deeper than taste, to that power within us which spiritualizes matter, and communes with God through His work, and not for their paltry market value.

Many persons lose all enjoyment of many flowers by indulging false associations. There be some who think that no *weed* can be of interest as a flower. But all flowers are weeds where they grow wildly and abundantly; and somewhere our rarest flowers are somebody's commonest. Flowers growing in noisome places, in desolate corners, upon rubbish, or rank desolation, become disagreeable by association. Roadside flowers, ineradicable, and hardy beyond all discouragement, lose themselves from our sense of delicacy and protection. And, generally, there is a disposition to undervalue *common* flowers. There are few that will trouble themselves to examine, minutely, a blossom that they have seen and neglected from their childhood; and yet if they would but question such flowers, and commune with them, they would often be surprised to find extreme beauty where it had long been overlooked.

If a plant be uncouth, it has no attractions to us simply because it has been brought from the ends of the earth and is a "great rarity;" if it has beauty, it is none the less, but a great deal more attractive to us, because it is common. A very common flower adds generosity to beauty. It gives joy to the poor, the rude, and to the multitudes who could have no flowers were nature to charge a price for her blossoms. Is a cloud less beautiful, or a sea, or a mountain, because often seen, or seen by millions?

At any rate, while we lose no fondness for eminent and accomplished flowers, we are conscious of a growing respect for the floral democratic throng. There is, for instance, the mullein, of but little beauty in each floweret, but a brave plant, growing cheerfully and heartily out of abandoned soils, ruffling its root about with broad-palmed, generous, velvet leaves, and erecting therefrom a towering spire that always inclines us to stop for a kindly look. This fine plant is left, by most people, like a decayed old gentleman, to a good-natured pity. But in other countries it is a *flower,* and called the "American velvet plant."

We confess to a homely enthusiasm for clover,—not the white clover, beloved of honey-bees,—but the red clover. It holds up its round, ruddy face and honest head with such rustic innocence! Do you ever see it without thinking of a sound, sensible, country lass, sun-browned and fearless, as innocence always should be? We go through a field of red clover, like Solomon in a garden of spices.

There is the burdock too, with its prickly rosettes, that has little beauty or value, except (like some kind, brown, good-natured nurses) as an amusement to children, who manufacture baskets, houses, and various marvelous utensils, of its burrs. The thistle is a prince. Let any man that has an eye for beauty take a view of the whole plant, and where will he see more expressive grace and symmetry; and where is there a more kingly flower? To be sure, there are sharp objections to it in a boquet. Neither is it a safe neighbor to the farm, having a habit of scattering its seeds like a very heretic. But most gardeners feel toward a thistle as boys toward a snake; and farmers, with more reason, dread it like a plague. But it is just as beautiful as if it were a universal favorite.

What shall we say of mayweed, irreverently called dog-fennel by some? Its acrid juice, its heavy pungent odor, make it disagreeable; and being disagreeable, its enormous Malthusian propensities to increase render it hateful to damsels of white stockings, compelled to walk through it on dewy mornings. Arise, O scythe, and devour it!

The buttercup is a flower of our childhood, and very brilliant in our eyes. Its strong color, seen afar off, often provoked its fate; for through the mowing-lot we went after it, regardless of orchard-grass and herd-grass, plucking down its long, slender stems crowned with golden chalices, until the father covetous of hay shouted to us, "Out of that grass! out of that grass! you rogue!"

The first thing that defies the frost in spring is the chickweed. It will open its floral eye and look the thermometer in the face at 32°; it leads out the snow-drop and crocus. Its blossom is diminutive: and no wonder, for it begins so early in the season that it has little time to make much of itself. But, as a harbinger and herald, let it not be forgotten.

You can not forget, if you would, those golden kisses all over the cheeks of the meadow, queerly called *dandelions*. There are many green-house blossoms less pleasing to us than these. And we have reached through many a fence, since we were incarcerated, like them, in a city, to pluck one of these yellow flower drops. Their passing away is more spiritual than their bloom. Nothing can be more airy and beautiful than

5

the transparent seed-globe—a fairy dome of splendid architecture.

As for marigolds, poppies, hollyhocks, and valorous sunflowers, we shall never have a garden without them, both for their own sake, and for the sake of old-fashioned folks, who used to love them. Morning-glories —or, to call them by their city name, the convolvulus —need no praising. The vine, the leaf, the exquisite vase-formed flower, the delicate and various colors, will secure it from neglect while taste remains. Grape blossoms and mignonnette do not appeal to the eye; and if they were selfish no man would care for them. Yet because they pour their life out in fragrance they are always loved, and, like homely people with noble hearts, they seem beautiful by association. Nothing that produces constant pleasure in us can fail to seem beautiful. We do not need to speak for that universal favorite—the rose! As a flower is the finest stroke of creation, so the rose is the happiest hit among flowers! Yet, in the feast of ever blooming roses, and of double roses, we are in danger of being perverted from a love of simplicity, as manifested in the wild, single rose. When a man can look upon the simple, wild rose and feel no pleasure, his taste has been corrupted.

But we must not neglect the blossoms of fruit-trees. What a great heart an apple-tree must have! What generous work it makes of blossoming! It is not content with a single bloom for each apple that is to be; but a profusion, a prodigality of blossom there must be.

The tree is but a huge boquet. It gives you twenty times as much as there is need for, and evidently because it loves to blossom. We will praise this virtuous tree. Not beautiful in form, often clumpy, cragged, and rude; but it is glorious in beauty when efflorescent. Nor is it a beauty only at a distance and in the mass. Pluck down a twig and examine as closely as you will; it will bear the nearest looking. The simplicity and purity of the white expanded flower, the half open buds slightly blushed, the little pink-tipped buds unopen, crowding up together like rosy children around an elder brother or sister, can any thing surpass it? Why here is a cluster more beautiful than any you can make up artificially even if you select from the whole garden! Wear this family of buds for my sake. It is all the better for being common. I love a flower that all may have; that belongs to the whole, and not to a select and exclusive few. Common, forsooth! a flower can not be worn out by much looking at, as a road is by much travel.

How one exhales, and feels his childhood coming back to him, when, emerging from the hard and hateful city streets, he sees orchards and gardens in sheeted bloom,—plum, cherry, pear, peach, and apple, waves and billows of blossoms rolling over the hill sides, and down through the levels! My heart runs riot. This is a kingdom of glory. The bees know it. Are the blossoms singing? or is all this humming sound the music of bees? The frivolous flies, that never seem to be thinking of any thing, are rather sober and solemn here. Such a sight is equal to a sunset, which is but a blossoming of the clouds.

We love to fancy that a flower is the point of transition at which a material thing touches the immaterial; it is the sentient vegetable soul. We ascribe dispositions to it; we treat it as we would an innocent child. A stem or root has no suggestion of life. A leaf advances toward it; and some leaves are as fine as flowers, and have, moreover, a grace of motion seldom had by flowers. Flowers have an expression of countenance as much as men or animals. Some seem to smile; some have a sad expression; some are pensive and diffident; others again are plain, honest, and upright, like the broad-faced sunflower and the hollyhock. We find ourselves speaking of them as laughing, as gay and coquettish, as nodding and dancing. No man of sensibility ever spoke of a flower as he would of a fungus, a pebble, or a sponge. Indeed, they are more life-like than many animals. We commune with flowers—we go to them if we are sad or glad; but a toad, a worm, an insect, we repel, as if real life was not half so real as imaginary life. What a pity flowers can utter no sound! A singing rose, a whispering violet, a murmuring honeysuckle! O, what a rare and exquisite miracle would these be.

When we hear melodious sounds,—the wind among trees, the noise of a brook falling down into a deep leaf-covered cavity—birds' notes, especially at night; children's voices as you ride into a village at dusk, far from your long absent home, and quite home-sick; or a flute heard from out of a forest, a silver sound rising up among silver-lit leaves, into the moon-lighted air; or the low conversations of persons whom you love, that sit at the fire in the room where you are convalescing;—when we think of these things we are apt to imagine that nothing is perfect that has not the gift of sound. But we change our mind when we dwell lovingly among flowers; for, they are always silent. Sound is never associated with them. They speak to you, but it is as the eye speaks, by vibrations of light and not of air.

It is with flowers as with friends. Many may be loved, but few much loved. Wild honeysuckles in the wood, laurel bushes in the very regality of bloom, are very beautiful to you. But they are color and form only. They seem strangers to you. You have no memories reposed in them. They bring back nothing from Time. They point to nothing in the future. But a wild-brier starts a genial feeling. It is the country cousin of the rose; and that has always been your pet. You have nursed it, and defended it; you have had it for companionship as you wrote; it has stood by your pillow while sick; it has brought remembrance to you, and conveyed your kindest feelings to others. You remember it as a mother's favorite; it speaks to you of your own childhood,—that white rosebush that snowed, in the corner, by the door; that generous bush that blushed red in the garden with a thousand flowers, whose gorgeousness was among the first things that drew your childish eye, and which always comes up before you when you speak of childhood. You remember, too, that your mother loved roses. As you walked to church she plucked off a bud and gave you, which you carried because you were proud to do as she did. You remember how, in the listening hour of sermon, her roses fell neglected on her lap—and how you slyly drew one and another of them; and how, when she came to, she looked for them under her handkerchief, and on the floor, until, spying the ill-repressed glee of your face, she smiled such a look of love upon you, as made a rose for ever after seem to you as if it smiled a mother's smile. And so a wild rose, a prairie rose, or a sweet-brier, that at evening fills the air with odor, (a floral nightingale whose song is perfume,) greets you as a dear and intimate friend. You almost wish to get out, as you travel, and inquire after their health, and ask if they wish to send any messages by you to their town friends.

But no flower can be so strange, or so new, that a friendliness does not spring up at once between you. You gather them up along your rambles; and sit down to make their acquaintance on some shaded bank with your feet over the brook, where your shoes feed their vanity as in a mirror. You assort them; you question their graces; you enjoy their odor; you range them on the grass in a row and look from one to another; you gather them up, and study a fit gradation of colors, and search for new specimens to fill the degrees between too violent extremes. All the while, and it is a long while, if the day be gracious and leisure ample, various suggestions and analogies of life are darting in and out of your mind. This flower is like some friend; another reminds you of mignonnette, and mignonnette always makes you think of such a garden and mansion where it enacted some memorable part; and *that* flower conveys some strange and unexpected resemblance to certain events of society; this one is a bold soldier; that one is a sweet lady dear;—the white flowering blood-root, trooping up by the side of a decaying log, recalls to your fancy a band of white bannered knights; and so your pleased attention strays through a thousand vagaries of fancy, or memory, or vaticinating hope.

Yet, these are not home flowers. You did not plant them. You have not screened them. You have not watched their growth, plucked away voracious worms, or nibbling bugs; you have not seen them in the same places year after year, children of your care and love. Around such there is an artificial life, an associational beauty, a fragrance and grace of the affections, that no wild flowers can have.

It is a matter of gratitude that this finest gift of Providence is the most profusely given. Flowers can not be monopolized. The poor can have them as much as the rich. It does not require such an education to love and appreciate them, as it would to admire a picture of Turner's, or a statue of Thorwaldsen's. And, as they are messengers of affection, tokens of remembrance, and presents of beauty, of universal acceptance, it is pleasant to think that all men recognize a brief brotherhood in them. It is not impertinent to offer flowers to a stranger. The poorest child can proffer them to the richest. A hundred persons turned together into a meadow full of flowers would be drawn together in a transient brotherhood.

It is affecting to see how serviceable flowers often are to the necessities of the poor. If they bring their little floral gift to you, it can not but touch your heart to think that their grateful affection longed to express itself as much as yours. You have books, or gems, or services, that you can render as you will. The poor can give but little, and do but little. Were it not for flowers they would be shut out from those exquisite pleasures which spring from such gifts. I never take one from a child, or from the poor, that I do not thank God in their behalf for flowers!

And then, when Death enters a poor man's house! It may be, the child was the only creature that loved the unbefriended father—*really* loved him; loved him utterly. Or, it may be, it is an only son, and his mother a widow—who, in all his sickness, felt the limitation of her poverty for her darling's sake as she never had for her own; and did what she could, but not what she would, had there been wealth. The coffin is pine. The undertaker sold it with a jerk of indifference and haste, lest he should lose the selling of a rosewood coffin, trimmed with splendid silver screws. The room is small. The attendant neighbors are few. The shroud is coarse. O! the darling child was fit for whatever was most excellent, and the heart aches to do for him whatever could be done that should speak love. It takes money for fine linen; money for costly sepulture. But flowers, thank God, the poorest may have. So, put white buds in the hair—and honey-dew, and mignonnette, and half blown roses, on the breast. If it be spring, a few white violets will do; and there is not a month till November, that will not give you something. But if it is winter, and you have no single pot of roses, then I fear your darling must be buried without a flower; for flowers cost money in the winter!

And then, if you can not give a stone to mark his burial-place, a rose may stand there; and from it you may, every spring, pluck a bud for your bosom, as the child was broken off from you. And if it brings tears for the past, you will not see the flowers fade and come again, and fade and come again, year by year, and not learn a lesson of the resurrection—when that which perished here shall revive again, never more to droop or to die.

II.

DEATH IN THE COUNTRY.

WOODSTOCK, CONN., *July* 28, 1851.

THERE is something peculiarly impressive to me in the old New England custom of announcing a death. In a village of but a few hundred inhabitants, all are known to each. There are no *strangers*. The village church, the Sabbath school, and the district school have been channels of intercommunication; so that one is acquainted with not only the persons, but, too often, with the affairs, domestic and secular, of every dweller in the town.

A thousand die in the city every month, and there is no void apparent. The vast population speedily closes over the emptied space. The hearts that were grouped about the deceased doubtless suffer alike in the country and in the city. But, outside of this special grief, there is a moment's sadness, a dash of sympathy; and then life closes over the grief as waters fill the void made when a bucketful is drawn out of the ocean!

There goes a city funeral! Well, I wonder who it is that is journeying so quietly to his last home? He was not in my house, nor of my circle; his life was not a thread woven with mine; I did not see him before, I shall not miss him now. We did not greet at the church; we did not vote at the town meeting; we had not gone together upon sleigh-rides, skatings, huskings, fishings, trainings, or elections. Therefore it is that men of might die daily about us, and we have no sense of it, any more than we perceive it when a neighbor extinguishes his lamp. And when one is buried—ah, a city burial! Amidst drays and carts, in the thunder of a million wheels, a few carriages fall behind a grim and heathenish hearse, black as midnight; for hearses are made, as all our funeral habits are, to express but one unbroken sorrow, as if a Christian heart had but that experience! It is a shame that eighteen hundred years of Christianity yet leave Death grim and dismal as a devil's cave. To be sure there is sorrow, but there is sorrow *ended* as well as begun; there is release, there is rest, there is victory, as well as bereavement. And yet, no badge of hope, not one sign of cheer, not a color or insignia of immortal joy and beauty, mingles with the black crape and plumes of Christian heathenism about the tomb! But I wander. When the procession starts, it moves through the crowded street scarcely attracting a look. No one asks the useless question, *Who is it?* No one knows or cares. There it goes—a black pilgrimage through a dusty, roaring street, wending its way toward Greenwood. When the city is well nigh cleared, then begins a gentle funeral trot, as if the attraction of the grave accelerated our pace as we drew nearer. Blessed portal! only within these bounds do we seem to receive from nature those lessons of death which we refuse to learn of Christianity. The very hills of life are here! Yonder, where men live, is only noise and dust, heat and smoke, canker and care! But here every curve and slope speaks beauty and peace. Almost only here the sun falls tranquilly, and flowers thrive, and winds make harps of every tree, and birds, unblemished and unterrified, rejoice. Surely these are the vales that speak of life! One must needs smile, and, in spite of our perverse education, feel some joy as we lay down the weary body to its rest. One enters Greenwood with a sense of relief. The air changes at the gate. We leave our burdens outside. But when we have laid the dust within its parent's bosom, we emerge into the world again as into a prison. It is a blessed contrast to have so much peace and so deep a beauty close by the city, silently putting life to shame, and winning grief thitherward, as if to the bosom of a parent!

It was upon the very day that we arrived in Woodstock, upon this broad and high hill-top, in the afternoon, as we were sitting in ransomed bliss, rejoicing in the boundless hemisphere above, and in the beautiful sweep of hills feathered with woods, and cultivated fields ruffled with fences, and full, here and there, of pictures of trees, single or in rounded groups: it was as we sat thus, the children, three families of them, scattered out, racing and shouting upon the village green before us, that the church bell swung round merrily, as if preluding, or clearing its throat for some message. It is five o'clock—what can that bell be ringing for? Is there a meeting? Perhaps a preparatory lecture. It stops. Then one deep stroke is given, and all is still. Every one stops. Some one is dead.

Another solemn stroke goes vibrating through the crystal air, and calls scores more to the doors. Who can be dead? Another solitary peal wafts its message tremulously along the air; and that long, gradually dying vibration of a country bell—never heard amid the noises of the air in a city—swelling and falling, swelling and falling; aerial waves, voices of invisible spirits communing with each other as they bear aloft the ransomed one!

But now its warning voice is given. All are listening. Ten sharp, distinct strokes—and a pause; some one is ten years old of earth's age. No; ten more follow—twenty years is it? Ten more tell us that it is an adult. Ten more and ten more, and twice ten again, and one final stroke count the age, *seventy-one!* Seventy-one years? Were they long, weary, sorrowful years? Was it a corrugated wretch who clung ignobly to life? Was it a venerable sire, weary of waiting for the silver cord to be loosed? Seventy-one years! Shall I see as many? And if I do, the hill-top is already turned and I am going down upon the further side! How long to look forward to! how short to look back upon! Age and youth look upon life from the opposite ends of the telescope: it is exceedingly long, it is exceedingly short! To one who muses thus, the very strokes of the bell seem to emblem life. Each is like a year, and all of them roll away as in a moment and are gone.

III.

INLAND *vs.* SEASHORE.

WOODSTOCK, CONN., *August*, 1851.

MY DEAR BROTHER STORRS:—Your first letter from Newport was pleasant to read. I rejoiced in your pleasure, but was quite aroused by your *heresies.* I do not mean any unsoundness of faith, but of taste. Do you not set forth the joys of a fashionable and crowded watering-place in terms that would draw thither a very recluse? I take up arms for the true country;—the pure and undefiled place of Nature!

Pray tell me whether there is in Newport such a thing as *quiet?* How many people have you there, every one on the search for amusement? Do you ever get rid of noise, or crowds, or excitements? You only exchange hot and dusty excitement, for excitements with sea-breezes. Can you find a place out of doors to be alone in for half-an-hour? You can not go out of doors without meeting somebody. Somebody is liable to be acquainted with you at every turn. Something is always "going on" in town. You are as much in society and as little with Nature as if in the old, thundering city.

But here, in this quiet, hill-top town, is the profoundest peace. The clouds in the air are hardly more alone than we. We have the plenitude of Nature in some of her loveliest aspects, and it requires an effort to get into company as great as for you to get out of it. A man may sink down within himself in the profoundest meditation. Nobody calls to see you. Nobody knows that you are here. You float, like a mote in sunbeams, where you will, up or down, hither or thither, without contact and in silence. The whole air is marvelous by its stillness. It is still in the morning, at noon, at sunset, at dark, and still all night. Early in the morning, from four to five, the birds say their matins. (Alas! Jenny Lind, you would be no bird here!) The stalwart lord of the barnyard starts up and challenges a hundred other cocks and cockerels of each degree. Then come the obstreperous children and coaxing nurses. These noises over, you have had the last of it. Nothing else makes a noise in this village.

Indeed, this is quite a wonder of a village to all who love quiet and a beautiful prospect. Its like I do not know anywhere. It is a miniature Mount Holyoke; and its prospect, the Connecticut Valley in miniature. It is placidly spread upon a hill-top so high up that dust, sound and insects have forsaken it, or never found their way hither. It is marvelous how a village can exist without any apparent trades. But, as far as I can perceive, there are no occupations here of any sort. There is a blacksmith's shop, which never makes a noise, and that is all. No carpenter's shop, nor cabinet-makers, nor turners; no hatters, saddlers, watchmaker or shoemaker, that I can see. No houses are building; we hear no trowel clinking, or muffled hammer-stroke; there is no mortar-making—no piles of brick or lumber.

The town was *finished* long ago: and all workmen of every sort seem to have gone off and left dear old Woodstock all to itself. Even travelers leave our solitude unbroken. There is no tavern on the street; and the two little tranquil stores might plant corn up to their very door steps without much fear of its being trodden down. Once in a while, toward evening, a farmer's wagon skirts along the edge of the green. Such a sight brings us to the windows. But it is a short and headlong drive, as if the rider felt guilty for disturbing the peace, or raising a dust, even for a moment. Some twenty houses, white and yard-inclosed, stand modestly apart, and back from the long, broad village-green which they inclose but do not shut in. This village-green is neither a circle, square, parallelogram, nor polygon, but a space sloping chiefly from north to south, and in some places eastward and westward, with no shape at all, but coming nearer than to any thing else to the form of an elongated flat-iron. For a long time, seeing no people in the street, no one going in or coming out of the doors, no persons in the window, or even smoke in the chimneys, neither babies, boys, nor maidens, being anywhere discernible, I supposed, for the first week, that only old people lived here,—nice, tidy, quiet old people, such as I saw on Sundays keeping themselves awake in church by nibbling fennel or caraway. I was mistaken. Familiarity has enabled me to detect signs of life in all its varieties. But the habit of the place is to be quiet. I wonder whether the children cry or not? I wonder if the sober, tranquil people ever made a noise in their life? How long is it since they subsided and tranquilized?

The air breathes as if it were iced sherbet. You have a distinct luxury in each particular breath. You halt voluntarily and cultivate inspiration. The sun, that rages in the valleys below, and wilts down the crowds in the sweltering cities, here walks in cool brightness through the heavens, tempering the air to that delicious point at which the chill is lost, but heat has not begun. *Your* coolness is all imported. You are hot in that pent-up, narrow-streeted, rackety Newport, and cooled only by the sea-breeze. Coolness with you is a thing inserted. But here it is indigenous. It belongs to the very texture of the air. You may have the sea-shore, waves and surf, storms once in a while, bathing and fishing—all, except the last, boisterous. Beside, you have the buzzing enthusiasm of thousands around you. Your pulse never gets down, your eye never cools. Why, my dear fellow, you see persons from the city every day! You get the papers the very day of their publication! Do you call that the country?

As for me, if I please to bathe, I have a little lake down yonder. Just now there is not a ripple on its surface—a falling insect here and there dimples it, and a fish, in taking in the petty Jonah, increases the dimple to a circlet. When, wading on the silver sand, I at length have depth to plunge, the ripple runs half across to yonder shore. Fishing? yes, I go down with great possessions of various tackle; but the perch are small, pickerel scarce, and pout only go out at dusk; so that one forgets his line, and falls off into a dream, or rows about the tranquil river, along the fringe of bushes, then among lily-pads, then toward the mouth of the *inlet*, then along the shaded edge, where deep, dark pine-woods forever murmur. Now and then a fish leaps up and falls back with a plash. Or your oar, poised for a second, sheds musical pearls into the pure lake, or the cracking of sticks tells you that a cow breaks through the thicket to drink—two cows evidently in the water, one drinking upward and the other downward, lip to lip! These are our bathings and fishings. By the way, those white pond-lilies! Is there another flower, its adjuncts also considered, so exquisitely beautiful. The rare form of its elongated cup, the interior coronet of stamens and pistils, delicately gold-colored, the green and pink-edged sepals, its delicious fragrance, make it a very queen. It chooses some nook or bay along the lake's edge, spreads out its large shield-like leaf, and floats its snow-white blossom on the surface. Flowers growing from the soil are full beautiful, but flowers growing out of crystal water are beyond all words of beauty.

In the morning, look out eastward. A vale with every conceivable undulation stretches full thirty miles from north to south. It lies almost under you. It is so near that you see the farm-houses, the orchards, the groups of trees, the corn-fields, the yellow rye, and the now half-ripe oats. It is not an even, level valley, but a collection of wide swells or rolls of land setting in on the north, and but half commingling when they reach the lake right over opposite to us. Indeed, so broken and stony are the features, that it would not be a valley at all if it were not for the hills that shut it in on either side. And these hills are made up of multitudes of little hills piled together in every way that is beautiful. The little stream, that finds its course through the valley among mounds and rounds and hillocks, seems uncertain of its way, and sets trees and bushes along its banks, for fear of forgetting where to flow. The brook has fairly reflected itself in the air—for see that film of silver mist, thin as gauze, hanging above the stream, clear down to the lake!

O, see the lake!—or, rather, see the robes of mist that hide it! The sun is at them. They are wreathing, moving, lifting up, and moving off, sun-colored in their depths, but silver-edged! Now the water reflects the morning. At noon it will be breezy, and whitish, or steel-gray. At night it will be black as ink. In the early part of the day the lakelet speaks of life; but at twilight it seems to think of death.

"But what do you do for amusement?" Why, sir, we do *not* receive company, or make calls, or ride about among a caravan of dandy vehicles, or "go with the multitude" in a-swimming, or anything else that implies excitement or company. Be it known, however, that we have a select few here, to whom *quiet* is enjoyment. We look at the picture-gallery of God in the heavens, with never two days' pictures alike; we sit down with our books on the brow of the breezy hill, under an old chestnut tree, and read sometimes the book, sometimes the landscape, sometimes the highland clouds; we wait till the evening sun begins to emit rose-colored light, and then we take rides along the edges of woods, upon unfrequented roads, across suspicious bridges, along forest paths leading no one knows where, and coming out just at the very spot we did *not* expect. In this perilous journeying we often breathe our horse while we collect flowers, leaves, mosses, and grasses; and we get home at the most urgent moment of sunset, just in time to go up into the observatory and see the wide and wonderful glory, of which for a moment we utter exclamations—"Look at that islet of fire," "and that deep crimson bank," "and that exquisite blue between those rifts of fire," "and that dove-colored cloud with a bronze-colored molding and fringe!" But words are foolish! And we sink away to silence, and only gaze and think!

But, on other days we vary the entertainment; for there is an inexhaustible variety. Behold us then—the ladies incipiently Bloomerized—wending afoot along the road leading out of town westward. Before we are half out of sight of the houses, the road is lined with blackberries. The high-blackberry is yet holding back, but the low-blackberry, trailing all over the banks and covering the rocks, is in high condition. How large and plump are these unhandled berries! It is a marvel how such little mouths as I see can get a whole one in. We are soon satisfied. Now for boquets of wayside flowers. Spireas, one, two, three, four species! Golden rod, a lingering bud or two on the wild rose; and here are *pussies,* as the children call the velvet little mulberry-shaped posies: and here are flowering grasses, and rushes, and ferns, and green leaves diverse and innumerable;—and a leaf is as pretty as a flower, any day, if you will only think so. Here, too, is the trailing strawberry, whose vine, inwoven with buds of spirea, will make your lady a queen-like coronet.

And now we come to the forks of the road, and yonder is a whortleberry patch! Even at a table, in a saucer, with cream and spoon, berries are not to be despised. But the bush is the only fit table, your hand the best spoon, and your exhilaration the richest cream. Commend me to a rocky hill-side, full of crickets, grasshoppers, butterflies, and birds, with blue berries, whortleberries, and, about the edges of the field, blackberries, millions and millions more than you, and all the village boys, and all the country girls, and all the little birds in the air or out of the woods, can eat! By the way, have you locusts, and chirping crickets, and stridulous grasshoppers, in Newport? A few crickets, perhaps, in the ashes, or cracks of the hearth, which you hunt with brush and broom, as soon as their shrill song disturbs you. But grasshoppers, brown, green, and gray, you have not in Newport, I know. You can not sit upon a gray, shelving rock, ruffled about with bushes, half of them in flower, and the rest full of berries, covered but in nowise cushioned with filmy lichens, and see grasshoppers, those speculators of the pasture, which jump first, and consider afterwards where they shall land. There goes one upon a spider's web, half broken through by its sprawling descent. Unwelcome morsel! It is doubtful which is most alarmed, spider or grasshopper.

Doubtless you have human spiders and webs, and entangled insects about you, in that fashionable watering-place.

There are a world of things to be considered on the way home. Mosses must be gathered; new flowers are espied; a deal of engineering is required to scale the fences; and I have never seen a lady tottering on a stone fence, anxiously securing her skirts, with reef and double reef, across whose mind convictions did not flash in favor of Bloomerism. Then this piece of twilight wood must be threaded, the golden-freckled ground admired, and the long shadows which it flings across the road and upon the meadow observed; and when, at length, you are safely home again, and daintily refreshed on the whitest bread, the freshest butter, and berries of your own picking, you sit an hour in the cool, shady veranda, and think it must be eleven o'clock, but find by your watch that it is only eight, you protest that never were days so long, never days so full of joy, deep and quiet, and never nights of unwinking sleep so refreshing.

I have it in my heart to tell you of our experiences in country thunder-storms; of sunsets gorgeously following storms; of moonlight scenery; of village scenes and country customs, awakening in us that were country bred, thousands of dear recollections of youth and home. But I spare you! I trust that you sinned in your enthusiasm for Newport through ignorance. I should be loth to think you so hardened in your desire to build there three tabernacles for the trine-editorship of *The Independent.* I will therefore wait to see if you recant your theses of heresy. But if you again shall declare them, and post them on the broadside of *The Independent*—as Luther did his on the church-door—it will then be time to bring up these other forces.

Of one thing I am sure, that your children have not half the chance in a fashionable watering-place that ours here have, for frolic and health, in this little serene village-wilderness. Here they are, perched like eagles on a cliff, and I am delighted to see how much children sympathize with landscape beauty, sunsets, cloud-flocks, and all the variable phases of Nature. But this long, sloping green, and the rounded sides of the almost precipitous hill which the village crowns, are their chief joy. All day long they are abroad, and the darkness hardly drives them in. Bad company is impossible where there is *no* company. All day long they race and chase, or go a-berrying, or gather under the shade of orchards or elms to relate marvelous stories; or they dig profound wells, in which, for lack of water, they impound solemn toads; they hunt hen's nests; and the lesser urchins disturb the gravity of old matronly hens by sundry attempts at catching them. They gather about the cow at milking, or drive her to pasture, or ride the horses to water; and once in a week they proudly vex the mill-pond with hook and line, and astonish their simple parents with two perch and four roach, caught, strung, sandy and dry! They have no time for quarreling, and it seems impossible for them to devise any mischief meritorious of a whipping.

But, good-bye, my dear friend! May I live to see you again and grasp your hand in fellowship of our common work.

P. S. At length I have discovered a cabinet-maker's shop! but there was nothing going on therein.

IV.

NEW ENGLAND GRAVEYARDS.

WOODSTOCK, CONN., *August* 30, 1853.

WHEN this reaches you, I shall have spent six successive Sabbaths in the State of Connecticut—the longest period of sojourn within this, the State of my birth, for twenty-five years. During this quarter of a century, she has partaken largely of the changes that have gone on throughout New England. Her old towns have grown rusty, and lie up upon her high places to the coolness of summer, and to the roaring winds of winter, in a tranquillity which would soothe the progressive fears of the most rooted conservative. Young men, as soon as they attain their majority, push off to the West or South, or to the nearest manufacturing village or railroad depot. Thus, the uplifted towns, seen afar, upon their mighty hills, lie like a dream; while their offspring villages in the valleys below whirl like a top with enterprise. The gods of the valley are mightier in New England than the gods of the hills; the loom is too strong for the plow. Indeed, *farmers' boys* are the most profitable crop that New England farms can now produce. To ride about these endlessly diversified hills, and marvel at their beauty, and rejoice in their associations, is, I am persuaded, a much easier way of spending time than to subdue them, and compel them to render up remunerating harvests. One would think that there had been, at some time, a hailstorm of granite bowlders, and a rain of small stones to boot, along these hills. I have seen a number of farms on which must have originated the affecting stories of sheep having their noses sharpened to get the grass between the stones, and grasshoppers clinging to mullen stalks with tears in their eyes from very hunger. And yet it is surprising to see how much soil labor has redeemed from rock and stone, and smoothed and enriched into deep and mellow tilth. The rugged pastures which inclose many of these beautiful farms are samples of what the farms once were, and a gauge of the degree of labor which they have cost. A highly cultivated farm is *always* an object of beauty; but in the rocky parts of New England, a fine farm has a *moral* beauty; it is an enduring mark and measure of indomitable industry. And the best of all is, that, while the men make the farms, the farms thus make the men. There is scarcely a homestead to be met, far or near, that has not reared some man who is or has been distinguished in public life. Nor can I think of a worthier aim, during the summer vacations of professional men, than to return to their native places, and gather up the memorials of past days, and in the lives, customs, and familiar events of the past and passing generations, furnish materials for history. Why should not all the old mansions and farm-houses be secured by daguerreotype, before they crumble? "Lossing's Field Book of the Revolution" is, on this account, worthy of all praise. But why should the memorials of only our revolutionary worthies be preserved? Why not the birth-places of eminent civilians, clergymen, inventors, schoolmasters, and of all others who have worthily served their generation? Dr. Sprague, of Albany, has in preparation the lives of the most noted American clergymen, now deceased,—a work which we believe, from a slight taste which we have privately had, will be of the highest interest. Why should there not be illustrations, so easily and cheaply procured, of their residences, birth-houses, their churches, and of their monuments or simple tomb-stones; and if there is none even of these, then of the spots or graveyards where they lie?

By the by, speaking of graveyards, one can not but be pained at the desolation of these places in so many New England towns. Once decently buried, and a stone erected, the labor of love ends, and the memorials are given over to the elements. It is painful to me, for the most part, to walk through the New England graveyards, always excepting the noble cemeteries which within a few years have begun to spring up near the larger towns and cities. The fences are dilapidated, the head-stones broken, or swayed half over, the intervals choked up with briers, elders, and fat-weeds; and the whole place bearing impress of the most frigid indifference. Yet, nowhere on earth is death more solemn than in New England, nor the remembrance of the dead more ineffaceable. Nowhere else is man valued so highly, or his loss more universally felt. But there seems to be little thought of anything that is not in some way connected with practical utility. If the departed could be made one whit happier,—if it were dreamed that the beautifying of the grave would even be noticed by those whose bodies sleep there,—nowhere else in the world would loving care continue to be lavished upon the inclosing soil, more than in New England. But the habits of the people make a thorough separation between the living and the dead. The theology has entered into the practical ways of life. The dead are utterly gone. God has them in another world. Their state is fixed and unalterable. So thinking, it seems of but little worth to garnish their sleeping places. But in part, this neglect in New England is owing to a want of education and of a love of the graceful and the beautiful. It is a pain to us to tread these places. Were I buried here, it seems as if my bones would pluck at these disgraceful weeds and thistles, should they penetrate the mold above my head. I can not help feeling that it is a shame and disgrace that the only places in thrifty New England where weeds are allowed to grow unmolested are graveyards, where the bodies of our sweet children, where father and mother, brother and sister, husband and wife, rest till the resurrection. Cows and horses are often allowed to pasture on the graves; thus saving the expense of mowing, beside a clear gain in grass! One of the finest orchards in Sherburne, Mass., is that which flourishes upon the old town graveyard (now private property). The remains of a succession of their former pastors, and one president of Harvard College, lie under the roots of these profitable trees.

It is impossible that pleasant associations can exist with the place of burial under such circumstances. The grossest dreads hedge about the spot which a Christian faith should hallow and enrich. Who would not shrink from being buried under wild parsneps, burdocks, blackberry bushes, and hardhack? It were better to be burned, or to sink to the bottom of the sea! One loves to wander through Greenwood, and think of such a resting-place for his body when life is done. Those quiet rounds and hills, sacred from carelessness or intrusion, over which trees cast their checkered shadows, and sing their music, how cheering and how refining are such associations! They tempt us frequently thither. Our children are pleased to go. Death begins to be more easily thought of. It becomes associated with themes which often inspire and sanctify the imagination. Christ, the Victor and Redemptor—our own victory and redemption; heaven, and renewed friendship, higher loves, and inconceivable joys;—these themes find in such places an easy association with our thoughts, and life becomes dignified by the estimate which we place upon death. Besides, it is a blessed attainment when we can so associate the truths of God's word with natural objects, that one is, in a manner, reading his Bible in flowers, in forests, in sunlight, and at twilight, always, everywhere, and in every thing. It is a blessed thing to have converted death into a joy; yea, to kindle up in its portals a light that shines backward upon our path of life, and cheers us onward toward it, as if it were, as it is, our home and glory. For death is the coming of the Son of Man. A Christian ought not to be afraid of his Father's bosom.

But how should one not shrink from burial if he sees that all who have gone before him are cast out into a place of desolation, where friends will not choose to come, or will come to wade through matted grass and tangled weeds, and push away bush and brier to read his decaying name; and hasten away, dreading the cheerless day that shall bring their bodies, too, to the home of the refuse and worn out! O! may the sun pierce through the shade of trees, dear to many birds, to fall in checkered light upon my grave! I ask no stone or word of inscription. May flowers be the only memorials of my grave, renewed every spring, and maintained through the long summer!

To a certain extent this matter will be reformed by the selection of grounds in imitation of our suburban cemeteries. But this should not hinder an immediate attention to the simple burial-grounds which must long be the only resting-places for the departed of our villages. And although any one who has Christian refinement will feel an interest in mending the grossness of prevalent custom, is it not a peculiarly fit labor of love for *woman?* The ladies of any parish have but to determine that the resting-places of their ancestors shall bud and blossom as the rose, and it will be done. Let clean and sufficient fences be made; let the borders and paths be planted with shade trees; let the side-paths be lined with roses, vines, and free-growing shrubs; let the grass be shorn at least every month; let measures be taken to erect again the drooping head-stones of the ancient dead. and, if needful, retrace the effaced letters; for all these things are within the reach of every village parish in New England.

We stood with peculiar pleasure, but a few days ago, in the burial-place of the family of UNCAS, in Norwich, Conn., upon the banks of the Yantic. Blessed be the hands that traced that inclosure, and builded the simple shaft of granite that bears the only word "UNCAS." About fifty descendants, even to the last of his noble line, lie sleeping about him. At but a little distance is the ground where the Indians buried their sachems. Bringing them up the cove in their canoes, they ascended a dark and beautiful ravine to the broad bluff-head, and there laid them down in burial upon its level circuit. This very ground is now the property of Ik Marvel, (the pleasant author of much summer literature,) upon which he proposes erecting his dwelling. At first one reluctates at such a use. Yet, as all other Indian haunts are now possessed by streets and dwellings—No, we are not satisfied, after all, that it should be so. But, if it must be, we are thankful that a genial soul, alive to all the associations of the place—finding inspiration in them—perhaps embalming their histories in his literary works, will rear his mansion over the dust of many generations of the mighty men of the forest. Perhaps, as he sits in thoughtful twilight, reflecting over the graves of those who once were chiefs among their fellows, but who now have faded away to a mere memory, he may be inspired to associate his labors with the moral growth of his age, that so *his* memory shall never fade, but stand in freshness and glory, even after the trump shall have called forth his reanimated dust, and that of his dusky predecessors, to the morning of ordeal and of glory.

I must reserve for a separate letter some few words about Norwich, the most picturesque of all the towns of Connecticut.

V.

TOWNS AND TREES.

NORWICH, CONN., *August* 30, 1851.

THERE are hundreds of villages in Connecticut that are beautiful in various degrees and by different methods; some by the width of prospect, some by their mountain scenery, some by their position on the water, and some, nestled away from all the world, find their chief attractions in their deep tranquillity. But in every place the chief beauty must be in what Nature has done, or in what man has done *naturally.* The rocks, hills, mountains; the innumerable forms of water in springs, rills, rivulets, streams, estuaries, lakes or ocean; but above all the *trees*—these create beauty, if it exist at all. It is rare that any place combines to a great degree the several specialities mentioned. A place that is inland, and yet on the seaboard—that has bold, precipitous rocks close at hand, and at the same time is spread out upon a champaign—that unites the refinements belonging to society in large towns with the freshness and quiet of a secluded village, imbosomed in trees, full of shaded yards and gardens, broad, park-like streets, soon opening out into romantic rural roads among pine woods along the rocky edges of dark streams—such a place, especially if its society is good, if its ministers, teachers, civilians, and principal citizens, are intelligent and refined, and

6*

its historical associations abundant and rich—must be regarded as of all others the most desirable for residence. And such a place is Norwich, Connecticut!

The river Thames is formed by the junction of the Yantic and the Shetucket. Upon the angle of these three streams stands the town. The Shetucket is a black water in all its course, and near to Norwich it has a bed hewed out of rocks, and cliffs for banks. The Yantic is a smaller stream, rolling also over a rocky channel, with a beautiful plunge, just above the town, of seventy-five feet. The Thames is not so much a river as a narrow arm of the sea, thrust far up inland as if to search for tributary streams. These ribbon-like bays mark the whole northern coast of Long Island Sound. The Thames is navigable for large steamers to its point of formation. The conformation of the ground on which Norwich stands is entirely peculiar. Along the water it is comparatively low, affording a business plane, and a space for railroad necessities. The whole ground then rises with sudden slope, lifting the residences far up out of the dust and noise of business into an altitude of quiet. But what is the most remarkable is, that a huge broad-backed granite cliff of rocks bulges up in the very midst of the city, cutting it in two, extending backward half a mile, and leaving the streets to sweep around on either side of it. This masterly old monarch looks down a hundred feet perpendicular, on the eastern side, upon the streets below, its bare rocks and massive ledges here and there half hid by evergreens, and in spots matted with grass, and fringed with shrubs. On the western side the slope is gradual, and it is cut half way down to the Yantic by a broad street, nobly shaded with stalwart elms, and filled with fine family residences. As one winds his way from the landing up the curving street, about the base of the rock on the eastern side, at evening especially, in twilight, or with a tender moonlight, this wild uplifted cliff—in the very heart of a city, with forest trees rooted almost plumb above his head—has a strange and changeable uncertainty, at one moment shining out distinctly, and at the next dim and shadowy; now easily compassed by the eye, and then glancing away, if he have imagination enough, into vast mountain spaces. This singular rocky ridge trends toward the north, and gradually loses itself in the plain on which stands Norwich Old Town. There is thus brought together, within the space of a mile, the city, the country, and the wilderness. The residences are so separated from the business part of the town, that one who comes first into the upper part of the city, and wanders about under its avenues of mighty elms, and among its simple old houses, or its modern mansions, would take it to be a place of elegant repose, without life or business. But if he first lands below, amid stores and manufacturing shops, as for several years we did, he might go away thinking Norwich to be a mere hammering, rumbling place of business. Indeed, there are three towns in one. The streets skirting the water form a city of business; the streets upon the hill, a city of residences; a mile or two back is the old town, a veritable life-like picture of a secluded country village of the old New England days. What could one want better for a place of retirement? An hour's ride brings you to the seaside: to boats, fishing, lounging and looking, whether in storm or calm. You may go by cars to old New London, or by boat to Stonington, and then by yacht or other craft to Block Island, or anywhere else you please. There are places for fish—black fish, blue fish, speckled bass, porgies, weak-fish, etc.; there are places for surf-bathing, with waves tempered to all degrees of violence, and to every tone from whispering to thunder. If your mood does not take you seaward, half an hour will suffice to bear you inland, among bold and rocky hills, cleft with streams, full of precipitous ravines, and shaded with oaks and evergreens. Or, if you do not wish to roam, you may ascend the intra-urban mountain—the Tarpeian Rock of Norwich, or its Mount Zion, whichever your associations prefer to call it—and from its pinnacles overlook the wide circumjacent country. If you happily own a house upon the western side of Washington street,—or, better yet, if you own a friend, who owns the house, and feels lonesome without *you*,—then you can have the joys of the breezy wilderness at home. For, if you will go back through the garden, and then through a little pet orchard, you shall find the forest-covered bank plunging two or three hundred feet down toward the Yantic; and there, hidden among shrubs and wild flowers, oaks and elms, you hear no din of wheels or clink of shops, but only the waving of leaves and the sport of birds.

But if there were none of these rare conjunctions

of hill, rock, and plain, river and sea, Norwich would still be a beautiful place by virtue of its trees, and especially of those incomparably most magnificent of all earthly trees, elms! A village shaded by thoroughly grown elms can not but be handsome. Its houses may be huts; its streets may be ribbed with rocks, or channeled with ruts; it may be as dirty as New York, and as frigid as Philadelphia; and yet these vast, majestic tabernacles of the air would redeem it to beauty. These are temples indeed, living temples, neither waxing old nor shattered by Time, that cracks and shatters stone, but rooting wider with every generation and casting a vaster round of grateful shadow with every summer. We had rather walk beneath an avenue of elms than inspect the noblest cathedral that art ever accomplished. What is it that brings one into such immediate personal and exhilarating sympathy with venerable trees! One instinctively uncovers as he comes beneath them; he looks up with proud veneration into the receding and twilight recesses; he breathes a thanksgiving to God every time his cool foot falls along their shadows. They waken the imagination and mingle the olden time with the present. Did any man of contemplative mood ever stand under an old oak or elm, without thinking of other days,—imagining the scenes that had transpired in their presence? These leaf-mountains seem to connect the past and the present to us as mountain ridges attract clouds from both sides of themselves. Norwich is remarkably enriched by these columnar glories, these mysterious domes of leaf and interlacing bough. No considerable street is destitute of them, and several streets are prolonged avenues of elms which might give a twinge of jealousy to old New Haven herself—elm-famous! Norwich Old Town, however, clearly has the pre-eminence. Its green is surrounded by old Revolutionary elms of the vastest stature, and of every shape and delineation of grandeur. How a man can live there and ever get his eyes to the ground, I can not imagine. One must needs walk with upturned face, exploring these most substantial of all air castles. And when pausing underneath some monumental tree, he looks afar up, and sees the bird-population, that appear scarcely larger than humming-birds, dimly flitting about their secure heritage and sending down a chirp that loses itself half way down to a thin whistle, it seems as though there were two worlds—he in one and they in another. Nearly before the fine old-fashioned mansion where Lydia Huntly (Mrs. Sigourney) was brought up are two gigantic elms—very patriarchs, measuring at the base more than eighteen feet in circumference. An old man of a hundred years, a member of Dr. Bond's society, relates that his father selected these trees from the forest, and *backed* them into town and planted them here. His name should be written on a tablet and hung upon their breasts! The two elms next south from these, though not as aged as they, may, we think, be regarded as models of exquisite symmetry and beauty. One might sit by the hour and look upon them as upon a picture.

No other tree is at all comparable to the elm. The

ash is, when well grown, a fine tree, but clumpy; the maple has the same character. The horse-chestnut, the linden, the mulberry, and poplars, (save that tree-spire, the Lombardy poplar,) are all of them plump, round, fat trees, not to be despised, surely, but representing single dendrological ideas. The oak is venerable by association, and occasionally a specimen is found possessing a kind of grim and ragged glory. But the elm, alone monarch of trees, combines in itself the elements of variety, size, strength, and grace, such as no other tree known to us can at all approach or remotely rival. It is the *ideal* of trees; the true Absolute Tree! Its main trunk shoots up, not round and smooth, like an over-fatted, lymphatic tree, but channeled and corrugated, as if its athletic muscles showed their proportions through the bark, like Hercules' limbs through his tunic. Then suddenly the whole idea of growth is changed, and multitudes of long, lithe branches radiate from the crotch of the tree, having the effect of straightness and strength, yet really diverging and curving, until the outermost portions droop over and give to the whole top the most faultless grace. If one should at first say that the elm suggested ideas of strength and uprightness, on looking again he would correct himself, and say that it was majestic, uplifting beauty that it chiefly represented. But if he first had said that it was graceful and magnificent beauty, on a second look he would correct himself, and say that it was vast and rugged strength that it set forth. But at length he would say neither; he would say both; he would say that it expressed a beauty of majestic strength, and a grandeur of graceful beauty.

Such domestic forest treasures are a legacy which but few places can boast. Wealth can build houses, and smooth the soil; it can fill up marshes, and create lakes or artificial rivers; it can gather statues and paintings; but no wealth can buy or build elm trees—the floral glory of New England. Time is the only architect of such structures; and blessed are they for whom Time was pleased to fore-think! No care or expense should be counted too much to maintain the venerable elms of New England in all their regal glory! No other tree more enjoys a rich loam and moist food. In summer droughts, if copious waterings were given to the finer elms, especially with diluted guano water, their pomp would be noticeably enhanced. But, except in moist places, or in fields where the plow has kept the surface stirred, we noticed that elms were turning yellow, and thinning out their leaves.

VI.

THE FIRST BREATH IN THE COUNTRY.

SALISBURY, CONN., *August*, 1853.

ONCE more we find ourselves at home among lucid green trees, among hills and mountains, with lakes and brooks on every side, and country roads threading their way in curious circuits among them. All day long we have moved about with dreamy newness of life. Birds, crickets, and grasshoppers, are the only players upon instruments that molest the air. Chanticleer is at this instant proclaiming over the whole valley that the above declaration is a slander on his musical gifts. Very well, add chanticleer to cricket, grasshopper, and bird. Add, also, a cow; for I hear her distant low, melodious through the valley, with all roughness strained out by the trees through which it comes hitherward. O, this silence in the air, this silence on the mountains, this silence on the lakes! The endless roll of wheels, the audible pavements, the night and day jar of city streets, gives place to a repose so full and deep, that, by a five-hours' ride, one is born into a new world. Across the street the woods begin; the real woods, that man never planted nor pruned, and that pride and avarice have saved from being plucked away. For, the property adjacent has long been wished for building lots, but the owner has that pride of land which leads him to refuse to part with an acre. Thus the forest stands, which, otherwise, would long before this have given way to yards and gardens. And there we stroll; or lie down upon the dethroned leaves that have had their day, and look up upon the reigning leaves, endless and multitudinous, that wink and quiver to every breeze, or idly spot the blue sky when the wind hushes. It is no ordinary forest. It covers some thirty or forty acres. The lower part is quite level, and covered with oaks. Then come sudden and very severe hills, bolted up so perpendicularly that, but for grooves and water-cut passages, not more than five or six yards wide, you could hardly climb them. Masses of granite rock are flung up here and there in vast heaps, their sides mossed over, the splits and rifts feathered out with ferns, with here and there a bush for a captain. Over behind the woods, there comes down a brook from the mountains, rushing like a courier fierce with news, which it quite forgets to tell, and tempering its zeal along a level meadow, it goes across the road bent on industry. A few miles below it works at a mill as steadily as if it were not a wild and mountain-born brook. The woods are full of hemlock, pine, and spruce; of laurel and ground-pine; of all manner of leaves and flowers; and not least for beauty, the finely-cut ferns, with delicate palms. All this, and a good deal more, for we have not spoken of a diamond spring under a rock, like an eye overhung by a shaggy brow, or of a pretty school-house on the road-edge of the wood, or of a huge rock balanced so as to seem falling, while yet it is firm:—

all this we have within a stone's throw of our dwelling, and it is just nothing to the abundance of attractions in the neighborhood.

The early morning, and the two hours before sunset, we give to riding and gazing. The middle of the day is given to keeping still. To those who have lived in intense excitements, there is something exquisitely enjoyable in mere quiet. Simple village sights, and village sounds, bring with them full-measured pleasure. Hours pass lightly away while you sit at your window, looking at everything and at nothing,—a passive recipient of all the impressions which the great out-of-doors can make upon you. Let me recount a half-hour's sights.

It is a very beautiful day. The sun is warm but the air is cool. Some very dreamy clouds are drifting about without any will of their own, and with no settled purpose. Now and then they half obliterate the sun, and make us look up from our book to see what is the matter. In a minute they bring him back again with a sudden dash of light, as if his eye flashed at the indignity of a vail. In the garden, under my window, crickets chirp and chirp, so long and steadily, that chirping seems to be the most of their housekeeping. A puff of air lifts the broad maple leaves, and shakes out a murmurous noise from them, and then flies off, leaving them motionless and silent. The far mountains seem wrapt in a Sabbath. The near hills are green beyond all greenness of any summers save such as this, that has had a shower for every week, and for almost every day. The fountains are full, the rills are brooks, the brooks are streams, the streams rivers.

What does a man think of in one of these mid-day summer hours? He reads a little, but is easily inveigled by the first side suggestion, and is flying off in every capricious fantasy. In full chase, through the door-yard, three children-boys are vociferous. In the next yard a young man lies flat on the grass under the tree. In front of the store stands an always-laughing or whistling colored man; just now he is cracking nuts with his teeth. Somebody casts a jest at him from out the store, and he laughs the whole air full. Now he is making all the motions of a fiddler; now he is drumming on his chair, and now he starts off whistling homeward for his dinner. "Well, Mott, whistling again—I always hear you whistling, but never saw you cry." Stopping the shrill tune, and sliding into the freest and cheeriest laugh that ever pulsated in the air, he answers, "Why, sir, I never cried in my life." I believe him. Careless, contented, luxuriously at ease when he has a dollar in his pocket, willing to work when that is gone, he is, on all hands, admitted to be the happiest man in town.

There goes the blacksmith—a jolly fellow. Hard work makes him fat. I do not know about the hard work—but the flesh is obvious. I can hear the anvil ring, and the hammer clink—so, his journeyman is at work. Here passes a new carriage. Somebody has come to town. I wonder who it is. The neighbors wonder who it is. It rolls through the town, and leaves nothing behind but a cloud of dust and much curiosity.

There troop the three most roguish boys that ever made parents scold and laugh. They have nothing to do but to set each other on to mischief. They pull off buds from the unblossomed rose-bushes; they pick cucumbers by the half-bushel that were to have been let alone; they break down rare shrubbery to get whips, and instead get whippings; they kill the guinea-pigs; chase the chickens; break up hen's nests; get into the carriages and wagons only to tumble out, and set all the nurses a-running; they study every means of getting under the horses' feet, and, as the more dangerous act, they are fond of tickling their hind legs, and pulling at their tails; they fill the already fed horses with extra oats, causing the hostler to fear for his charges' health, since he refuses oats at the next regular feeding; they paddle in all the mud on the premises; sit down in the street and fill their pockets with dirt; they wet their clothes in the brook, tear them in the woods, lose their caps a dozen times a day, and go bare-headed in the blazing sun; they cut up every imaginable prank with their long-suffering nurses when meals are served, or when bed-time comes, or when morning brings the washing and dressing. They are little, nimble, compact skinfuls of ingenious, fertile, endless, untiring mischief. They stub their toes, or cut their fingers, or get stung, or eat some poisonous berry, seed or root, or make us think that they have, which is just as bad; they fall down stairs, or eat green fruit till they are as tight as a drum; and yet there is no peace to us without them, as there certainly is none with them. Mischievous darlings! Joyful plagues! Loving, rollicking, laughing rogues!

Our house is girded about on the west with vigorous maples. No shade-tree is cleaner or more dense. Its form can not vie with the elm. It is round and heavy. Its foliage is black-green. The leaves are quite star-like. Few are the places through which the now westward-going sun can pierce. But through one or two of these it is casting on my paper a mottled radiance, that, as the leaves move to the breeze, runs up and down like a kitten playing with my pen. There is something solemn about a maple. The elm is airy, open, dome-like. Through it you can see the skies, and for this reason, as well as from its arched and hanging boughs, it is a cheerful, inspiring and companionable tree. The maple is opaque. Therefore, and especially as the light fades at evening, it stands like a globe of vegetable darkness.

However, we are not out now on a tree-errand; and all these remarks are thrown in accidentally and for nothing. By stage we will take you with us to see sights worth seeing; you shall go to Bashe-Byshe, to Mount Prospect, to the Dome, to Bald Peak, and to Monument Hill; you shall stroll along the valley of the Housatonic, to the Falls at Canaan; you shall go a-trouting up and down meadow and mountain brooks, and catch perch and pickerel in the twin lakes, Washinee and Washining, than which more beautiful can not be found in the state.

Here, then, for a few weeks we shall forget the city and lay aside its excitements, and bathe with a perpetual lavation in the bright, cool mountain air.

When one is young, and not yet entered on life, the heart pants for new things and for excitements. But after one has taken the burden upon his back, and lived amidst cares that never rest, but beat upon the shore like an unquiet surf, then nothing is so luxurious as the calm of a country neighborhood.

Nor is the only experience that of pleasure. There is ample space for retrospection, a mental state which is almost denied to public men in the life of a city No man in a city parish, driven by new demands each hour, has leisure to go a-gleaning over harvested fields. He must plow again, sow again, reap again. But now, at this distance, and separated from all daily solicitation, one can review the whole year; and if done with any worthy standard, it can not fail to furnish food for the most earnest reflection, and for the most solemn resolutions for the future.

VII.

TROUTING.

WHERE shall we go? Here is the More brook, the upper part running through bushy and wet meadows, but the lower part flowing transparently over the gravel, through the pasture grounds near the edge of the village. With great ingenuity, it curves and winds and ties itself into bow-knots. It sets out with an intention of flowing toward the south. But it lingers on its errand to coquette with each point of the compass, and changes its mind, at length, just in time to rush eastward into the Housatonic. It is a charming brook to catch trout in, when you can catch them.; but they are mostly caught. Nevertheless, there are here in Salisbury, as in every village, those mysterious men who are in league with fish, and can catch them by scores when no one else can get a nibble. It is peculiarly satisfactory to one's feelings to have waded, watched, and fished with worm, grasshopper, and fly, for half a day, for one poor feeble little trout, and four *dace,* and at evening to fall in with a merry negro, who informs you, with a concealed mirth in his eye, and a most patronizing kindness, that he has been to the same brook, and has caught three dozen trout, several of them weighing half-a-pound! We will not try that stream to-day.

Well, there is the Candy brook. We will look at that. A man might walk through the meadows and not suspect its existence, unless through the grass he first stepped into it! The grass meets over the top of it, and quite hides it through the first meadow; and below, through that iron-tinctured marsh land, it expands only a little, growing open-hearted by degrees across a narrow field; and then it runs for the thickets—and he that takes fish among those alders will certainly earn them. Yet, for its length, it is not a bad brook. The trout are not numerous, nor large, nor especially fine; but every one you catch renews your surprise that you should catch *any* in such a ribbon of a brook.

It is the upper part of the brook that is most remarkable, where it flows through mowing meadows, a mere slit, scarcely a foot wide, and so shut in by grass, that at two steps' distance you can not tell where it flows, though your ear hears the low sweet gurgle of its waters down some pet waterfall. Who ever dreamed of fishing in the grass? Yet, as you cautiously spy out an opening between the red-top and foxtail, to let your hook through, you seem to yourself very much like a man fishing in an orchard. One would almost as soon think of casting his line into a hay-mow, or of trying for a fish behind winrows or haycocks in a meadow! Yet, if the wind is only still, so that the line shall hang plumb down, we can, by some dexterity, drop the bait between grass, leaves, and spikes of aquatic flowers. No sooner does it touch the invisible water than the line cuts open the grass and rushes through weeds, borne off by your speckled victim.

Still further north is another stream, something larger, and much better or worse according to your luck. It is easy of access, and quite unpretending. There is a bit of a pond, some twenty feet in diameter, from which it flows; and in that there are five or six half-pound trout who seem to have retired from active life and given themselves to meditation in this liquid convent. They were very tempting, but quite untemptable. Standing afar off, we selected an irresistible fly, and with long line we sent it pat into the very place. It fell like a snow-flake. No trout should have hesitated a moment. The morsel was delicious. The nimblest of them should have flashed through the water, broke the surface, and with a graceful but decisive curve plunged downward, carrying the insect with him. Then we should, in our turn, very cheerfully, lend him a hand, relieve him of his prey, and, admiring his beauty, but pitying his untimely fate, bury him in the basket. But he wished no translation. We cast our fly again and again; we drew it hither and thither; we made it skip and wriggle; we let it fall plash like a blundering bug or fluttering moth; and our placid spectators calmly beheld our feats, as if all this skill was a mere exercise for their amusement, and their whole duty consisted in looking on and preserving order.

Next, we tried ground-bait, and sent our vermicular hook down to their very sides. With judicious gravity they parted, and slowly sailed toward the root of an old tree on the side of the pool. Again, changing place, we will make an ambassador of a grasshopper. Laying down our rod, we prepare to catch the grasshopper. That is in itself no slight feat. At the first step you take, at least forty bolt out and tumble headlong into the grass; some cling to the stems, some are creeping under the leaves, and not one seems to be within reach. You step again; another flight takes place, and you eye them with fierce penetration, as if thereby you could catch some one of them with your eye. You can not, though. You brush the grass with your foot again. Another hundred snap out, and tumble about in every direction. There are large ones and small ones, and middling-sized ones; there are gray and hard old fellows; yellow and red ones; green and striped ones. At length it is wonderful to see how populous the grass is. If you did not want them, they would jump into your very hand. But they know by your looks that you are out a-fishing. You see a very nice young fellow climbing up a steeple stem, to get a good look-out and see where you are. You take good aim and grab at him. The stem you catch, but he has jumped a safe rod. Yonder is another creeping among some delicate ferns. With broad palm you clutch him and all the neighboring herbage too. Stealthily opening your little finger, you see his leg; the next finger reveals more of him; and opening the next you are just beginning to take him out with the other hand, when, out he bounds and leaves you to renew your entomological pursuits! Twice you snatch handfuls of grass and cautiously open your palm to find that you have *only* grass. It is quite vexatious. There are thousands of them here and there, climbing and wriggling on that blade, leaping off from that stalk, twisting and kicking on that vertical spider's web, jumping and bouncing about under your very nose, hitting you in your face, creeping on your shoes, or turning summersets and tracing every figure of parabola or ellipse in the air, and yet not one do you get. And there is such a heartiness and merriment in their sallies! They are pert and gay, and do not take your intrusion in the least dudgeon. If any tender-hearted person ever wondered how a humane man could bring himself to such a cruelty as the impaling of an insect, let him hunt for a grasshopper in a hot day among tall grass; and when at length he secures one, the affixing him upon the hook will be done without a single scruple, with judicial solemnity, and as a mere matter of penal justice.

Now then the trout are yonder. We swing our line to the air, and give it a gentle cast toward the desired spot, and a puff of south wind dexterously lodges it in the branch of the tree. You plainly see it strike, and whirl over and over, so that no gentle pull will loosen it. You draw it north and south, east and west; you give it a jerk up and a pull down; you try a series of nimble twitches; in vain you coax it in this way and solicit it in that. Then you stop and look a moment, first at the trout and then at your line. Was there ever anything so vexatious? Would it be wrong to get angry? In fact you feel very much like it. The very things you wanted to catch, the grasshopper and the trout, you could not; but a tree, that you did not in the least want, you have caught fast at the first throw. You fear that the trout will be scared. You cautiously draw nigh and peep down. Yes, there they are, looking at you and laughing as sure as ever trout laughed! They understand the whole thing. With a very decisive jerk you snap your line, regain the remnant of it, and sit down to repair it, to put on another hook, you rise up to catch another grasshopper, and move on down the stream to catch a trout!

Meantime, the sun is wheeling behind the mountains, for you are just at the foot of the eastern ridge of Mount Washington (not of the White Mountains, but of the Taconic range in Connecticut). Already its broad shade begins to fall down upon the plain. The side of the mountain is solemn and sad. Its ridge stands sharp against a fire-bright horizon. Here and there a tree has escaped the axe of the charcoalers, and shaggily marks the sky. Through the heavens are slowly sailing continents of magnificent fleece mountains—Alps and Andes of vapor. They, too, have their broad shadows. Upon yonder hill, far to the east of us, you see a cloud-shadow making gray the top, while the base is radiant with the sun. Another cloud-shadow is moving with stately grandeur along the valley of the Housatonic; and, if you rise to a little eminence, you may see the brilliant landscape growing dull in the sudden obscuration on its forward line, and growing as suddenly bright upon its rear trace. How majestically that shadow travels up those steep and precipitous mountain sides! How it scoops down the gorge and valley and moves along the plain!

But now the mountain-shadow on the west is creeping down into the meadow. It has crossed the road where your horse stands hitched to the paling of a deserted little house.

You forget your errand. You select a dry tufty knoll, and lying down you gaze up into the sky. O! those depths. Something within you reaches out and yearns; you have a vague sense of infinity—of vastness—of the littleness of human life, and the sweetness and grandeur of divine life and of eternity. You people that vast ether. You stretch away through it and find that celestial city beyond, and therein dwell O how many that are yours! Tears come unbidden. You begin to long for release. You pray. Was there ever a better closet? Under the shadow of the mountain, the heavens full of cloudy cohorts, like armies of horsemen and chariots, your soul is loosened from the narrow judgments of human life, and touched with a full sense of immortality and the liberty of a spiritual state. An hour goes past. How full has it been of feelings struggling to be thoughts, and of thoughts deliquescing into feeling. Twilight is coming. You have miles to ride home. Not a trout in your basket! Never mind, you have fished in the heavens, and taken great store of prey. Let them laugh at your empty basket. Take their raillery good-naturedly; you have certainly had good luck.

But we have not yet gone to the brook for which we started. That must be for another tramp. Perhaps one's experience of "fancy tackle" and of fly-fishing might not be without some profit in moral analogies; perhaps a mountain stream and good luck in real trout may afford some easy side-thoughts not altogether unprofitable for a summer vacation. At any rate it will make it plain that oftentimes the best part of trout-fishing is not the fishing.

VIII.

A RIDE.

COME, if you are a-going to-day, it's high time you were off. It's four miles to the mountain road, and then a stiff pull up the hills. Is the lunch in the basket? Have you got all your rig? Well, good morning all! And here we are under way. The sky is full of slowly-opening, rolling, evasive fleece-clouds, that never do what you think they are a-going to, and always develop with unexpected shapes and effects. So you get and lose the sunshine by turns, and go along a checkered road just under the Taconic range. First you have on your right the swampy meadows, full of rank grasses, clumps of alders. Here and there little arboral villages of hemlock, a fringe of bushes and trees wind circuitously through the four-mile stretch, having in charge a brook, whose fair face the sun is not to gaze at too broadly, but only in golden glances, softened and tempered to mildness by the leafy bath of lucid green through which it passes.

Birds are busy as you ride along, and they have an intuitive knowledge that you are not to disturb them. They scarcely rise from the bush. Black-winged yellow-birds are harvesting the thistle-tops; king-birds, perched upon the corner stakes of the rail fence, wait till you are fairly up to them, and then with a fling and a measured circuit, they alight upon another stake four or five panels ahead. Crows, briskly flying through the air, are too intent for breakfast to spend time in cawing. Now and then, a kingbird makes a dash at them, and drives them up or down with unwonted nimbleness. Striped squirrels run along the fence, their pouches protuberant with prudent stores. The grasses and leaves, as you look aslant upon them, glitter with dewdrops; and all about you those nocturnal architects, spiders, have spread forth their crystal palaces, which glitter and quiver along every thread with jewel-drops.

This is called the under-mountain road. You would know why if you were on it. The mountains are not of the giant species, but they are much too large for hills. They range along on the west side of the Housatonic valley about twelve or fifteen miles. Their sides are not perpendicular except in two or three places. They slope toward you with almost every possible variation, giving your eye many and diverse pathways to the summit, up through gorges, ravines, and almost valleys. You of course know that mountains, which have the firmest features and the most fixed forms of nature, are yet of a more variable expression than any thing in the world except the ocean and the air. Lakes, trees, meadows, and men, have moods and changeable expressions; but mountains, beyond all other natural objects, are subject to moods. Every change of temperature, every change of hour throughout the day, every change of cloud or sun, is reflected upon the mountains. They are the grand expositors of the atmosphere. Sometimes they stand in dreamy mood, hazy, indistinct, absent-minded. All inequalities seem effaced. The lines of depression or the bulges of rock are lost, and they lie in airy tranquillity, as if God had sloped them from base to summit with an even line. Perhaps the next morning all reserve is gone. They have traveled up toward you. They seem close at hand. Every line is sharp, and there is no longer any dreamy expression, but one of earnest out-looking. They gaze down on you. There is a dark, solemn, positive expression, as if they had come to judgment with you. Mountains are the favorite grounds for shadows. They lie patiently still while clouds amuse themselves with painting every possible form and shape upon their huge sides; and they even choose to make their own shadows rather than to have none. A mountain-shadow, when the sun is in the west—a somber sheet of transparent darkness, cast loosely and mysteriously down from cliff to base—is a very witch with the imagination. One's thoughts play with it, rushing in and out, as we have seen swallows at Niagara dashing in and out of the thunder-mists of the Horse-shoe Falls.

But no effects are finer than those which sometimes are seen at or near sunset, when the heavens are full of white-gray and blue-gray clouds. The light which reveals them is entirely reflected down from the clouds, and from different strata and with different intensities. It is of all other light that which gives the utmost distinctness in contrast with the most perfect obscurity.

The nearest point to you will be black with purple darkness, and swell up into an unfamiliar grandeur which effaces all your former knowledge of it. Whether the mountain is a cloud or the cloud a mountain; whether there is a change going on, and the rocky top is melting away and mistily exhaling, or the mists are condensing and hardening into rock, you can not tell. But right out against this Obscure stands another section, so astonishingly revealed that you can trace its anatomy almost to the minutest line. Every swell or scoop, all the ribs and bones, the petty ridges and hollows, the whole wavy surface of the four-mile slope, is as distinct as the wrinkles on your own hand. Between these extremes is every possible gradation. Never long alike in any feature, but changing with the ever-changing cloud, you can not but feel that there is some mysterious connection between cloud-mountains and earthy rock-mountains. Those airy hills, are they the spirit-forms which come into visible communion with their yet earth-bound brethren? Do these things symbol forth the communion of spirits disembodied with spirits embodied? And are these evanescent hues, these strange effects of light, these systems of opal-shadows, analogous to all those openings and shuttings of heart, those lights and darks of imagination, which come upon us in the experiences of life?

We are at the foot of the hill. It is well that we have a good horse, for it will be a stiff pull, such as would appal dainty riders. It is the old road up the mountain; and is now principally used in hauling charcoal. It is seldom repaired, and in many places, particularly at the steepest parts, all that could be washed away has gone long ago, leaving nothing but ledges of rock, and loose round stones, from the size of a hen's egg upward, indefinitely. Now we come to the first pitch. Loose the check-rein, and give the horse his own way. See how bravely he makes at the hill, quickening his step, and breaking into a series of jumps; the wagon clatters and shakes, and bounds hither and thither, as if it were a great horse-rattle! There! stop and breathe your nag; pat him and praise him; he understands you perfectly, and enjoys applause just as much as if he had but two legs instead of four.

Do you notice what a profusion of growth there is about you, and what a fulness of health and perfection of green every vegetable has? Perpetual moisture, and a right proportion of light and shade give here the best conditions of growth. The asters are beginning to fringe the way. Golden rod, one of the most regal of all late summer plants, waves its plumy head. Its little arching boughs, feathered with gold, light up the way-side, shine along the fence corners, and glow in patches all through the field; it follows you up the mountain-sides, glittering along the edges of the laurel-bush, splendidly pictured on the deep green and varnished leaves. A young leaf of the laurel, just come of age, in a favorable spot, is the perfection of leaves!

However, we must not run off into these things. Come, Charley, away with you: and away it is, sure enough; bounce, clatter, thwack, up here, down a little there, over this side, over upon that, and at length, at full jump, up another pitch steeper than the last. Now, while he breathes, you may see that the next rise is steeper yet, and the next steeper than that; and if you could see around that turn of the road, as you will full soon enough, you would find another steeper than all of them put together. There is no more riding for the present. We must take it afoot, leaving the horse only an empty wagon to draw. For little silver-threaded streams are coming down the side of the rocks at every few rods; there is also such variety and beauty of leaf, and withal, such a hearty smell of the woods, that with occasional peeps at the distant country through forest and meadows, you find enough to tempt you to leisurely ascent; to say nothing of other reasons for it which your feet find out.

Now, then, we have come to the turn, right up to the left. Indeed, it *is* right up. When we first tried this road we had a heavier carriage and stopped it at this point. We will stop, again, but not for the same reason. Do you hear that noise? Yes! a storm is coming up—or is it the wind in the forest trees? It is neither; but the sound of a water-fall, mellowed to a deep, grand murmur. Fasten the horse, and let us turn off and see it; it is but a few moments' walk, but is worth many hours if you could not reach it sooner. There it opens! It is but a few feet wide; it drops a hundred feet right over the mountain's edge, to begin with, and white as snow; then it lovingly embraces an insensible rock, and dashes down beyond it a double fall, whiter than before.

Emboldened by its success, it now commences every species of fantastic caper that ever entered the imagination of a mountain brook. It comes together and then widens over that shelving rock, rushing down into a crystal pool; then, like a watery hand, at the exit it divides into five fingers, each sparkling with myriads of diamonds. The alacrity with which the separated currents make haste to get together again after this feat, is amusing;—the whirls, the side quirks, the petty impetuosities, the splitting and uniting, the plunging and emerging, until the distributed waters impool themselves once more, and look back upon you with a grave and a placid face, as if they asked your forgiveness for past levity, and your pity for the serious experience which now awaits them below. For we are on the upper brink of another series of long down-plunges, each one of which would be enough for a day's study. Below these are cascades and pools in which the water whirls friskily around like a kitten running earnestly after its tail. But we will go no further down. These are the mountain jewels; the necklaces which it loves to hang down from its hoary head upon its rugged bosom.

Shall we take out our tackle? That must be a glorious pool yonder for trout! No, my friend, do not desecrate such a scene by throwing a line into it with piscatory intent. Leave some places in nature to their beauty, unharassed, for the mere sake of their beauty. Nothing could tempt us to spend an hour here in fishing;—all the more because there is not a single trout in the whole brook. Indeed, this is an extemporaneous affair. Come here next week and there will be scarcely a drop of water. It is a mere piece of amusement which storms get up for the occasion. After heavy rains you may find it worth seeing, never else.

Let us return. Now, well-rested Charley, let us put at that grand ascent. Nothing loath, he canters up with such right good will that we must run too, over stones, up this bank, down that gully, bearing to the right over that ledge, close up to the left from that gully, round that point; and, yonder is the top—not of the mountain, but of our journey. Now get in, and we will take the left fork of the road, leaving that log cabin, locked-up, to its solitude, that stands by the other (and regular) mountain road. We now wind pleasantly round the side of the mountain's upper cone, having a deep, gorge-like valley on our left, at the bottom of which roars one of the most romantic of all mountain streams—*Sage's Brook,* by name. Trotting along your leaf-covered path, turning out, as best you may, for the heavy charcoal carts, whose home you have invaded, we will stop about two miles up, and leaving our horse to his oats in a rude stable, we will take our lunch, and go afoot along the road, till it crosses the upper part of Sage's Brook. Now rig out your rod. Among the bushes on the right see that stagnant stretch of water. It is the last place one would think of approaching for trout. Let us try. Here comes one; there is another; another, and another. Well, at length let us count—forty-two as sure as there is one—and that without moving from one spot. However, a little below this, a clerical friend, of this vicinity, took *eighty trout* out of one pool! To be sure they are small, but they are *trout,* and can afford to be small, they are so sweet and hard and every way good. Indeed, while we are up here we conceive a great contempt for those fat pound trout that feed in meadow brooks! Who would wish them that could have mountain trout? We always prefer these small but superb fish—until we get down to the meadows. A half-pound trout, at the end of one's line, may produce a change in his mind.

By following down this stream till it begins its descent on the east front of the mouutain, you will enter a gorge, called Sage's Ravine, which, if you love solitude, wildness, and beauty, will be worth all the pains you may take to climb through it. If it were possible, we should love to make the passage once in every month of the year. It is best entered from below. One requires a good foot, a strong hand, and a cool head, and then there is but little danger. It has been attempted successfully by ladies, and not one who ever explored it will regret the risk. And no one exploring the scenery in the vicinity of Salisbury should leave Sage's Ravine unvisited.

IX.

THE MOUNTAIN STREAM.

TROUTING in a mountain brook is an experience of life so distinct from any other, that every man should enjoy it once at least. That being denied to most, the next best that I can do for you, reader, is to describe it. So, then, come on.

We have a rod made for the purpose, six feet long, with only two joints, and a reel. We will walk up the mountain road, listening as we go to the roar of the brook on the left. In about a mile the road crosses it, and begins to lift itself up along the mountain side, leaving the stream at every step lower down on your right. You no more see it flashing through the leaves; but its softened rush is audible at any moment you may choose to pause and listen. When the wind moves through the whole mountain side of trees, you think it to be the rush of the brook down some rock. But, when you stand to look down through some more open glade, and see the misty current, far down, changing like a wild dream, through woods the most strange and contrary, it seems to you as if its sound was the voice of all the woods sunk down to the bottom of the valley, and murmuring up to you, in soft and sad complaint.

But you must see one thing before you wet the soles of your feet in the brook. Select a point from which you may look three miles down through the vast hollow, whose sides are mountains clad with forests. These huge trees you look down upon as if they were grass. When the winds move them, to the eye the swaying is like the shadowy roll of winds over a wheat field. The trees around us, handled by winds, have a slow and majestic swaying. Can it be that so grave a movement here, is represented far down yonder by that mere shivering and silvery trembling of the leaves? Can you look upon this gorgeous summer richness and imagine a winter storm raging at the gorge? Clouds scowling down, snow let loose from them, and whirled through the bare-branched trees, and then eddying down into dark clefts and frozen corners? Who can look at the one scene, winter or summer, and fully think of the other? Yet both reign alternately here. They who have come forth from towns and cities only in summer, to see the country, know little of the grandeur of mountains in winter.

But we must return from this dream. A hot August day inclines one to reflect upon ice and snow.

We will put into the brook just below a smart foamy fall. We have on cow-hide shoes, and other rig suitable. Selecting an entrance, we step in, and the swift stream attacks our legs with immense earnestness, threatening to take us off from them. A few minutes will settle all that, and make us quite at home. The bottom of the brook is not sand or gravel, but rocks of every shape, every position, of all sizes, bare or moss-covered. The stream goes over them at the rate of ten miles an hour. The descent is great. At every few rods cascades break over ledges, and boil up in miniature pools below. The trees on either side shut out all direct rays of the sun, and for the most part the bushes line the banks so closely, and cast their arms over so widely, that they create a twilight—not a gray twilight, as of light losing its luster, but a transparently black twilight, which softens nothing, but gives more ruggedness to the rocks, and a somber aspect even to the shrubs and fairest flowers.

It is a great matter to take a trout early in your trial. It gives one more heart. It serves to keep one about his business. Otherwise, you are apt to fall off into unprofitable reverie; you wake up and find yourself standing in a dream, half-seeing, half-imagining, under some covert of over-arching branches, where the stream flows black and broad among rocks, with moss green above the water and dark below it.

But let us begin. Standing in the middle of the stream, your short rod in hand, let out twelve to twenty feet of line, varying its length according to the nature of the stream, and, as far as it can be done, keeping its position and general conduct under anxious scrutiny. Just here the water is mid-leg deep. Experimenting at each forward reach for a firm foot-hold, slipping, stumbling over some uncouth stone, sliding on the moss of another, reeling and staggering, you will have a fine opportunity of testing the old philosophical dictum, that you can think of but one thing at a time. You *must* think of half a dozen;—of your feet, or you will be sprawling in the brook; of your eyes and face, or the branches will scratch them; of your line, or it will tangle at every step; of your far-distant hook and dimly-seen bait, or you will lose the end of all your fishing. At first, it is a puzzling business. A little practice sets things all right.

Do you see that reach of shallow water gathered to a head by a cross-bar of sunken rocks? The water splits in going over upon a slab of rock below, and forms an eddy to the right and one to the left. Let us try a grasshopper there. Casting it in above, and guiding it by a motion of your rod, over it goes, and whirls out of the myriad bubbles into the edge of the eddy, when, quick as a wink, the water breaks open, a tail flashes in the air and disappears, but re-appears to the instant backward motion of your hand, and the victim comes sklittering up the stream, whirling over and over, till your hand grasps him, extricates the hook, and slips him into the basket. Poor fellow! you *want* to be sorry for him, but every time you try you are glad instead. Standing still, you bait again, and try the other side of the stream, where the water, wiping off the bubbles from its face, is taking toward that deep spot under a side rock. There! you've got him! Still tempting these two shores, you take five in all, and then the tribes below grow cautious. Letting your line run before you, you wade along, holding on by one branch and another, fumbling with your feet, along the jagged channel, changing hands to a bough on the left side, leaning on this rock, stepping over that stranded log. Ripping a generous hole in your skirt as you leave it, you come to the edge of the petty fall. You step down, thinking only how to keep your balance, and not at all of the probable depth of water, till you splash and plunge down into a basin waist-deep. The first sensations of a man up to his vest pockets in water are peculiarly foolish, and his first laugh rather faint. He is afterward a little ashamed of the alacrity with which he scrambles for the bank. A step or two brings him to a sand-bank and to himself. But while *you* are in a scrape at one end of your line, a trout has got into a worse one at the other. A little flurried with surprise at both experiences, you come near losing him in the injudicious haste with which you overhaul him.

But see what a stately aster has ventured in hither In these black shades, through which the sun seldom penetrates, there is yet the light of flowers. What place *is* so dark that there is no light, if you only wait till the eye is used to its minute quantity? and what place is so rugged and so homely that there is no beauty, if you only have a sensibility to beauty? But, by this flower, and by more which I dimly see through the bushes, and lower down, I judge that the forest is thin, and that we are coming to a more open space. The stream sweeps grandly about an angle, and we open upon a bright, half-sunlighted reach of water.

You emerge from a long shadowy archway of leaves and trees, and stand in the mouth of its darkness to look down upon that illuminated spot. The leaves, struck with light from above, are translucent in all their softer parts, while their opaque frame-work seems like pencil lines finely drawn upon their surface. The sunlight comes checkering through the leaves. They, moving to a gentle wind, seem to shake it off from themselves. It falls upon the uncovered surface of the whirling brook, and flashes back in inconstant and fragmentary glances. The very gravel glows beneath the lucid water. The moss upon the upheaved stones has a golden greenness as if it exhaled about itself an atmosphere of color. The rocks that creep down to the bank, covered too with moss-plush, take, in spots, a stray reflected light, and seem to be luminous rather than illuminated. A hemlock tree by the bank is covered to its top with a grape-vine, from among whose broad palms it shoots out its arms and finely cut foliage in vivid contrast. It is a green tent: a hollow spire. I would that it stood in my door-yard, close by that cottage which shines in the edge of that grove of old trees that I see in my imaginary grounds. This stream, too, ought to flow just behind that grove; and that gigantic grandly unshaped rock, which has been heaved out of its bed at some far distant day, and cast down here, crashing like a thunderbolt,—O yes, I must have that in my grounds too;—but, just here my foot slipped from the unsteady stone, and the vision burst like one of the bubbles at my feet,—as fair and as fragile.

But look down below, through this sapphire and emerald atmosphere, and see the dark arches into which the stream presses headlong. The descent is greater there. And the water makes haste into the shadows while the trees frown upon it, and, as it wheels for a plunge, casts up pearl-drops that even in that gloom seem to emit a pale light. One could stand here by the hour. This rush of wild waters about your feet; this utter lawlessness of power and beauty, so solitary, with such instant contrasts, with the sound of waters beneath and of leaves above, and you, alone and solitary, standing in the fascination until you seem to become a part of the scene. A strange sensation steals over you, as if you were exhaling, as if you were passing out of yourself, and going into diffusive alliance with the whole scene! You reel and start and wake up, saying, Well! well! this is not trouting; and start off, forgetful of stones, crevices, slippery moss, and snags, as if you were in a level road. You are brought to a consciousness at your third step by a slip, a plunge, a full tumble, and find yourself, in the most natural manner, upon your hands and knees, making one more water-fall. You cannot help laughing at your ludicrous posture, the water damming itself up upon you as unceremoniously as if you were a log, and making a pet eddy in the neighborhood of your breeches pocket. You even stop to sup up a mouthful of drink, and wish that somebody that knew you could only be peeping through the bushes at your predicament, they would get a great deal of innocent happiness at your expense, but not at your damage.

Gathering up your awkward body you go dripping along down the stream, through the radiant spots into the dark, up to the falls, over which you peer, and, learning discretion from experience, you deem it best to take the shore and walk around the fall. You are repaid for the trouble by three trout, neatly slipped out of their aqueous nest into your willow basket. Stepping in again, you pursue your way with various experience for a quarter of a mile, when you enter a narrow gorge. The rocks come down in a body to the stream on either side. There are no side bushes. The way opens up through the air, far above you, to the receding mountain sides, upon which stand yet a few pines, spared of the axe, memorials of a vast brotherhood long since chopped away by the inexorable charcoalers. The very stream seems to take something of dignity from its surroundings. It gathers its forces, contracts its channels, darkens its surface, and moves down to a succession of falls, over which one feels no disposition to plunge. And so, climbing along the edges of the rock, prying into each crevice with your toes, grasping twig and root, bush or stem, you perch yourself mid-way, where you may see the fall above you, and the fall below you. Here you dream for a half hour—a waking, gazing dream. You study each shoot and indentation of the water—its bursts of crystal drops—ever changing, yet always the same. On the far side come down sheaves of water-stems. Nowhere is the water visible, and if you did not see the twinkling drops cast out their flash, you would think it a long harvest-shock, in some fairy field where grain bore diamonds transparent and colorless; from side to side, from top to bottom, within and without, it is struck through and through with air-mixed drops, so that it shoots down from top to bottom like a flow of pearls and crystals.

The gulf beneath is ragged and ugly. Freshets in spring carrying the winter out of the mountains, ice and half-dissolved snow, surging white in black and furious waters, tear up, and carry over these cliffs, mighty trees. They plunge headlong, sticking fast where they strike, gaunt, upright, till time and the elements strip them of bark and make them spectral and shadowy to all who look down upon them in that cavernous hollow, as I do now.

How rich and various are the mosses in this ravine. You sit down upon their moist plush, and find miniature palms and fern-like branches, and all manner of real or fanciful resemblances. The flowers too, those humble friends, have not forsaken this wild glen. They have crept up to drink at the very edge of the water; they hang secure and fearless from crevices on the face of the perpendicular rocks, and everywhere different species are retreating to their seed-forms or advancing to their bud, or are shaking their blossoms to the wind which comes up from the gorge below.

Here indeed is good companionship—here is space for deep and strange joy. If the thought of the city intrudes it seems like a dream; it can hardly be real that there can be stacked houses, burning streets, reeking gutters, everlasting din of wheels, and outcry of voices, or that you were ever hustled along the uproarious streets! In this cool twilight, without a voice except of wind and waters, where all is primeval, solitary, and rudely beautiful, you seem to come out of yourself. Your life lifts itself up from its interior recesses, and comes forth. Your own nature—your longings—your hope and love—your faith and trust, seem to live with quiet and unshrinking life; neither ruffled nor driven back, nor overlaid by all the contacts and burdens of multitudinous life in the city. O! why may not one carry hence that freshness which he feels—that simplicity, that truthfulness to what is real, and that repugnance to all that is sham? Why may not one always find the way to heaven and to spiritual converse, as short and as facile as it is in these lonely mountains?

It was in such places that Christ loved to stray. It was in such places that he spent nights in prayer. I never linger long in such scenes without a thought of his example, and a sympathetic understanding of why it should be so. Christ's love of nature, his constant allusions to flowers, his evident familiarity with solitudes, as if he was never so little alone as when separated from all men, mark any degree of the same relish in us as a true and divine taste.

But we must hasten on. A few more spotted spoils are awaiting us below. We make at the brook again. We pierce the hollow of over-hanging bushes, we strike across the patches of sun-light, which grow more frequent as we get lower down toward the plain; we take our share of tumbles and slips; we patiently extricate our entangled line, again and again, as it is sucked down under some log, or whirled around some network of beechen roots protruding from the shore. Here and there, we half forget our errand as we break in upon some cove of moss, where our dainty feet halt upon green velvet, more beautiful a thousand times than ever sprung from looms at Brussels or Kidderminster.

At length we hear the distant clatter of mills. We have finished the brook. Farewell—wild, wayward, simple stream! As many as are all the drops that have flowed in your channels since we came, so many thoughts and joys have flowed down through our soul! In a few moments you will be grown to a huge mill-pond; then at work upon its wheel; then, prim and proper, with ruffles of willow and aquatic bushes on each side, you will trip through the meadows, clatter across the road, and mingle with the More-brook, flow on toward the Housatonic—and be lost in its depths and breadths. For who will know thy mountain-drops in that promiscuous flood? Or who, standing on its banks, will dream from what scenes thou hast flowed, through what beauty—thyself the most beautiful?

X.

A COUNTRY RIDE.

MEN never will see the country who fly through it at the rate of thirty or forty miles an hour. The usual path of railroads never lies through the most interesting portions. The very best method of traveling is upon horseback. Next best, if you are strong and hearty, or if you wish to become so, is foot-traveling. The pedestrian is, in all respects, the most independent, and the best prepared to explore in detail.

If you are on horseback, you can do more in a shorter period. You abbreviate the time and labor of passing over the intermediate space between you and the points of interest. Besides, there is more company in a spirited horse a thousand times than in a foolish man. You sit in your saddle at ease, giving him his own way, the bridle loose, while you search on either side the various features of the way. Your nag becoming used to you and you to him, a sympathetic connection is established, and he always seems to do, of his own reflection, just what you wish him to do. Now a leisurely swinging walk, now a smart trot, then a spirited bit of a canter, which imperceptibly dies out into an amble, a pace, and then a walk again. When you rise a hill to overlook a bold prospect, can anybody persuade you that your horse does not enjoy the sight too? His ears go forward, his eye lights up with a large and bright look, and he gazes for a moment with equine enthusiasm, till some succulent bough or grassy tuft converts his taste into a physical form. A good horse is a perfect gentleman. He meets you in the morning with unmistakable pleasure; if you are near the grain-bin, he will give you the most cordial invitation, if not to breakfast with him, at least to wait upon him in that interesting ceremony. His drinking is particularly nice. He always loves running water, in the clearest brook, at the most sparkling place in it. No man shall make me believe that he does not observe and quietly enjoy the sun-flash on the gravel beneath, and on the wavy surface above. He arches down his neck to the surface, his mane falls gracefully over his head, he drinks with hearty earnestness, and the throbbing swallows pulsate so audibly and musically that you feel a sympathetic thirst. Now he lifts his head, and looks first up the road to see who is coming, and then down the road, at those work-horses, turned loose, affecting gayety with their old stiff legs and hooped bellies, and then, with a long breath, he takes the after-drink. Once more lifting his head, but now only a few inches above the surface, the drops trickle from his lips back to the brook. Finally, he cleanses his mouth, and chews his bit, and plays with the surface of the water with his lithe lip, and begins to paw the stream.

Guiding him out, you propose to yourself a real boy's drink. Selecting a favorable place, on a dry bank, where the stones give you a suitable rest, you lie flat down, at full length, and begin. Your luck will depend upon your judgment of places and skill of performance. Should you be too dignified to lie down, you will probably compromise and kneel, awkwardly protruding your head to the edge, where a little pool breaks over a rim of rock; thus you will be sure to send the first drops down the wrong way. Musical as is crystal water softly flowing over silver gravel, between fringed banks, its passage down the breathing tubes is anything but musical or graceful; and you will have an episode with your handkerchief behind the bushes —coughing, crying, being greatly exercised in various ways. But if you are willing to be a real boy (and no one is a real man after he has lost out all the boy), then you must lie level with the stream, careless of grass or gravel, and apply your lips gently, just above the point of the ripple, where it breaks over the gravel, and you shall quietly and relishfully quench your thirst. If you be handsome, or think yourself so, you can regale your eyes, too, with a fair face, seen in that original mirror in which, long before quicksilver or polished metal, Adam and Eve made their toilet. There is yet another mode: with both your hands form a cup, by lapping the little finger of the left hand upon the corresponding part of the right, and then curving the whole in a bowl-form. A little practice will enable you to lift and drink from this ruby goblet with great ease, where the ground does not permit recumbency. A good pair of hands, such as ours, ought to hold two large and one small mouthfuls. But that will depend somewhat on the size of the mouth.

But it was not to tell you how to drink, nor how our good and companionable horse drinks, that this sheet was begun; but to urge those who can command leisure in September or October, avoiding all beaten paths of pleasure, to make a tour through the mountain country of western Connecticut and Massachusetts. If you are young, and not abundant in means, and can get a friend to accompany you, go afoot. If you are able, go on horseback. If you wish to take your wife, your mother, or a sister, then a light, four-wheeled, covered buggy is to be elected. If there be three or four of you, take two horses and a two-seat light carriage, with a movable top.

Limit your articles of dress to a few, and those not easily torn or soiled; for it is good and most morally wholesome for Americans once in a while to dress and to act, not upon the rule of "What will people think?" but according to their own real necessities and convenience. And, above all, let every woman have a bloomer dress, for the sake of foot-excursions. In the city or town, our eye is yet in bondage to the old forms. But in the country, where the fields are to be traveled, the rocks climbed, brooks crossed and recrossed, fences scaled, bushes and weeds navigated, a woman in a long dress and multitudinous petticoats is a ridiculous or a pitiable object. Something is always catching; the party is detained till each woman can gather up her flowing robes, and clutch them in her left hand, while a shawl, parasol and bonnet-strings fill up the right hand. Thus she is engineered over and around the rocks or logs; and, in spite of all pains and gallantry, returns home bedrabbled and ragged. A bloomer costume leaves the motion free, dispenses with half the help from without, and avoids needless exposure of one's person. If, ignorant of what is best, a fair friend is caught in the country without such suitable dress, she is to be pitied, not blamed. But where one may have them, and rejects them for field-excursions as unbecoming and ridiculous, let me assure such foolish persons that it is the only dress that is really decent. I should think less of one's judgment and delicacy who, after a fair trial of both dresses, in an excursion requiring much field-walking, was not heartily converted to the theory of Bloomerism and to its practice in the country.

Having dispatched preliminaries, we are now ready for our tour. If one has not leisure for detailed explorations, and can spend but a week, let him begin, say at Sharon, or Salisbury, both in Connecticut, and both accessible from the Harlem railroad. On either side, to the east and to the west, ever-varying mountain-forms frame the horizon. There is a constant succession of hills swelling into mountains, and of mountains flowing down into hills. The hues of green in trees, in grasses, and in various harvests, are endlessly contrasted. There are no forests so beautiful as those made up of both evergreen and deciduous trees.

At Salisbury, you come under the shadow of the Taconic range. Here you may well spend a week, for the sake of the rides and the objects of curiosity. Four miles to the east are the Falls of the Housatonic, called Canaan Falls, very beautiful, and worthy of much longer study than they usually get. Prospect Hill, not far from Falls Village, affords altogether the most beautiful view of any of the many peaks with which this neighborhood abounds. Many mountain-tops of far greater celebrity afford less various and beautiful views. Near to it is the Wolf's Den, a savage cleft in the rocks, through which you grope as if you had forsaken light and hope for ever. On the west of Salisbury you ascend Mount Riga to Bald Peak, thence to Brace Mountain, thence to the Dome, thence to that grand ravine and its wild water, Bash-Bish—a ride, in all, of about eighteen miles, and wholly along the mountain-bowl. On the eastern side of this range, and about four miles from Norton's house, in Salisbury (where you will of course put up), is Sage's Ravine, which is the antithesis of Bash-Bish. Sage's Ravine, not without grandeur, has its principal attractions in its beauty; Bash-Bish, far from destitute of beauty, is yet most remarkable for grandeur. Both are solitary, rugged, full of rocks, cascades, grand waterfalls, and a savage rudeness tempered to beauty and softness by various and abundant mosses, lichens, flowers and vines. I would willingly make the journey once a month from New York to see either of them. Just beyond Sage's Ravine, very beautiful falls may be seen, after heavy rains, which have been named *Norton's Falls.*

Besides these and other mountain scenery—to which,

if described, we must give a separate letter—there are the Twin Lakes on the north of Salisbury, and the two lakes on the south, around which the rides are extremely beautiful. But they should always be afternoon rides; for these discreet lakes do not choose to give out their full charms except at about an hour before sunset. The rides in all this neighborhood are very fine, and a week at Salisbury (if the weather be fine and your disposition reasonable) will be apt to tempt you back, again and again.

From Salisbury to Great Barington the road lies along the base of the mountains, and, indeed, is called the under-mountain road. Great Barington is one of those places which one never enters without wishing never to leave. It rests beneath the branches of great numbers of the stateliest elms. It is a place to be desired as a summer residence.

Next, to the north, is Stockbridge, fàmed for its meadow-elms, for the picturesque scenery adjacent, for the quiet beauty of a village which sleeps along a level plain, just under the rim of hills. If you wish to be filled and satisfied with the serenest delight, ride to the summit of this encircling hill-ridge, in a summer's afternoon, while the sun is but an hour high. The Housatonic winds, in great circuits, all through the valley, carrying willows and alders with it wherever it goes. The horizon, on every side, is piled and terraced with mountains. Abrupt and isolated mountains bolt up here and there over the whole stretch of plain, covered with evergreens. Upon the northern ridge, lived the worthy Dr. West, known and honored among New England theologians. It is but recently that his old house was demolished. And this very spot we came near purchasing for a summer house.

But Stockbridge is memorable to us, chiefly, as the residence of Jonathan Edwards, once a missionary among the Indians. The colonial government, with singular wisdom, established among the Indians a desirable system of culture. Families of the utmost integrity were selected to live among them and teach them in mechanic arts, husbandry, and various social civilization. A religious teacher was also put in charge of their moral and spiritual interests. And among these missionaries, Jonathan Edwards, after his dismission from Northampton, as a man too progressive in his tendencies, was by far the most remarkable. The house, where he lived, and in which he wrote his world-renowned treatise on the Will, still stands strong, and fair for another hundred years' existence. The very place where he sat to write this work—then a little writing closet, now a portion of the parlor—is to be seen by all who have curiosity in such matters. We often ride through this beautiful village in summer, and never, without driving down to the Edwards house, and going back in imagination to the simplicity and the humble devotedness of this man, in a field apparently the least fitted for one of his philosophic tastes. He seemed unconscious of greatness. He was not pestered, as smaller men are, with great solicitude lest they should be found in a field too small for the eminence of their gifts. Around about Stockbridge are many charming rides, and places of curiosity for all to visit. An excellent hotel is kept, and is usually well filled in summer with refugees from the arid city.

Going north four or five miles, we come to Lenox, known for the singular purity and exhilarating effects of its air, and for the beauty of its mountain scenery. As it is to be hereafter our summer home, we shall be regarded as a partial witness in its favor. But, if one spends July or October in Lenox, they will hardly seek another home for summer. The church stands upon the highest point in the village, and if, in summer, one stands in the door, and gazes upon the vast panorama, he might, without half of the Psalmist's devotion, prefer to stand in the door of the Lord's house, to a dwelling in tent, tabernacle, or mansion. Close by, and equally eminent, and rich in prospect, lies the village graveyard. No dark and sickly fogs ever gather at evening about it. It lies nearer heaven than any place about. It is good to have our mortal remains go upward for their burial, and catch the earliest sounds of that trumpet which shall raise the dead!

Some talk has been made of rebuilding the church lower down in the village. Long may the day be distant when it shall be done! The brightest thing in the village is the church upon the hill! It was in the adjacent burial-ground that Mrs. Fanny Kemble Butler desired to rest when her work on earth was over. "I will not rise to trouble any one if they will let me sleep there. I will ask only to be permitted, once in a while, to raise my head, and look out upon this glori ous scene!" May she behold one so much fairer, that this scenic beauty shall fade to a shadow!

From Salisbury to Williamstown, and then to Bennington in Vermont, there stretches a county of valleys, lakes and mountains, that is yet to be as celebrated as the lake-district of England and the hill-country of Palestine.

XI.

FAREWELL TO THE COUNTRY.

SALISBURY, CONN., *Sept.* 16, 1853.

DURING two summers we have found a home in this hill-country. We have explored its localities in every direction. The outlines of its horizon, its peaks and headlands, its mountains and gorges, its streams and valleys, have become familiar to us. It is a sad feeling that we have in going away.

Nature makes so many overtures to those who love her, and stamps so many remembrances of herself upon their affections, and draws forth to her bosom so much of our very self, that, at length, the fields, the hills, the trees, and the various waters, become a journal of our life. In riding over from Millerton to Salisbury (six miles), for the last time, probably, for years, we could not but remark what a hold the face of the country had got upon us. This round hill on the left, as we draw near the lakes, it is *our* hill! Hundreds of times we have greeted it, and been greeted; we have bounded over it; in imagination we have built under those trees, and welcomed friends to our air-cottage. How often, at sunset, have we looked forth north, east, south and west, and harvested from each direction great stores of beauty and of joy. As we wound around its base, a three-quarter's moon shining full and bright, the two lakes began to appear in silver spots through the trees.

When we reached the summit of the road, they opened in full, and glimmered and shone like molten silver. For more beautiful sheets of water, and more beautiful sites from which to look at them, one may search far without finding.

During a few days' absence the first frost has fallen. The Reaper then has come! And this is the sharp sickle whose unwhetted edge will cut all before it! We had, before this, noticed the blood-red dogwood in the forests, and a few vines that blushed at full length, with here and there a maple in swamp-lands, that were prematurely taking bright colors. But now all things will hasten. Two weeks, and less, will bring October. That is the painted month. Every green thing loves to die in bright colors. The vegetable cohorts march glowing out of the year in flaming dresses, as if to leave this earth were a triumph and not a sadness. It is never Nature that is sad, but only we, that dare not look back on the past, and that have not its prophesy of the future in our bosoms. Men will sit down beneath the shower of golden leaves that every puff of wind will soon cast down in field and forest, and remember the days of first summer and the vigor of young leaves; will mark the boughs growing bare, and the increasing spaces among the thickest trees, through which the heavens every day do more and more appear, as their leaves grow fewer and none spring again to repair the waste—and sigh that the summer passeth and the winter cometh. How many suggestions of his own life and decay will one find!

But there is as much of *life* in autumn as of death, and as much of creation and of growth as of passing away. Every flower has left its house full of seeds. No leaf has dropped until a bud was born to it. Already, another year is hidden along the boughs; another summer is secure among the declining flowers. Along the banks the green heart-shaped leaves of the violet tell me that it is all well at the root; and in turning the soil I find those spring beauties that died, to be only sleeping. Heart, take courage! What the heart has once owned and had, it shall never lose. There is resurrection-hope not alone in the garden-sepulchre of Christ. Every flower and every tree and every root are annual prophets sent to affirm the future and cheer the way. Thus, as birds, to teach their little ones to fly, do fly first themselves and show the way; and as guides, that would bring the timid to venture into the dark-faced ford, do first go back and forth through it, so the year and all its mighty multitudes of growths walk in and out before us, to encourage our faith of life by death; of decaying for the sake of better growth. Every seed and every bud whispers to us to secure, while the leaf is yet green, that germ which shall live when frosts have destroyed leaf and flower.

Is there any thing that the heart needs more than this? Is there any thing that can comfort the heart out of which dear ones have fled, as birds flying out of and forsaking the trees where they were wonted to sit and sing, but the assurance of their speedy re-coming? They are not silent everywhere because they do not speak to us here. Their feet still walk, though no footfall may be in our houses. Thine, O Death, was the furrow; we cast therein our precious seed. Now let us wait and see what God shall bring forth for us. A single leaf falls—the bud at its axil will shoot forth many leaves. The husbandman bargains with the year to give back a hundred grains for each one buried. Shall God be less generous? Yet, when we sow, our hearts think that beauty is gone out, that all is lost. But when God shall bring again to our eyes the hundred-fold beauty and sweetness of that which we planted, how shall we shame over that dim faith, that having eyes saw not, and ears heard not, though all heaven and all the earth appeared and spake, to comfort those who mourn. And yet! and yet!—something sinks heavily down and weighs the heart too hardly. The future is bright enough; but, the *Now!*

This glorious vision, this hope and everlasting surety of the future, how shallow were life without it, and how deep beyond all fathoming with it! The threads that broke in the loom here shall be taken up there. The veins of gold, that penetrate this mighty mountain of Time and Earth, shall then have forsaken the rock and dirt, and shine in a sevenfold purity. All those wrongly estranged and separated, and all who, with great hearts, seeking good for men, do yet fall out and contend, and all they who bear about hearts of earnest purpose, longing to love, and to do, but hindered and baulked, and made to carry hidden fire in their souls that warms no one, but only burns the censer, and all they who are united for mutual discomfort, and all who are separated that should have walked together, and all that inwardly or outwardly live in a dream all their days, longing for the dawn and the waking,—to all such how blessed is the dawn of the Resurrection! The stone is rolled away, and angels sit upon it; and all who go groping toward the grave to search for that which is lost, shall hear their voices teaching them that Heaven harvests and keeps whatever of good the earth loses.

But we began to write for the sake of saying farewell to old Salisbury and to all its beautiful scenery. The enjoyment which one receives in an eight weeks' communion with such objects as abound here can not be measured in words. We are not ashamed to acknowledge that our last ride through the familiar places was attended with an overflow of gratitude, as intelligent and distinct as ever we experienced toward a living person. Why not? Did not God create the heavens and the earth full of benefactions? Did he not set forth all enchantments of morning and evening, all processes of the seasons, to be almoners of His own bounty? God walks through the earth with ten thousand gifts which he finds no one willing to receive. Men live in poverty, in sadness and dissatisfaction, yearning and wishing for joy, while above them and about them, upon the grandest scale, with variations beyond record, are stores of pleasure beyond all exhaustion, and incapable of palling upon the taste. When our heart has dwelt for a long time in these royalties, and has been made rich with a wealth that brings no care, nor burden, nor corruption, and that wastes only to burst forth with new treasures and sweeter surprises, we can not forbear thanksgiving and gratitude which fills the eye rather than moves the tongue. It is not alone thanks to God. By a natural process the mind gives sentient life to His messengers, and regards them as the cheerful and conscious stewards of divine mercy, and thanks them heartily for doing what God sent them to do. Nor can we forbear a sense of sorrow that that which was meant for so great a blessing to all men should be wasted, upon the greatest number of men, either because they lack education toward such things, or lack a sensibility which produces enjoyment without an education.

If there were an artist to come among us who could stand in Metropolitan Hall in the presence of a living assemblage, and work with such marvelous celerity and genius, that in a half-hour there should glow from his canvas a gorgeous sunset, such as flushes the west in an October day; and then, when the spectators had gazed their fill, should rub it hastily out, and overlay it, in a twenty minutes' work, with another picture, such as God paints rapidly *after* sunset—its silver white, its faint apple-green, its pink, its yellow, its orange hues, imperceptibly mingling into grays and the black-blue of the upper arch of the heavens, to be rubbed out again, and succeeded by pictures of clouds —all, or any, of those extraordinary combinations of grandeur, in form and in color, that make one tremble to stand and look up; these again to be followed by vivid portraitures of more calm atmospheric conditions of the heavens, without form or vapor; and so on endlessly,—such a man would be followed by eager crowds, his works lauded, and he called a god. He *would* be a god. Such *is* God. So he fills the heavens with pictures, strikes through them with effacement that he may find room for the expression of the endless riches of the divine ideas of beauty and majesty. "The heavens declare the glory of God, and the firmament showeth his handiwork." The Psalmist then boldly personifies days and nights, as if they were sentinels and spectators, each as it passes from his watch rehearsing what it had seen: "Day *unto* day uttereth speech, and night *unto* night showeth knowledge."

We are thankful that our incarceration in the city, though it shuts out all these things, can not efface the memory of a summer's happiness. *That* glows and lives again, and will be a sweet twilight on our path, till another season and another vacation.

XII.

SCHOOL REMINISCENCE.

It was our misfortune, in boyhood, to go to a District School. A little, square, pine building, blazing in the sun, stood upon the highway, without a tree for shade or shadow near it; without bush, yard, fence or circumstance to take off its bare, cold, hard, hateful look. Before the door, in winter, was the pile of wood for fuel; and there, in summer, were all the chips of the winter's wood.

In winter we were squeezed into the recess of the furthest corner, among little boys, who seemed to be sent to school merely to fill up the chinks between the bigger boys. Certainly we were never sent for any such absurd purpose as an education. There were the great scholars; the school in winter was for *them*, not for us piccaninies. We were read and spelled twice a day, unless something happened to prevent, which *did* happen about every other day. For the rest of the time we were busy in keeping still. And a time we always had of it. Our shoes always would be scraping on the floor, or knocking the shins of urchins who were also being "educated." All of our little legs together (poor, tired, nervous, restless legs, with nothing to do!) would fill up the corner with such a noise, that every ten or fifteen minutes the master would bring down his two-foot hickory ferule on the desk with a clap that sent shivers through our hearts to think how that would have felt if it had fallen somewhere else; and then, with a look that swept us all into utter extremity of stillness, he would cry, "Silence! in that corner!" Stillness would last for a few minutes; but, little boys' memories are not capacious. Moreover, some of the boys had great gifts of mischief, and some of mirthfulness, and some had both together. The consequence was, that just when we were the most afraid to laugh, we saw the most comical things to laugh at. Temptations which we could have vanquished with a smile out in the free air, were irresistible in our little corner where a laugh and a stinging slap were very apt to woo each other. So, we would hold on, and fill up; and others would hold on and fill up too; till, by and by, the weakest would let go a mere whiffet of a laugh, and, then, down went all the precautions, and one went off, and another, and another, touching off the others like a pack of fire-crackers! It was in vain to deny it. But, as the process of snapping our heads and pulling our ears went on with primitive sobriety, we each in turn, with tearful eyes and blubbering lips, declared "we didn't mean to," and that was true; and that "we wouldn't do so any more," and that was a fib, however unintentional; for we never failed to do just so again, and that about once an hour all day long.

Besides this, our principal business was to shake and shiver at the beginning of the school for very cold; and to sweat and stew for the rest of the time, before the fervid glances of a great box iron stove, red hot. There was one event of great horror and two of pleasure; the first was the act of *going to school*, in which is to be comprised the leaving off play, the face-washing and clothes-inspecting, the temporary play-spell before the master came, the outcry, "There he is—the master is coming," the hurly-burly rush, and the noisy clattering to our seats. The other two events of pleasure were the play-spell and the dismission. O, dear! can there be any thing worse for a lively, mercurial, mirthful, active little boy, than going to a winter district-school? Yes. Going to a summer district-school! There is no comparison. The last is the Miltonic depth below the deepest depth.

A woman kept the summer school, sharp, precise, unsympathetic, keen and untiring. Of all ingenious ways of fretting little boys, doubtless her ways were the most expert. Not a tree was there to shelter the house. The sun beat down on the shingles and clapboards till the pine knots shed pitchy tears, and the air was redolent of warm pine-wood smell. The benches were slabs with legs in them. The desks were slabs at an angle, cut, hacked, scratched, each year's edition of jack-knife literature overlaying its predecessor, until in our day it already wore cuttings and carvings two or three inches deep. But if *we* cut a morsel, or stuck in pins, or pinched off splinters, the little sharp-eyed mistress was on hand, and one look of her eye was worse than a sliver in our foot, and one nip of her fingers was equal to a jab of a pin;—for we had tried both.

We envied the flies—merry fellows, bouncing about, tasting that apple skin, patting away at that crumb of bread; now out the window, then in again; on your nose, on your neighbor's cheek, off to the very school-ma'am's lips, dodging her slap, and then letting off a real round and round buzz, up, down, this way, that way, and every way. O, we envied the flies more than any thing, except the birds. The windows were so high that we could not see the grassy meadows; but we could see the tops of distant trees, and the far, deep, bounteous blue sky. There flew the robins; there went the bluebirds, and there went we. We followed that old Polyglott, the skunk-blackbird, and heard him describe the way they talked at the winding up of the Tower of Babel. We thanked every meadow-lark that sung on, rejoicing as it flew. Now and then a "chipping-bird" would flutter on the very window-sill, turn its little head sidewise, and peer in on the medley of boys and girls. Long before we knew that it was in Scripture, we sighed—O, that we had the wings of a bird—we would fly away and be out of this hateful school. As for learning, the sum of all that we ever got at a district-school would scarcely cover the first ten letters of the alphabet. One good, kind, story-telling, Bible-rehearsing aunt at home, with apples and gingerbread premiums, is worth all the school-ma'ams that ever stood by to see poor little fellows roast in those boy-traps called district-schools.

But this was thirty-five years ago. Doubtless it is all changed long since then. We mean *inside;* for certainly there are but few school-houses that we have seen in New England whose outside has much changed. There is a beautiful house here in Salisbury, Conn., just on the edge of the woods. It is worth going miles to see how a school-house *ought* to look. But generally the barrenest spot is chosen, the most utterly homely building is erected, without a tree or shrub; and there those that can do no better, pass the pilgrimage of their childhood education.

We are prejudiced, of course. Our views and feelings are not to be trusted. They are good for nothing except to show what an effect our school-days left upon *us*. We abhor the thought of a school. We do not go into them if we can avoid it. Our boyhood experience has pervaded our memory with such images as breed a private repugnance to district-schools, which we fear we shall not lay aside until we lay aside everything into the grave. We are sincerely glad that it is not so with everybody. There are thousands who revert with pleasure to those days. We are glad of it. But we look on such persons with astonishment.

XIII.

THE VALUE OF BIRDS.

SPORSTMEN, BEWARE.—The last Legislature enacted that it shall not be lawful in the State of New Jersey for any person to shoot, or in any other manner to kill or destroy, except upon his own premises, any of the following description of birds: the night or mosquito hawk, chimney swallow, martin or swift, whippoorwill, cuckoo, kingbird or bee martin, woodpecker, claip or highhole, catbird, wren, bluebird, meadow lark, brown thresher, dove, fire-bird or summer redbird, hanging bird, ground robin or chewink, boblink or rice bird, robin, snow or chipping bird, sparrow, Carolina lit, warbler, blackbird, bluejay, and the small owl. The penalty is five dollars for each offence, or for the destruction of the eggs of such birds.—*Tribune.*

WHAT is a bird good for? What dainty sentimentalism has set a stupid Legislature at such enactments?

Not so fast. Although we should greatly respect a Legislature that had the humanity to think of birds among other constituent bipeds, yet experience has taught farmers and gardeners the economic value of birds.

There are no such indefatigable entomologists as birds. Audubon and Wilson never hunted for specimen birds with such perseverance as birds themselves exhibit in their researches. They depasture the air, they penetrate every nook and corner of thicket, hedge and shrubbery, they search the bark, pierce the dead wood, glean the surface of the soil, watch for the spade-trench, and follow the furrow for worms and larvæ. A single bird in one season destroys millions of insects for its own food and for the supply of its nest. No computation can be made of the insects which birds devour. We do not think of another scene more inspiriting than the plowing season, in this respect. Bluebirds are in the tops of trees practicing the scales, crows are cawing as they lazily swing through the air toward their companions in the tops of distant dead and dry trees; robins and blackbirds are wide awake, searching every clod that the plow turns, and venturesome almost to the farmer's heels. Even boys relent, and seem touched by the birds' appeal to their confidence, and, until small fruits come, spare the birds. Bob'o'links begin to appear—the buffoon among birds, and half sing and half *fizzle.* How our young blood sparkled amid such scenes, we could not tell why; neither why we cried without sorrow or laughed without mirth, but only from a vague sympathy with that which was beautiful and joyous.

Were there ever such neat scavengers? Were there ever such nimble hunters? Were there ever such adroit butchers? No Grahamitic scruples agitate this seed-loving and bug-loving tribe. They do not show their teeth to prove that they were designed for meat. They eat what they like, wipe their mouths on a limb, return thanks in a song, and wing away to a quiet nook to doze or meditate, snug from the hawk that spheres about far up in the ether.

To be sure, birds, like men, have a relish for variety. There are no better pomologists. If we believed in transmigration we should be sure that our distinguished fruit-culturists could be traced home. *Longworth* was a brown-thresher; *Downing* a lark, sometimes in the dew and sometimes just below the sun; *Thomas* was a plain and sensible robin; junior *Prince* was a bob'o'link, irreverently called skunk-blackbird; *Ernst* a dove; *Parsons* a woodpecker; *Wilder* a kingbird. We could put our finger, too, upon the human blackbird, wren, bluejay, and small owl, but prudence forbids; as it also does the mention of a certain clerical mocking-bird that makes game of his betters!

But we wander from the point. We charge every man with positive dishonesty who drives birds from his garden in fruit-time. The fruit is theirs as well as yours. They took care of it as much as you did. If they had not eaten egg, worm, and bug, your fruit would have been pierced and ruined. They only come for wages. No honest man will cheat a bird of his spring and summer's work.

XIV.

A ROUGH PICTURE FROM LIFE.

It is a fine thing to be a conservative of the benevolent class. Inheriting a fine old mansion, amid orchards, and gardens, and lawns, and surrounded by old trees, whose mighty arms waved joyfully when he was born, and have discoursed noble music to his ear ever since —the happy, kind, even-minded dreamer dreads all change. His nest is snug, and he is afraid to lose a single egg by the hand of thievish innovation. In the sunny parlor he reads his daily conservative journal, ratifies its curses, and thinks he hates all whom it stigmatizes. His sides grow fat, his face grows round, his head grows bald, his heart grows mellow to all who know its sunny side.

Meanwhile, the schools must be supported—yes, schools are ancient institutions, and he patronizes schools. The academy must be built—and there are century-old precedents for academies—so he approves of them. All the boys are exhorted to go to school, and all the maidens are there to keep the boys out of mischief. Now it will never do to educate Yankee lads and lasses, if it is a sin to think, and if thinking errs when it leads to action. Accordingly, so many girls are growing up who, finding themselves able to govern their parents, aspire to be teachers of schools; and so many inventive, thinking boys are brewing schemes and improvements, that, in a half-score of years, our kind old conservative finds much mysterious mischief abroad. Where it could have come from, he can not imagine. There are new fashions and new architecture, new halls and new churches, new ministers and new lawyers.

Meanwhile, the neighboring valley, child of a mountain-gorge a little back, and borrowing its brook, has shown signs of evil. A dam has raised the brook to an ominous pond, which trout scorn and frogs love. Gaunt mills go up, shanties abound, Irish fairies are digging under ground and over ground, in the water and out of the water, powder drilled into rocks is splitting them open with surprise. Alas! there is no more quiet for our kind old heart; his walks are circumscribed, his influence wanes, his prejudices grow, his quails and his partridges, his spring blackbirds, his bluebirds and robins, are driven into close quarters or utterly dispersed.

Ten thousand daily feelings vex his soul. The factory-village eats up his quiet. Its roughness, its various impertinences, its night and day clatter, all offend him. He retreats more desperately to his paper, and holds back with all his might.

But time has a temptation for him that he did not estimate. His own grounds are wanted. Through that exquisite dell which skirts along the northern side of his estates, where he has wandered, book in hand, a thousand times, monarch of squirrels, bluejays and partridges, his only companions and subjects—are seen peering and spying those execrable men that turn the world upside down, civil engineers and most uncivil speculators. Alas! the plague has broken out. His ground is wanted—is taken—is defiled—is daily smoked by the passage of that modern thunder-dragon, dragging its long tail of cars. A jury of his own townsmen, after gravely estimating the case and considering his demand for ten thousand dollars damages, frankly admit the claim, but offset it with a judgment that his property is increased in value at least twenty thousand. But that will never pay for his robins, his quails, his autumnal quiet, his evening strolls and his trout brook. They have spoiled one of God's grandest pictures by slashing it with a railroad, but declare that the frame has been enough improved to make up for the picture.

Who that has a spark of nature or the love of nature in him, would not be a conservative? After this we quite enjoy to hear him drub the world in general and all modern improvements in particular. Nevertheless his sturdy son, stealing upon paternal pride, and very quietly and reverently governing his governor, has persuaded the sale of a few lots. You know the rest. A man may, peradventure, withstand an Eve in Paradise; an Abdiel may be found; but a man proof against speculations in town lots, which to-day are worth a hundred dollars and to-morrow a thousand, you may search the earth through and you shall not find.

And so this place is gone. The old mansion, driven up more sharply every year, has lost its orchard, has lost its meadows, has lost that long slope, has a rail fence crooking like a serpent through the middle of its gardens, with a hundred Irish imps whooping in and out of shanties on the other side, where the old mulberry tree stood and the best currant bushes grew that ever hung with fruit like drops of blood. At last, the poor stately old house, standing askew by reason of the streets that have cut in on every side, goes, like its master, to ruin.

For such conservatives we have a genuine sympathy. There is something very natural in the whole process; and the appeal is rather to our pity than our censure.

XV.

A RIDE TO FORT HAMILTON.

It is difficult to choose between the scenery of the ocean side and inland scenery, if one were to have the liberty of but one of them. Both of them take hold of the imagination with great power; both are stimulating and yet soothing. But they act upon the mind in very different ways.

The power of the mind to animate natural objects with its own emotions, and gradually to clothe external objects with the attributes and experiences of the soul, is well known. The place where any event in our history has occurred becomes a memorial of the feelings which that event excited in us. The walk which for years our feet have trod in hours of meditation, is no longer a dry path, half leaf-covered, obscure among the underbrush, or sinuous along the summit of the overlooking bluff. It has become intrusted with our deepest sensations. It speaks to us, and we talk with it. It is a journal of our gradual experiences. A rock, under whose sides we have been wont to commune with God, and dream of the future, can never assume a merry face or an irreverent demeanor. The home-trees, under which we sit with daily friends, become social and familiar; those which our solitude seeks out, and under which we take refuge from men, whose whispering boughs charm our cares, or whose silence descends from far-up branches, to quiet our fears or sorrows—become sacred companions. Thus, too, certain places—bends in a river, nooks in a mountain side, clefts in rocks, sequestered dells—have their imputed life. Whenever we come back to these places it is as when one reads old letters, or a journal of old experiences, or meets old friends, that bring thronging back with them innumerable memories and renewed sensations of pleasure or sadness.

The ocean can not produce such effects. Whatever may be the sources of its power, it does not depend upon association. The ocean has no permanent objects. The waves of yesterday are gone to-day; and the calm of to-day will be tumultuous to-morrow. The very effect of the sea, in part, depends upon its exceeding changeableness. Upon what can we hang our associations? The line of coast supplies a partial resource, but the sea none. It has no nooks, or dells, or caves, or overhanging rocks, which, once formed, abide for ever. It has no perpetual boughs or enduring forests. Its mountains are liquid, and flow down in the very same moment that they lift themselves up. The wide and whole sea, as a great One, to be sure, comes to us always the same; but its individual features are always strangers. Its waves are always new waves; its ripples are always formed before us; its broad and uncrested undulations are fresh and momently produced. If we go down to the shore to mourn for those who shall not come forth from the deep till the archangel's trump shall bring forth its dead, though we shed daily tears for weary months, they treasure up no associations in the rolling waters or bright-glancing calms. If the place becomes sacred, it is the shore, the surrounding rocks or sand-hills, and not the ever-born, ever-dying waves.

The operation of these causes extends to level country scenery. The mind seldom wishes to trust much to a level and insipid country. The inhabitants of such plains form but feeble local attachments. But those who are mountain-born become so intensely attached to their familiar places, that when removed from them, home-sickness becomes a disease, and preys upon the frame like a fever or a consumption.

The scenery of the sea addresses itself to a different part of our being. It speaks more to the imagination than to the affections, giving fewer objects for analysis or examination; for ever throwing off the eye by revolutions of form and changeableness, and refusing to become familiar in those patient and gentle ways of companionship that venerable forests and benignant mountains assume. The sea is not a lover and friend, but an inspirer and an austere teacher. Trees soothe us and comfort us by sympathy. We still stand in our sorrows, or yearnings, or sadness; but they speak to us with ten thousand airy voices or melodious whisperings, and, mingling better thoughts and faith with our fretful experience, they sweeten the heart without washing away its thoughts with utter forgetfulness.

But the sea forces life away from us. We stand upon its shore as if a new life were opening upon us, and we were in the act of forgetting the things that are behind, and reaching forth unto those which are before and beyond. The unobstructed distance, the far horizon line, on which the eye only stops, but over which the imagination bounds, and then first perceives plainly where the eye grows dim; the restless change, the sense of endless creative power, the daily and sometimes hourly change of countenance, that makes you think that the ocean revolves deep experiences in its bosom, and reveals distinctly upon its mutable face expressions of its peace, or sorrow, or joy, or struggle and rage, or victory and joyfulness;—these are phenomena that excite us, and carry us away from life, away from hackneyed experiences. When we retire from the seaside we come back to life as if from a voyage, and familiar things have grown strange.

A frequent and favorite ride, with us, is to Fort Hamilton. It lies, in part, upon the Long Island side of New York Bay and the Narrows, and terminates a little beyond the Fort, where, between the dim sand-points of Coney Island on the left, and the Hook on the right, the ocean stretches out itself.

It is an autumnal day; the leaves are changed, but not fallen. The air is mild and genial. The carriage stands at the door; the mother is ready, the friends are waiting, and Charley paws impatiently. Away we go rattling over the noisy pavement, enduring rather than enjoying, till we reach the toll-gate. This passed, the fresh sea-smell comes across the Bay, and we look out upon heaps of seaweed on our right, odorous in its peculiar and not disagreeable way. The bay is specked with sails. Staten Island stands boldly up on the far side, a noble frame to so beautiful a picture as New York Bay.

The wheels roll softly over the smooth causeway till we enter the street of Gowanus, when again we quake and shake for a long mile over execrable pavements, poorly laid at first, and through daily use, grown daily worse. For, O my friends, this is Death's highway. Here, through almost every hour of the day, he holds his black processions to Greenwood. And now we reach the corner which leads to the Funeral Gate; this is the corner guarded with oysters, liquor and cakes, on one side, and a thriving marble-cutting, monument-making business, on the other. It is quite American. One reflects with peculiar emotions upon these happy national conjunctions of dissipation, commerce, and death-rest. But, after all, is not this an unconscious type of life? Is there not every day, if we would see it, just as terrible a mingling of things sacred and profane? And yet it is painful always and increasingly, that there is not in the public mind enough of taste, or of sentiment, or of superstition, to keep the sordid hucksters from shoving their bar and booth up to the very cheeks of death and the grave! Or, must the last sounds that smite the dead man's coffin bear witness of the spirit of that great, sordid den from which he has departed and is departing?

Cut away, then, mason, as the mother follows her babe to its peaceful bed; tempt her with your marble cherubs, set your lambs in inviting array, and coax her sorrow to buy an angel, or a marble mourner! How grateful to a sorrowful heart to see that you have been expecting him, that you have reckoned that it would come to this soon! You are all ready for a bargain, just as the undertaker was before you. The undertaker has his ostentatious coffins, his show-windows, brilliant with decorated coffins, where a man is tempted to stop and examine the latest fashion of a coffin—a perfect gem of a thing. One can refresh himself at a hundred places in the city with such agreeable sights, and have explanations thrown in for nothing. If your vanity is susceptible, it will be gratifying to know that a connoisseur of coffins thinks and assures you that you would make one of the most genteel corpses. Pah! the clink of hammers on marble is harsh discord. This money-making out of sorrow and death; this driving a trade upon the occasions of others' misery, over griefs that dissolve the very heart, how it adds an element of horror to all the other pangs of bereavement!

Neither will we turn in at the second entrance, which is for company who come to gaze. It is Death's ground. All over it he has set up his banners of Victory. What has the heart to do there? Why should we wish to see the weakness, the dishonor of our mortal bodies? Was it not enough to pray with vain anguish for their life; to struggle with both oars against the stream that was sweeping them down toward death, and be yet borne downward? Was not the darkness, the stillness, the burden of lonesomeness, the changed aspect of men and the world, the thrusting in upon us by invisible power of huge and dark distresses, enough? Why should we go in to weep afresh? to wish that we were dead? to hear the trees sigh, and the song of birds changed, so that their very glee is sad to the ear? How morbid is life when the light is black, and flowers are mockers, and leaves are hoarse, and birds and every living thing and the whole atmosphere are but a brooding of sorrow! Then let us hasten past the great bosom of Greenwood and leave her alone to nurse the dead.

We are for other scenes; for now we come to a little rustic church on the right, around which we turn and hasten toward the water. The way is narrow, the road smooth, the sides hedged with trees and bushes, and many evergreens intermixed. We emerge. There lies the narrowing Bay. Up through the Narrows come the weary ships that have struggled bravely with the ocean, and are come home to rest. They look grateful. Their sails are loosely furled. They submit themselves to steam-tugs with a resigned air, as if it was fit, after so great a voyage, that they should rest from toil. Down come ships from the city, some with sails and some towed, but all eager, fresh painted, vigorous in aspect, and ready to pitch into storm and spray. Little boats skip about like insects. Sloops and schooners, with snow-white sails, are busying themselves with just as much self-respect and look of usefulness as if they had the tunnage of the hugest ship!

As we draw near the Fort, the lower bay opens.

Shadows divide the light into sections along the surface. The whole expanse is full of little undulations that quiver and gleam, as if from beneath the water myriads of fire-fish flashed their light. But all these things we see the more thoroughly when we return.

Now the eye searches the horizon. There are the faint ships dying out of sight, outward bound. That speck yonder, far in the horizon, is not a ship—but a mote such as dances before the eye strained to penetrate an empty distance. Yet a little while, and it has the semblance of a cloud. It gathers substance before you, and, ere long, swells its airy proportions into the undoubted form of a ship carrying every bit of sail that can be made to cling to the spars!

We turn the carriage from the road; we grow silent and thoughtful; we gaze and think. We fly away from the eye, and see the world beyond the horizon; we hover over ships upon the equator, we outrun the Indiaman, and double the Horn; we dart away westward and overlook that garden of islands, the Pacific! If one speaks, the charm breaks, the fairies fly, the vision is gone, and we are back again! Now you may see that noblest of all ocean sights, for beauty, a full-rigged ship under full sail! A man that can look upon that and feel nothing stir within him, no glow, or imagination, or sense of beauty, may be sure that something important was left out in his making.

If you come down here a hundred times, it is never twice alike. The diversity is endless. Its population of sails changes; every veering of the wind, every mood of the atmosphere, every mutation of clouds, every changing hour of the sun, give new aspects. It arouses in you an idea of infinity. As you look, the serene ocean of ether and the tremulous ocean of water, both and alike, give inspirations. You forget; you let go of care; you drop sorrows; all threads of thought snap in the loom, and the shuttle carries a new yarn, and the fabric stretches out a new pattern. God's truths, that came near to fading out among the clang of men and the fictions of the real, gain form and power. The Invisible grows more real than the substantial. Nothing seems so wild and extravagant as human life; nothing so sweet as flying away from it. The soul hears itself called from the other world. Nor does it require that supremest architect, the imagination, to fashion forth the illustrious gate and the blessed City;—not, if your ride be at evening, and the sun sets enthroned among high-piled and multitudinous clouds. Then the eye beholds things unutterable to the tongue.

How restful is all this! Irritableness and impatience are gone. The woes and frets of life are not then hard to be borne. To live for the things which occupy God; to lift up our fellow-men, through all the round of human infirmities; to build the substantial foundations of life, to enrich the conditions of society, to inspire better thoughts, to fashion a noble character, to stand with Gospel trumpet and banner, and see flocking toward it troops of regenerated men, who, ere long, shall throng about our Lord, the Christ of God;—these seem, then, neither unsubstantial ambitions nor impracticable works. At other times, among giddy excitements, nothing seems so unsubstantial and visionary as the impress of your labor upon human hearts. But now, and here, nothing seems so real as that which God gives the soul power to do upon the soul.

The tide that came down with us is returning. Ships that dashed out toward the sea are slowly coming up to their anchor, and swinging around toward the city. Let us return, for we have flowers to gather along the banks, and crimson leaves, and branches of cedar clustered full of pale blue berries, and creeping strawberry vines. We must clamber down, too, to the rocks, and let the water lick our feet; and gather a few choice pebbles, which our children, at least, will think pretty.

Slowly, and reluctantly, we travel homeward. We approach that sweet and restful ground of Greenwood. We fain now would draw near and enter in. It is no longer repugnant. We have sacred rights there, and anticipations of our own bodies slumbering there. That which we have committed in its mortal part to the earth, God will guard with sacred vigilance till the TIME comes. All the trees, rustling their leaves, are prophesying to our ears of the trees of life; and all the birds and flowers are witnesses of God's guardianship. "Shall not He, who careth for us, care for your children, which were, and are, his own children?" they say. "Yea," our hearts respond; "God hath them. No black wolf of Death shall break into that fold to ravish them again. God shall keep them till our coming." And with faith and hope, and serene content, we wend our way back to life and to work, now not burdensome, or hopeless.

XVI.

SIGHTS FROM MY WINDOW.

UPON what the window opens—whether upon a narrow, paved street of red houses, a back yard, a landscape, or upon such a noble sheet of water as always awaits my eyes from my rear windows—will make a great difference in the thoughts which spring up. It is a sad thing to look upon the life of the street in a city. The poor, the worse than poor, the degraded; unquiet faces of toiling women; ragged children; the feeble valetudinarian;—all these are human beings as much as the hearty, the prosperous, the gay and sanguine throng among whom they mix. Health has its near contrast; poverty is the shadow of wealth; and happiness and gayety are only golden spots upon toil and trouble—like sunbeams that reach through the gloom of thick forests, and checker the ground with unaccustomed light.

The problem of life and earthly destiny are painful, and draw out the weary thoughts through many a maze of questionings, from which they return without a sheaf, or a flower, and more in doubt than ever. I do not love the front windows.

But there lies New York Bay, spread wide abroad from my back windows. I sit in my window, and my thoughts fly over and bathe in the forever changing water, just as I daily see the gulls dip down into it and come up unwet. I walk on it, I hover over it; I go all about its rim—beginning with the far Jersey shore, right across the Battery down to Staten Island, and round again to my window. I have great times with those blue hills in the distance. They are moody fellows. Sometimes they sulk, and darken themselves, and hide in a smoky-obscure, so that whether they be clouds, or mountains, or only a forest, you can scarcely tell. Peradventure, the very next day they have dusted themselves, and swept down all the films, and stand right up to your eye, frank, apparent, and not ashamed of your gaze. Always, the first thing is to see what the hills are about.

To see the sun go down over those hills is a sight to make one's soul cry out to God! What else on earth is done as the sun performs his work? His highway is without an obstruction. Where grow the vines, O Vintner, from which stars hang and from whence light is pressed? He fills the whole heavens with light from his clusters as if it were a goblet. He casts forth his brightness upon the earth as if he were sowing it with seed, and spreading it double-handed, profuse, inexhaustible. In the morning he sends sheaves of light, as first-fruits of his coming, long before the sun-rising, and on retiring he leaves his way full of fruits for the evening to glean. Stars that come timidly out to see what he does, catch the inspiration, and themselves grow good and kind, sending forth a blessing to all that look for their coming.

Those blue hills know all these things, and gambol in the solar flood as dolphins in the deep—flushed with as many fabulous colors as they. Before the sun goes down, you can hardly look at them, as the hazy atmosphere, struck through with intense gold, flames about them, and only lets them be seen dimly as if standing in a blazing furnace.

But they are not harmed. For when the sun gets behind them, they stand forth against the sky, large, full, bold, and unconsumed. They are the last sights that die out of the heavens as night deepens and darkens.

Such sights as these do not rest in the eye alone. They enter the soul. They arouse thoughts that heal heart-sickness. Even before the light forsakes the horizon, you are already cleansed of life's daily grime and dust. That great round horizon!—it is whatever your imagination requires it to be. It is a zone belting the earth. Or it is a lucid rampart, a battlement of transparent stones. Or it is an ocean full of purple islands, whose near waters are crimson, but take orange hues as they recede, then sapphire, amid white and gray, and are carried up toward the vault with spangled blue and black. Upon such a ground as this Nature sets up and takes down her temple of clouds with wondrously facile architecture. There is no footstep left along that horizon, and no visible hand. But can any one look and not know that there is an enshrined spirit there? Is it not from out of such passes as these that angels come to guard our night watch? From those cliffs are there no slumberless eyes that gaze after us? Behind them dwell the unnumbered dead. Death? Translated into the heavenly tongue, that word means Life!

Therefore, there are some hours in which we feel called to pierce these outguards of heaven, and see that City beyond, from which the sun himself borrows his light. For, the moon borrows of a greater borrower—she, of the sun, and the sun of God! Why should we stand upon this side the entrance, falling down, like poor Mercy in Pilgrim's Progress, before the gate? Thought *may* enter, faith *does;* but the body, like an anchor, sticks fast to the earth, and brings back again the reluctant soul to her moorings.

Ten thousand stars stand meekly now in the heavens. Ten thousand sparkling stars are lit from beneath and rock themselves silently in the trembling waters. Yonder, too, lies that great city with a thousand shining eyes, couched down, but always watching, always murmuring, night and day, like some huge, muttering behemoth, waiting for its prey in the reeds by the seashore.

One who had lived within sound of the surf upon Long Island south shore, would think, if he sat for the first time by my window, in the night, and heard the dull, low, muffled roar of the city, that he was close upon the ocean. If I shut my eyes, I can imagine in this sound the sullen plunge of Niagara as it came through the night-air to my room in the hotel. Nor does the resemblance cease with the sound. It is the united roll of single wheels, crushing and jarring through all the streets of the vast city, that form this bass; just as it is but the singing of single drops in the choir of waves that makes the thunder of the ocean.

Morning, noon, night and midnight, you have still this continuous roar; distant and soft when the wind is from the east; near, and rushing right toward you, when the winds are from the west. But there is a rest even for New York. From midnight of Saturday till three o'clock of Monday morning, the Sabbath charms and hallows the air. The city sleeps like a laboring man after his toil. It is very impressive to stand upon a radiant Sabbath morning and feel the hush and solitude of a great motionless city! Silence always speaks of God. The gilded cross on the spire of Trinity, catching the earliest glow, shines like a star, as if, like that of Bethlehem, it would lead men to where the Saviour dwelt.

But, on other days, nothing can quiet the great voice of the city. All day and all night it sounds on. It is the cry of grief, the hearty shout of labor, laughter, rage and yells, sighs and whisperings, the tramp of feet, the clang of bells, the roar of wheels, all mingled into one deep vast sound, in which single sounds are lost, like so many drops in the ocean.

Then, there are the deep, measured strokes of the ponderous fire-bell, answered and echoed from bell to bell, all over the city. Now and then a beam of light shoots up upon the sky, and the city glows in its conflagration. Usually, fires would come and go unknown except to lookers on, were it not for the bells. They are smothered before they can break out. And all that the bell tells you is that, somewhere, in that great somber space, an army of men are fighting with flames.

Then the bell ceases, and you know that the flame is quenched, but the eye has seen nothing.

One sits at night and looks out upon that mysterious space, marked to the eye only by lights, gleaming singly, or in files, and imagines what scenes are transpiring before him. Should I pierce to that distant lamp, I should land in a wedding group—for it shines from a joyful mansion! Should I overleap that one, and go on to the chamber from which the next shines, there a child is dying, a mother is wailing. Should I strike through the shell to the living kernel, in one place, crimes would spring up disclosed; another line would reveal vices of unimagined grossness. I say to myself, as I look forth:—there, a mother sings her child to sleep; there, a virgin draws angels to her prayers; there, a wife waits for footsteps, which once were music, but which ere long will tread down her joys like trampled flowers; there, sorrow and want and despair work; there, the poor and failing seamstress draws the thread whose breaking will drop her into hopeless shame. In that great shadow are now working griefs and shames and joys, crimes and cruelties, virtues and secret heroism. Yonder is patience, and faith, and hope; there are laughing faces, frivolous hearts, tearless joys. There, too, are devout hearts, deep meditations, holy aspirations. Good and evil angels fly athwart that rack of smoke and vapor on errands of grace or mischief. Up through that pathless air are passing every hour scores of departing souls. And yet, I gaze upon the certainty and perceive nothing! I know, too, that there are in the depths of yonder obscure city sharp outcries, eager implorations, piercing shrieks, life-struggles;—but I hear not a lisp of them! I know that the tremendous drama of life is playing in every act, from beginning to exit, and I, the solitary spectator, sitting here, can see nothing, hear nothing; yet assuredly I know that it is all passing there!

But there is an eye from which darkness hides nothing. There is an ear to which every whisper of the Universe goes. Over the great city God watches. It is neither tangled nor confused to Him. To his piercing gaze stone and brick are transparent as crystal. Yea, the silence of the soul is audible. The secret intents of the heart are before him. The Lord shall watch the city, and when all other keepers fail, He shall keep it.

XVII.

THE DEATH OF OUR ALMANAC.

1853.

He died without a groan. He seemed as vigorous, only the day before, as the first day of his life; and held his own to the last moment. Were it not that another child of the same family, bearing the same general features, and apparently of the same temper, is ready to take his place, we should be inconsolable. For, no other friend have we to whom we can go for advice, as we could to him. He was, doubtless, somewhat of an Oriental turn of mind, and spoke mostly in figures. Yet his knowledge in various things was not small and was exceedingly practical. He held converse with the stars, and seemed to know what was going on among all the planets. He had a habit of looking after the sun, and had become so well acquainted with his favorite resorts that he could tell you what he would do and where he could be found for years to come. He knew all the coquettings of the sun and moon; and all the seasons at which the stars would play bo-peep with each other; and all the caprices of the moon, from her slyest glance to the fullest gaze of her maidenly face.

Although his thoughts seemed much on high, he also had much earthly lore. He was particularly fond of looking after the tides; he kept a calendar of various events and days, and notched the whole year upon his table.

We seldom took in hand an important matter without consulting him. We never found his judgment of events wrong. And now, his face and sides bear the marks of our regard.

These economical uses were but the "exterior knowledges" of our departed friend. Nothing pleased him better than, on some winter night, to be drawn forth, and held before the glowing fire, and persuaded into a spiritual converse. How many discourses has he thus uttered! Sometimes he would liken the year to human life, and draw the analogies of each month to corresponding periods in man's development and experience. At other times, he would divide the world's life into periods, and he always declared that the world was revolving through a vast year of its own—a period as long as the earth's whole existence—and that we were living the world's great month of March,—full of bluster and storm. You can no more know, said he once to us, the glory of the world as it shall be, from what it has been, than, from the scenes of February and March, you can suspect the contents of June and October.

On one occasion, our Almanac seemed unusually oracular. Laid on the shelf with several imaginative authors, he seemed to have felt their influence.

We were sitting in our scarlet chair, our feet upborne upon another, and pointed toward the fire, like artillery. We passed into an "impressible" state. The wind was rattling the windows on the back of the house, and whistling wild tones through the crevices; and, occasionally, we could hear the tide below rushing past the piers in the East River, and splashing sullenly against them. "Come," said we, "speak out. Under these names, January, February, March, April, how much is hid that the eye can not see? Uncover the months and interpret them." We touched the very chord. In a low and sweet way, he began to speak as if he were a harp, and as if the spirit of the year like a gentle wind was breathing through it.

"JANUARY! Darkness and light reign alike. Snow is on the ground. Cold is in the air. The winter is blossoming in frost-flowers. Why is the ground hidden? Why is the earth white? So hath God wiped out the past; so hath he spread the earth like an unwritten page, for a new year! Old sounds are silent in the forest, and in the air. Insects are dead, birds are gone, leaves have perished, and all the foundations of soil remain. Upon this lies, white and tranquil, the emblem of newness and purity, the virgin robes of the yet unstained year!

"FEBRUARY! The day gains upon the night. The strife of heat and cold is scarce begun. The winds that come from the desolate north wander through forests of frost-cracking boughs, and shout in the air the wierd cries of the northern bergs and ice-resounding oceans. Yet, as the month wears on, the silent work begins, though storms rage. The earth is hidden yet, but not dead. The sun is drawing near. The storms cry out. But the sun is not heard in all the heavens. Yet he whispers words of deliverance into the ears of every sleeping seed and root that lies beneath the snow. The day opens, but the night shuts the earth with its frost-lock. They strive together, but the Darkness and the Cold are growing weaker. On some nights they forget to work.

"MARCH! The conflict is more turbulent, but the victory is gained. The world awakes. There come voices from long-hidden birds. The smell of the soil is in the air. The sullen ice retreating from open field, and all sunny places, has slunk to the north of every fence and rock. The knolls and banks that face the east or south sigh for release, and begin to lift up a thousand tiny palms.

"APRIL! The singing month. Many voices of many birds call for resurrection over the graves of flowers, and they come forth. Go, see what they have lost. What have ice, and snow, and storm, done unto them? How did they fall into the earth, stripped and bare? How do they come forth opening and glorified? Is it, then, so fearful a thing to lie in the grave?

In its wild career, shaking and scourged of storms through its orbit, the earth has scattered away no treasures. The Hand that governs in April governed in January. You have not lost what God has only hidden. You lose nothing in struggle, in trial, in bitter distress. If called to shed thy joys as trees their leaves; if the affections be driven back into the heart, as the life of flowers to their roots, yet be patient. Thou shalt lift up thy leaf-covered boughs again. Thou shalt shoot forth from thy roots new flowers. Be patient. Wait. When it is February, April is not far off. Secretly the plants love each other.

"MAY! O Flower-Month, perfect the harvests of flowers! Be not niggardly. Search out the cold and resentful nooks that refused the sun casting back its rays from disdainful ice, and plant flowers even there. There is goodness in the worst. There is warmth in the coldness. The silent, hopeful, unbreathing sun, that will not fret or despond, but carries a placid brow through the unwrinkled heavens, at length conquers the very rocks, and lichens grow and inconspicuously blossom. What shall not Time do, that carries in its bosom Love?

"JUNE! Rest! This is the year's bower. Sit down within it. Wipe from thy brow the toil. The elements are thy servants. The dews bring thee jewels. The winds bring perfume. The earth shows thee all her treasure. The forests sing to thee. The air is all sweetness, as if all the angels of God had gone through it, bearing spices homeward. The storms are but as flocks of mighty birds that spread their wings and sing in the high heaven! Speak to God, now, and say, 'O, Father, where art thou?' And out of every flower, and tree, and silver pool, and twined thicket, a voice will come, 'God is in me.' The earth cries to the heavens, 'God is here.' And the heavens cry to the earth, 'God is here.' The sea claims Him. The land hath Him. His footsteps are upon the deep! He sitteth upon the Circle of the Earth!

"O sunny joys of the sunny month, yet soft and temperate, how soon will the eager months that come burning from the equator, scorch you!

"JULY! Rouse up! The temperate heats that filled the air are raging forward to glow and overfill the earth with hotness. Must it be thus in every thing, that June shall rush toward August? Or, is it not that there are deep and unreached places for whose sake the probing sun pierces down its glowing hands? There is a deeper work than June can perform. The earth shall drink of the heat before she knows her nature or her strength. Then shall she bring forth to the uttermost the treasures of her bosom. For, there are things hidden far down, and the deep things of life are not known till the fire reveals them.

"AUGUST! Reign, thou Fire-Month! What canst thou do? Neither shalt *thou* destroy the earth, whom frosts and ice could not destroy. The vines droop, the trees stagger, the broad-palmed leaves give thee their moisture, and hang down. But every night the dew pities them. Yet, there are flowers that look thee in the eye, fierce Sun, all day long, and wink not. This is the rejoicing month for joyful insects. If our unselfish eye would behold it, it is the most populous and the happiest month. The herds plash in the sedge; fish seek the deeper pools; forest-fowl lead out their young; the air is resonant of insect orchestras, each one carrying his part in Nature's grand harmony. August, thou art the ripeness of the year! Thou art the glowing center of the circle!

"SEPTEMBER! There are thoughts in thy heart of death. Thou art doing a secret work, and heaping up treasures for another year. The unborn infant-buds which thou art tending are more than all the living leaves. Thy robes are luxuriant, but worn with softened pride. More dear, less beautiful than June, thou art the heart's month. Not till the heats of summer are gone, while all its growths remain, do we know the fullness of life. Thy hands are stretched out, and clasp the glowing palm of August, and the fruit-smelling hand of October. Thou dividest them asunder, and art thyself molded of them both.

"OCTOBER! Orchard of the year! Bend thy boughs to the earth, redolent of glowing fruit! Ripened seeds shake in their pods. Apples drop in the stillest hours. Leaves begin to let go when no wind is out, and swing in long waverings to the earth, which they touch without sound, and lie looking up, till winds rake them, and heap them in fence corners. When the gales come through the trees, the yellow leaves trail, like sparks at night behind the flying engine. The woods are thinner, so that we can see the heavens plainer, as we lie dreaming on the yet warm moss by the singing spring. The days are calm. The nights are tranquil. The year's work is done. She walks in gorgeous apparel, looking upon her long labor, and her serene eye saith, 'It is good.'

"NOVEMBER! Patient watcher, thou art asking to lay down thy tasks. Life, to thee, now, is only a task accomplished. In the night-time thou liest down, and the messengers of winter deck thee with hoarfrosts for thy burial. The morning looks upon thy jewels, and they perish while it gazes. Wilt thou not come, O December?

"DECEMBER! Silently the month advances. There is nothing to destroy, but much to bury. Bury, then, thou snow, that slumberously fallest through the still air, the hedge-rows of leaves! Muffle thy cold wool about the feet of shivering trees! Bury all that the year hath known, and let thy brilliant stars, that never shine as they do in thy frostiest nights, behold the work! But know, O month of destruction, that in thy constellation is set that Star, whose rising is the sign, for evermore, that there is life in death! Thou art the month of resurrection. In thee, the Christ came. Every star, that looks down upon thy labor and toil of burial, knows that all things shall come forth again. Storms shall sob themselves to sleep. Silence shall find a voice. Death shall live, Life shall rejoice, Winter shall break forth and blossom into Spring, Spring shall put on her glorious apparel and be called Summer. It is life! it is life! through the whole year!"

We know not the temper of our Almanac for 1854. As yet, it is taciturn. But we have hopes that in the loss of our old friend, now silent and laid to rest, we shall not be left without a companion, as wise, as genial, and as instructive.

XVIII.

FOG IN THE HARBOR.

LATE in the fall, especially if the season be mild, we are visited by dense fogs. Not such as Londoners boast, in which men lose their way in the streets at mid-day, and shopmen light their gas—fogs that might almost be weighed and measured, or shoveled like snow. But we have fogs that serve every purpose of a new country.

The gay and the idle do not venture out. Only necessity draws men forth on such a day. People of leisure look listlessly out of the windows into the gray haze. As they look, the mist seems to darken into a form, and a man emerges, passes by, and disappears at a few steps into the cloud that broods the street. You hear footsteps across the way of invisible walkers. There goes one with a decisive plat, plat, plat, but not the shadowy film of a man can you see. A heavy and muffled footfall comes next, a fat woman in India-rubbers undoubtedly. A little child is coming now; pit, pat, pit, pat; it stops, perhaps to change the basket to the other arm. Away go the sightless feet again, pit, pat, quickening every step, and now running, clat, clat, clat, clat, till they are brought up with a smothered *bunt* and scuffle, telling you that somebody has been run into. There will be a dolorous story when somebody gets home, without doubt, and relates with great indignation how a dirty beggar boy almost knocked the breath out of him! And the beggar boy will regale his young friends with the amazement and vexation of the nicely dressed gentleman into whom he ran headlong!

Now and then, the mist holds up its skirts and the street for a minute is cleared; but soon the robe drops again, and the cloud trails its fleece along the very ground. People come in with hat and coat seeded all over with minute dew-drops. Everybody feels moist and clammy. The horses that go past in the middle of the streets are spectral, like outline pencil-drawings, not yet filled up and shaded.

But there are grander things than these; for, like every thing else in a pent up city, mist becomes insignificant and mean in the defiles of the streets.

Mists imbosom the whole great city yonder, which grinds and roars from out of it like a huge factory concealed by its own smoke.

Upon the bay it lays an embargo. Lighters and row-boats creep timidly along the wharves. Ships, ready for sea, lie still. Craft, great and small, hug the water in silence, and dare not stir. Ships and steamers come up from the ocean to the mouth of the harbor and dare not enter. Sea-sick and home-sick passengers sigh for cleansing winds. Pilots are as blind as other men. There are no stars, no sun, no headlands, no buoys. Tow-boats, having given the outward-bound ships a wide berth, are returning from their ponderous tasks, and timidly creeping homeward with slow wheels, revolving at half-stroke, probing the channel with sounding-lead, and often bewildered in their way.

It is the day for the Liverpool steamers. But they do not leave their pier. No storm could stay them, no violence of wind or force of wave. But this silent, formless, motionless mist, without weight, without power, lays its hands upon them and they are still. There is rest upon all the bay. Ships that should be on their way toward India, or the Horn, catch the refluent tide upon their bows, and listen to its gurgling as it splits and drives bubbling past on either side. Labor slackens along the wharves. Idle gangs of men may be heard in the distance, as if their laugh were just under your window. Noises are no longer swallowed up in a general clangor, but have individuality. A plank falls, and resounds like the explosion of a cannon. A shout rings through the air like a weird and ghostly thing. These sounds in the air, in broad daylight, made by persons near at hand, but invisible, produce a strange effect upon you.

Ferry-boats alone are doomed to ply their wonted tasks. Two great cities like New York and Brooklyn, which are the first and third in size in the Union, can not afford to have this liquid street stopped up by a fog. The boats must grope and creep. It is not among the least of New York sights to take a fog-trip upon a ferry-boat. The boats are loaded down with passengers who huddle together like sheep in a cold rain. The boat pushes boldly out, but is lost before it gets its length from the slip. The pilot knows the tide; he knows what crafts are anchored in the stream; but he does not know how the tide is placing him in reference to them. The hands are all on the alert. The pilots and extra officers are on the top, peering and watching, and seeking, like metaphysicians, to penetrate the misty-obscure. "There she is," suddenly cries one, "stop her, back her." There is a rumbling down below, as the engineer stops and reverses the engine. The white foam begins to sweep past the bow, showing that the wheels are revolving in an opposite direction. By this time, common eyes can see a spectral ship, with filmy masts, looming up right in the track of the boat. We are close upon her before the headway is checked, and we begin to draw off. Taking a new start, the boat aims again with her ears for the slip, and soon the gray masts of other craft shoot up from out of the white mist-bank. Again the engine stops. We creep up cautiously. We can hear voices, but see no forms. We have run two piers too far up, and must back out; then we run as far below; we must back again, and creep stealthily along, and at length we hit the mark.

In the night, when dense fogs prevail, the whole night long you hear the signal-bells tolling, and the steam-whistles of the boats calling to each other shrilly, like whistling quails in a forest. Now and then a single stroke upon a large *triangle* used upon the boats, tells you that they are signaling each other. Our dwelling, on the Heights, brings these night sounds drearily up to us. One can hardly help imagining that these are living beings, wandering about in the harbor, crying out to each other with wild implorations, all night, as if they were lost and called for help. Sometimes a trip, which usually requires five minutes, will be more than an hour long, and boats have sometimes got entirely lost, and landed their passengers half a mile from the proper place. One can not be familiar with such scenes without many suggestions of moral analogy. How many men of great strength and power are made helpless by ignorance, and spend their time in running in toward, and backing out from, their aims; how many men reason upon great questions of the Past and of the Future, in a mist as profound as that which bewilders these pilots, and find themselves running due south when they thought they were going north!

How nearly do all of us, in some respects, resemble these befogged coursers! The stream of life hides its further bank. We steer across it, scarcely knowing where we go. If the vapor lifts occasionally, to give an assurance to our faith, it soon lets down its robe again, and we run drowsily and unseeing upon the shores.

XIX.

THE MORALS OF FISHING.

JUNE 22, 1854.

THE following note came to us some weeks ago. But so grave a matter could not be digested as hastily as if it were a mere state paper or the programme of a revolution. It required, and has received, judicious reflection.

"NEW YORK, *May* 31, 1854.

"RESPECTED SIR:—I was arguing against *fishing*, for pleasure, with some young men, saying that they (fishes) were permitted to be caught only for food, and that they ought to have the liberty of the sea as much as they (the young men) the road, and further declared it kidnapping to catch them; — when they cited your example of catching fish. I could say not one word. What could I say against such authority?

"Sorrowfully, for the fishes, but taking this occasion to express my affection for you, I am, etc."

The writer argues against fishing for only pleasure. Of course, he exonerates all fishermen who fish for the New York and Boston markets, all fishermen on the British Coast and off Newfoundland, since they can hardly be presumed to fish for "pleasure." To stand for hours hauling up cod for market is sport nearly equal to drawing water at a fire out of a well fifty feet deep, with an old-fashioned well-sweep, or with a frozen rope. We presume, however, that when one is catching fish under a sense of duty, there will be no sin if he takes pleasure in it.

Neither will any blame attach to those luckless wights who have what is termed "fisherman's luck," which may be explained to be a whole day's tramp, in dismal weather, with very wet clothes, after fish that won't bite, with tackling that seems predetermined to vex you by breaking or snarling; a state of things which hunger and weariness seldom mend. In a hot day, after a misty morning has cleared up, and let the sun out to do his best, this experience may be varied by sitting in a boat upon a lake, sunk down between so many hills that not a breath of wind ever gets down to it. If you are a man of piscatory perseverance, you can philosophize upon the probable sensations of martyrs with whom slow fires are set to reason, for instance, upon the folly of dissent and heresy. No breadth of straw-brim can save you from the upward glances of the sun reflected from the water. Hands and wrists, face and neck, will furnish memorials of the sincerity of your pursuit. But, after such experience, is the man to have superadded the charge of inhumanity? Is it possible to treat a fish worse than he is treating himself?

These considerations aside, we will answer the question as it is usually put by the non-fishing philanthropist. It is not right to make up our enjoyment out of the suffering of any creature. If the pleasure of hunting or of fishing were in the excitement furnished by the creatures suffering, then it could no more be justified than any other form of torturing, as practiced hitherto, upon moral principles, for the good of men's souls. A benevolent man should find no pleasure in mere animal suffering.

But Isaac Walton would not accept the case thus put, as truly representing the facts. He would say, and all true sportsmen are scrupulously at agreement with him, that no man should take a single fish, or bag a single bird, beyond the number which can be used for food by himself or his friends. To fish all day in solitary lakes, or in the streams of the wilderness, when it is certain that not one in twenty of the trout taken can be used, is not any more a violation of humanity than it is of the public sentiment of all true sportsmen. A man who would stand at a pigeon-roost and fire by the hour into the dense mass of fluttering birds, only to kill them, is a butcher and a brute. We shall let him off from the severity of this sentence only by a confession that he is a fool, expressed by that universal formula of folly, "I did it without *thinking*."

Nothing is more clearly received as common-law among gentlemen, than that the suffering of the victim is *not* to be allowed to give pleasure. It is to be abridged in every way. And prolonged suffering, or needless suffering, is a fundamental violation of good rules. We fear that we must make an exception against those who follow hare or fox hunting.

The true source of enjoyment in field-sports is to be found in the exertion of one's own faculties, and especially in such a carriage of one's self as to be superior in sagacity and caution to the most wary and sharp-sighted of creatures. It is a contest between instinct and reason. And reason has, often, little to be proud of in the result.

But, aside from the pleasure which arises in connection with seeking or taking one's prey, we suspect that the collateral enjoyments amount, often, to a greater sum than all the rest. The early rising, the freshness of those morning hours preceding the sun, which few anti-piscatory critics know anything about; that wondrous early-morning singing of birds, compared to which all after-day songs are mere ejaculations;—for, such is the tumult and superabundance of sweet noise soon after four o'clock in summer mornings, that one would think that, if every dew-drop were a musical note, and the birds had drank them all, and were deliciously exhaling each drop as a silvery sound, they could not have been more multitudinous or delicious. Then, there is that incomparable sense of freedom which one has in remote fields, in forests, and along the streams. His heart, trained in life to play by jets, like an artificial fountain, to flow along the rigid banks of prescribed custom, seems, as he wanders along the streams, to resume its own liberty, and like a meadow-brook, to wind and turn, amid flowers and fringing shrubs, at its own unmolested pleasure.

One who believes that God made the world, and clearly developed to us his own tastes and thoughts in the making, can not express what feelings those are which speak music through his heart, in solitary communions with Nature. Nature becomes to the soul a perpetual letter from God, freshly written every day and each hour.

A little plant, growing in silent simplicity in some covert spot, or looking down from out of a rift in some rock uplifted high above his reach or climbing—what has it said to him, that he stops, and gazes as if he saw more than material forms? What is that rush of feeling in his heart, and that strange opening up of thoughts, as if a revelation had been made to him? Who, that has only a literal eye, could see anything but that solitary flower casting a linear shadow on the side of the gray rock?—a shadow that loves to quiver, and nod, and dance, to every step which the wind-blown flower takes? But this floral preacher up in that pulpit has many a time preached tears into my eyes, and told me more than I was ever able to tell again.

Indeed, in many and many a tramp, the best sporting has been done on my back. Flat under a tree I lay, a vast Brobdignag, upon whom grasshoppers mounted, and glossy crickets crept, harmless and unharmed, with evident speculation upon what such a phenomenon could portend. Along the stems creep aspiring ants, searching with fiery zeal for no one can even guess what. They race up that they may race down again. They are full of mysterious signs to each other. They knock heads, touch antennæ, and then off they rush fuller of minute zeal than ever.

The blue-jay is in the tree above you. The woodpecker screws round and round the trunk, hammering at every place like an auscult-doctor sounding a pa tient's lungs. Little birds fly in and out gibbering to each other in sweet detached sentences, confidentially talking over their family secrets, and expressing those delicate sentiments which one never speaks except in a whisper, and in twilight. When you rise, the birds flutter and fly, and clouds of insects flash off from you like sparks from a fire when a log rolls over.

The brook that gurgles past the tree, feeding its roots, and taking its pay in summer shadows, varied every hour, receives a portion of the off-jumping fry. For a grasshopper, unlike a bomb, goes off without calculating where it shall fall. Far off its coming shines. Before it had even touched the water, that bold trout sprung sparkling from the surface and sunk as soon, leaving only a few bubbles to float away. There! if the trout has a right to his grasshopper, have I not a right to the trout? I'll have him! After several throws, I find that it takes two to make a bargain.

At length one must go home. I never turn from the silence of the underbrush, or the solitude of the fields, or the rustlings of the forest, without a certain sadness as if I were going away from friends.

But we shall be deemed superficial if we leave it to be believed that this is a fair exposure of the joys of fishing. What have we said of mountain brooks, and the grandeur of dark gorges, where one is well nigh in a trance, and almost forgets to drop his bait; or does it mechanically, and draws forth a fish as if it were a very solemn deed. What have we said of sea-fishing, a snug boat, a smart breeze, a long and strong line ending with a *squid*. We sweep along the flashing waters as if racing. A blue-fish strikes the glittering, whirling squid, with a stroke that sends electricity along the line into the hands of him that holds it, as you would believe if you saw the sprightliness with which he hauls in his line. Back and forth you sweep the waters, your boat apparently as much alive as you are, and enjoying as much!

Then you lie under some fragment of a boat, or upon some dry seaweeds, while your distant dinner is sputtering and reeking in the kitchen of the rude hotel, used only in summer, by people seeking health or amusement, in out-of-the-way fishing places. O, how the heavens swell roundly out, and lift themselves up, with a wild attraction, that makes you gasp, as one sighs and gasps who is deeply thinking of some profound horror! The sea is running out in fiery lines, crossed by the sun, on every wave-swell; white sails lie cloudily against the distant horizon, and dim and spectre-like, as they are, how they open the whole world of islands and continents to the imagination, whence they come, or whither they are going. But the dinner-horn sounds, and sea, heavens, islands and continents, ships with homesick voyagers, sink down like a dream in the morning, and we make haste to the universally respected duty of eating. There is no prejudice against that. Sober men, careful, earnest men, yea, all of them eat, and as zealously as the flippant and the careless.

Then comes the going down of the sun. The boat puts us across to the main land. The wind has gone down. The surface is clear and level. Shadows from the land fall far over on the bay, and the light that yet plays upon the surface is ruddy and mellow. The oar is thoughtful, and dips and rises gently. At each pull the oarsmen pause, and musical drops, through which the light flashes, trickle back to the deep whence they had risen. Each drop is a sphere, and in each sphere might have arisen the mother of beauty, liquid Venus Anadyomene. And so came we into life, and so sink away from it, into the great Eternal Sea.

The day is over. The cars have received us. Our thoughts have dismissed all their fanciful forms. We talk of failures, of brilliant strokes of policy, of banks, and ships, of what this man is worth, and what his neighbor was worth just before he became worth nothing. In short, we are sensible again; fit to plod in the streets, so as to have good, sound, prudent men call us a safe and discreet man!

But to return to our correspondent. Will he be pleased to say to all disputants who quote our example, that we never fish except with a remote culinary inspiration; that we never catch more than will supply the reasonable wants of the family, and that, too often, unfortunately, we stop far short of that.

The gentle gurgling of the brook, what is it to a thoroughly practical man but a remembrancer of the savory simmering of the frying-pan? It couples the practical and domestic end of fishing with the physical and poetic excitement of the operation! Alas! that a world should be so barbarous as to condemn piscatory sports so long as they contribute to exercise taste, sentiment, and moral enjoyment; and that all objection ceases when a man can prove that he labored for his mouth alone. It is all right, if it was eating that he had in mind. The frying-pan is in universal favor. This is the modern image that fell down from heaven, which all men hold in reverence!

Inform your friends, if you please, that our skill in fishing is principally displayed upon paper; and that our excursions usually turn out to be a little of fishing, a good deal of wandering dreamily about, yet more of lying under trees, or of being perched up in some notch of a rock, or of silent sittings on the edge of ravines and trumpeting waterfalls. And, finally, inform them that we are guiltless of shooting, and seldom feel an impulse to explode powder, except when we see respectable city stupidities killing little singing-birds. We sometimes feel an inclination then to shoot the unmannerly fowler. No gentleman would shoot a singing-bird. And now, if our correspondent's friends *will*, in spite of his excellent dissuasions, still go a-fishing, our only wish is that after two seasons of fishing they may do what we have not done—catch so many fish as would, if sold at a fair price, pay the expense of *their tackle.*

XX.

THE WANDERINGS OF A STAR.

JULY 6, 1854.

WE reached Albany at 9 o'clock, and waited, inconveniently, till half-past ten, for the night express-train to start. We took a lonely walk along the streets, saw men as if they had been trees, looked upon glittering windows as a vain show, and speculated upon the sensations of a man in the midst of all the impulses of busy life but not affected by them, walking unmoved amid things which move others.

As the hour drew near for starting, we hastened back to the cars, took possession of the whole seat, meditating methods of extracting sleep out of a long night-ride. Every one seemed doing the same thing, namely, keeping people out of their seat. The cars on the night line were far from comfortable. There was no such amplitude of space as one gets upon the Erie road, no soft-embracing backs, enticing the spine and its terminal knob to rest; but narrow, pent-up seats, and backs invented to fit the wrong place. After all our goings out and comings in, we publicly declare it to be our faith, unbought by free ticket, or any privilege whatever, that the good broad-gauge Erie road is the only one on which comfort is indigenous. On all others it is a mere imitation. But, of narrow gauges, first in comfort is the Hudson River, on an express-train; for, the speed and the river prospect excite you beyond the notice of inconvenience. But to return.

We left Albany at half-past ten o'clock. At about eleven, the hum of conversation died away. Every one was busy with the unnatural problem of sleep. In the cars, stretching one's self out for balmy sleep, means, curling one's self up like a cat in a corner. Short limbs are a luxury when a man sleeps by the square inch. First, you lie down by the right side, against the window, till a stitch in your side, worming its way through your uneasy dream, like an awl, leads you to reverse your position. As you lean on the inside end of your seat, the conductor knocks your hat off, or uses your head as a support to his steps as he sways along the rocking passage. At length, with a groan which expresses the very feeling of every bone and muscle and individual organ in your body, you try to sit upright, and to sleep erect. But erect sleep is perilous, even when it is possible. You nod and pitch, you collapse and condense, and finally settle down in a promiscuous heap, wishing that you were a squirrel, or a kitten, and curiously remembering dogs that could convolute on a mat, and birds that could tuck their head under their wings, and draw their feet and legs up under their feathers. O! that I were round like a marble, and could be rid of protruding members! But such slumberous philosophy and somnolent yearnings for circular shapes die out as you sink again into a lethargy, until the scream of the whistle, the grinding of the brakes, the concussions and jerks, arouse you to the fact that you are stopping to wood and water, and that some surely insane person has come in at this station, and wishes a part of your seat! "No, sir! I am a sovereign squatter here. I claim a pre-emption right. I have staked off this seat, and after all that I have suffered, I shall not give it up to any body." So the wheezing obesity, at least 300 avoirdupois, goes on. A faint smile plays on my lips to think what a time somebody will have who takes that continent of flesh into his seat; for, in his despair, he will soon plunge into somebody's seat, like an over-setting load of hay. But the incomers walk disconsolately along, examining each side for a spot. It is quite easy to defend yourself against the pert and knowing. But that poor, pale, faint-looking woman, carrying a sleeping babe, that fears to disturb any one, —"Here, madam, sit down here—room enough—sit down, if you please." "But I fear, sir, I shall, with my babe—" "No, madam—no trouble—not if there were ten more children." Poor little thing, it sleeps amidst the night, and all this inconvenience and weariness of trouble, as a sea-bird sleeps in some grassy cove, on the swing of the black waters. By and by, you shall not sleep so. You shall grow up to bear your own troubles, and the storms that blow shall not be broken by a mother's bosom, but strike right into your own. You offer a part of your shawl; you insist that the child shall be divided, or the care of it, and by a quiet way you gradually get the little fellow wholly into your own lap, and press him to your heart, and drop down tears on him, God knows why! How it rests you to feel his sweet burdensomeness. The mother knows her child's safety, and drops asleep. It is a face with which sorrow has been busy. Perhaps she seeks her father's house again, from the grave of a buried husband. Or she may have gone eager to meet her young returning husband, from Californian adventure, only to learn that he died on the Isthmus—that mountain graveyard of so many thousands. But you ask no questions. About three of the morning she leaves. You carry the child, and give it to her; and as she turns and disappears into the somber-gray night, you hear the little fellow's voice chirruping, like a bird's startled note, as it dreams in the still night, and speaks in its sleep from out of leaves and darkness.

You return, and look for a moment at the grotesque appearance of a car full of sleeping and sleepless wretches. What persuasion could induce that pompous little man, bald-headed, round-faced, and rubicund, to put himself into such a ludicrous attitude, if he were awake? His feet sprawled forth, his body half sunk sideways, his head lolling back, his mouth wide open like a cannon! His good dame by his side looks like a bag of clothes, thrown loosely into a corner till the next morning. There sits a sandy-haired man, thin-visaged, keen-eyed, as still as if he were asleep, but as wide awake and perpendicular as if he were a light-house. By contrast everybody looks ten times sleepier than before, after you have looked at him. At length, the long nightmare wears itself out. Color begins to come into the cheeks of the morning. The air smells fresher. Birds are seen, and might be heard, if the huge Bird of Speed that whirls you along were not so noisy.

But, while thus speeding along, you suddenly check your headway, stop, switch off upon a side-track: the conductor walks through the cars, "Engine has burst a flue; stop here one hour, till we can get another from Rochester." Every body starts up, the cars swarm like bee-hives in a hot day, every body goes out and looks at the engine, and the grand fellow stands patiently to be looked at. I feel like taking off my hat in the presence of these monarchs of the road. It is at Palmyra. The village is half a mile back. I question the conductor, look at my watch, and march off in search of a breakfast. The first tavern has a specimen on the steps that discourages me; go on to the second, new, coldly clean, and desolate. Nothing is round, soft, cosy; the angles are sharp as razors; the colors are cold, and every thing is proper and stiff. They promise to get me a hasty breakfast. Three young fellows slyly slip into a room below, the landlord following. Hear a churning in the tumblers. They come up wiping their mouths, and looking happy. Table ready, cold meat left from yesterday, tasted it, and knew why they left it. Good tea, good butter and bread, and that is good enough for any body. Felt better. Angles not quite so sharp after all. The colors of the house warmed up a little. Walked back. Thanked the birds, thanked the grass, the bushes, and the river. Thanked the trees and the clouds. Sat down under the bridge and thanked God. Saw the waters move softly by.

Felt alone. Wished I had company. Concluded that nothing could be seen properly with less than four eyes. The willows swayed to the moving stream. The stream sped noiselessly over the rocky bottom. My thoughts swayed like the willow, and my feelings glided like the stream. At last the engine came. Had to wait yet for another train to pass, as there was but a single track. Off we went at freight-train speed. Being out of time, we were *irregular*, and had to wait for every thing on the road. There stood the grand express train, and the vast engine, waiting for freight trains and cattle trains, and peddling way trains to go by, just as many a noble man stands upon the path of life, silent and waiting, until the cumbrous baggage of life clears the track and lets him on. At length, at about two o'clock, we reached Buffalo, tired, dusty, sweaty, and eminently patient. Amid sentiments, high-soaring thoughts, and back-reaching remembrances and affections, there arose stern thoughts of dinner. These appetites are very humiliating weaknesses. That our grace depends so largely upon animal conditions is not quite flattering to those who are hyper-spiritual.

At half-past three we start for Erie, thinking, as we roared along the borders of the lake, towards Ohio, of the days of our childhood, when emigration first began, towards this, then, new wilderness. We thought of the terror with which our childish eyes saw the long string of movers' wagons filing through Litchfield, "going to Ohio," and of our oft retreat under the bed, and into dark cupboards, that we might not be pilfered and carried off to the West. In those days the church had special meetings when a family of their number was going to Ohio. The town took notice of their departure. Farewells were uttered as if the separation were eternal. The journey was one of months. Now Cleaveland is as near to Albany, as then Litchfield was to Hartford or New Haven.

Arrived at Erie, we put up at Brown's, but true to her reputation, Erie served us with a mob that night. Learning that several railroad men were staying at the hotel, the rioters gathered, with hootings and deceased eggs. But the room which they pelted proved to be the lodging of a gentleman from St. Louis, who was stopping over night with a sick wife. The landlord seemed greatly stirred, and said that he had never taken sides before in any of these difficulties, but he knew hereafter which side he was on. If he and other good citizens had known which side they were on much earlier, there would have soon been but one side to it. We left for Meadville, Pennsylvania, before breakfast, in a buggy. Pleasant road, fine weather, and a poor horse. We wound around among the Pennsylvanian hills, admiring the fertile farms, and feeling the force of the trees, and never before so much impressed with the endless resources of beauty to be found in mere foliage. The various hues of green in nature are so many and so shaded and contrasted, that a carpet might be woven of green alone, and yet range through a long scale almost from black to white.

About half way upon our journey, we struck upon

the edge of one of those ponds of the hill-country full of pickerels and white lilies. The first we could not see. But the last glittered like stars all over the edges of the pond. We were somewhat in haste. But what was time compared with lilies? There they lay holding up their exquisite cups—silver without and gold within—the gold embossed in white, and the white set in green. We grew zealous. But they were somewhat out of reach. The water was full of trunks of trees, roots, and decaying branches. The trunks would not bear up our weight. We stepped, and drew back. We ventured on to this larger log, and ventured off again in half the time. Difficulty whetted determination. We became lily-enthusiastic. We got rails down to the edge of the water, and by laying them across several contiguous logs, hoped their united floating power would buoy us up. Alas! no. We had no thought before of our weight in life. We were satisfied too, that walking on water was a thing most easily done in imagination; and if done well, to be tried in January rather than June. Having neither faith enough, nor any miracle, we were at our wits' end, and became more firmly convinced every moment that it was our duty to have those pond-lilies; all the more, because it seemed impossible, and because we were in a hurry and could not well afford the time necessary. Now in all such cases fanaticism is the only match for impossibility, and we were seized with floral fanaticism.

We pulled down logs, we packed more rails, we searched out more practicable places, we engineered, and by using a long pole, to relieve the trembling rails and sub-incumbent logs, of part of our weight, we reached the fleet of snowy blossoms, no longer to waste their sweetness on the aqueous air. Each flower meekly said, "Take me." With divided effort, to keep our trembling feet, to hold fast our pole slowly sinking in the ooze, we stooped over the darlings and one by one drew up the long stems, snapped by gentle pulling, till we had gathered a store of broadly open flowers, perfect and full; another abundance of half open flowers, beautiful, and to be more so; and yet another multitude of buds, that are but the promises that flowers make. As we drove on, we found a small boat lying near the edge, from which we could have gathered easily our treasures. But we were agreed that we would not have touched the boat even if we had known its presence, and that the sweet faces that we were bearing off were worth all the enterprise which we had put forth. Our errand was to Meadville Theological Seminary, whose president, Dr. Stebbins, was a college classmate. A pleasant day we had, and early departed for our home journey.

Thursday night saw us safely arrived at Painesville, Ohio, and in the hospitable mansion of our friend and parishioner, Mr. Charles Avery, who has taken unto himself this beautiful spot as a summer resort. And surely, a more quiet, tree-singing, restful spot could not well be found. The grounds are full of trees, the trees full of birds, and we that walk under them full of joy and gentle remembrances and yearnings. The house itself is a model of an old twenty-inch walled house, with deep windows, large rooms, and a hall through which a regiment of soldiers might march without touching. One wishes a summer-house to have a certain largeness—a sense of space, a feeling as if you lived in an out-of-doors with a roof on. And under these rustling, sighing leaves, where the light comes and goes to the opening and shutting of a thousand boughs, among which the wind wanders, we do now write, and cease from writing, this prolix epistle.

XXI.

BOOK-STORES, BOOKS.

May 25.

Nothing marks the increasing wealth of our times and the growth of the public mind toward refinement, more than the demand for books. Within ten years the sale of common books has increased probably two hundred per cent., and it is daily increasing. But the sale of expensive works, and of library-editions of standard authors in costly bindings, is yet more noticeable. Ten years ago, such a display of magnificent works as is to be found at the Appletons' would have been a precursor of bankruptcy. There was no demand for them. A few dozen, in one little show-case, was the prudent whole. Now, one whole side of an immense store is not only filled with most admirably bound library-books, but from some inexhaustible source the void continually made in the shelves is at once refilled. A reserve of heroic books supply the places of those that fall. Alas! Where is human nature so weak as in a book-store! Speak of the appetite for drink; or of a *bon-vivant's* relish for a dinner! What are these mere animal throes and ragings compared with those fantasies of taste, of those yearnings of the imagination, of those insatiable appetites of intellect, which bewilder a student in a great bookseller's temptation-hall?

How easily one may distinguish a genuine lover of books from the worldly man! With what subdued and yet glowing enthusiasm does he gaze upon the costly front of a thousand embattled volumes! How gently he draws them down, as if they were little children; how tenderly he handles them! He peers at the title-page, at the text, or the notes, with the nicety of a bird examining a flower. He studies the binding: the leather,—Russia, English calf, morocco; the lettering, the gilding, the edging, the hinge of the cover! He opens it, and shuts it, he holds it off, and brings it nigh. It suffuses his whole body with book-magnetism. He walks up and down, in a maze, at the mysterious allotments of Providence that gives so much money to men who spend it upon their appetites, and so little to men who would spend it in benevolence, or upon their refined tastes! It is astonishing, too, how one's necessities multiply in the presence of the supply. One never knows how many things it is impossible to do without till he goes to Windle's or Smith's house-furnishing stores. One is surprised to perceive, at some bazaar, or fancy and variety store, how many *conveniences* he needs. He is satisfied that his life must have been utterly inconvenient aforetime. And thus, too, one is inwardly convicted, at Appleton's, of having lived for years without books which he is now satisfied that one can not live without!

Then, too, the subtle process by which the man convinces himself that he can afford to buy. No subtle manager or broker ever saw through a maze of financial embarrassments half so quick as a poor book-buyer sees his way clear to pay for what he *must* have. He promises with himself marvels of retrenchment; he will eat less, or less costly viands, that he may buy more food for the mind. He will take an extra patch, and go on with his raiment another year, and buy books instead of coats. Yea, he will write books, that he may buy books. He will lecture, teach, trade; he will do any honest thing for money to buy books! The appetite is insatiable. Feeding does not satisfy it. It rages by the fuel which is put upon it. As a hungry man eats first, and pays afterward, so the book-buyer purchases, and then works at the debt afterward. This paying is rather medicinal. It cures for a time. But a relapse takes place. The same longing, the same promises of self-denial. He promises himself to put spurs on both heels of his industry; and then, besides all this, he will *somehow* get along when the time for payment comes! Ah! this SOMEHOW! That word is as big as a whole world, and is stuffed with all the vagaries and fantasies that Fancy ever bred upon Hope. And yet, is there not some comfort in buying books, *to be* paid for? We have heard of a sot, who wished his neck as long as the worm of a still, that he might so much the longer enjoy the flavor of the draught! Thus, it is a prolonged excitement of purchase, if you feel for six months in a slight doubt whether the book is honestly your own or not. Had you paid down, that would have been the end of it. There would have been no affectionate and beseeching look of your books at you, every time you saw them, saying, as plain as a book's eyes can say, "Do not let me be taken from you."

Moreover, buying books before you can pay for them, promotes caution. You do not feel quite at liberty to take them home. You are married. Your wife keeps an account-book. She knows to a penny what you can and what you can not afford. She has no "speculation" in *her* eyes. Plain figures make desperate work with airy "*somehows*." It is a matter of no small skill and experience to get your books home, and into their proper places, undiscovered. Perhaps the blundering Express brings them to the door just at evening. "What is it, my dear?" she says to you. "Oh! nothing—a few books that I can not do without." That smile! A true housewife that loves her husband, can smile a whole arithmetic at him in one look! Of course she insists, in the kindest way, in sympathizing with you in your literary acquisition. She cuts the strings of the bundle, (and of your heart,) and out comes the whole story. You have bought a complete set of costly English books, full bound in calf, extra gilt! You are caught, and feel very much as if bound in calf yourself, and admirably lettered.

Now, this must not happen frequently. The books must be smuggled home. Let them be sent to some near place. Then, when your wife has a headache, or is out making a call, or has lain down, run the books across the frontier and threshold, hastily undo them, stop only for one loving glance as you put them away in the closet, or behind other books on the shelf, or on the topmost shelf. Clear away the twine and wrapping-paper, and every suspicious circumstance. Be very careful not to be too kind. That often brings on detection. Only the other day we heard it said, somewhere, "Why, how good you have been, lately. I am really afraid that you have been carrying on mischief secretly." Our heart smote us. It was a fact. That very day we had bought a few books which "we could not do without." After a while, you can bring out one volume, accidentally, and leave it on the table. "Why, my dear, *what* a beautiful book! Where *did* you borrow it?" You glance over the newspaper, with the quietest tone you can command: '*That!* oh! that is *mine.* Have you not seen it before? It has been in the house these two months;" and you rush on with anecdote and incident, and point out the binding, and that peculiar trick of gilding, and every thing else you can think of; but it all will not do; you can not rub out that roguish, arithmetical smile. People may talk about the equality of the sexes! They are not equal. The silent smile of a sensible, loving woman, will vanquish ten men. Of course you repent, and in time form a habit of repenting.

Another method which will be found peculiarly effective, is, to make a *present* of some fine work, to your wife. Of course, whether she or you have the name of buying it, it will go into your collection and be yours to all intents and purposes. But, it stops remark in the presentation. A wife could not reprove you for so kindly thinking of her. No matter what she suspects, she will say nothing. And then if there are three or four more works, which have come home with the gift-book—they will pass through the favor of the other.

These are pleasures denied to wealth and old bachelors. Indeed, one cannot imagine the peculiar pleasure of buying books, if one is rich and stupid. There must be some pleasure, or so many would not do it. But the full flavor, the whole relish of delight only comes to those who are so poor that they must engineer for every book. They set down before them, and besiege them. They are captured. Each book has a secret history of ways and means. It reminds you of subtle devices by which you insured and made it yours, in spite of poverty!

XXII.

GONE TO THE COUNTRY.

Lenox, Mass., *July*, 1854.

At length the joyful day was come! Eagerly we escaped from the glow and rage of the town-heat, as if we had been flying from a burning city. We shut the door, and turned the key upon all our cares. For we always arrange to leave our burdensome affairs behind, and take nothing to the country with us but hilarious hearts, contentment, and eyes that never tire of the heavens, or the earth, that do indeed and forevermore show forth the glory of God!

The stalwart engine could not rush fast enough for our impatience. And when, at Bridgeport, we branched off upon the Housatonic Railway, and set our faces full toward the north, where the "hill-country" lay, and flitting through fields and patches of forest, our spirits rose at every mile.

The film fell from our eyes; no ceaseless tasks stood between us and nature; no prospective discourse, inwardly working, drew back our outward sight. We let go our whole routine of duties, and they sank down and faded away as dreams do from the face of the morning. It was all youth with us now. At Newtown our heart prompted us to get out, and take a first and loving look of the hills that here begin to show mountainous symptoms. They were doing extremely well. We gazed as long as the impatient engine would allow at their tree-tufted tops, their long green slopes, at the quiet intervales, in which were snugged away many dear homes and houses, and inhaled the new and perfumed air with a full recognition of its virtues. The very movement of the air upon our skin was pleasurable, as if spirits breathed upon us.

It was a day for traveling, cloudy but not sullen. The heaven was full of those spirit-like films and evanescent wreaths that go sailing about in an aimless way. Deeper in the vault lay those mysterious banks of vapor, brilliantly white upon their rounded outer edges, and shaded to gray and leaden black in the interior. They slowly changed from thrones to battlements; and from battlements to mountains. Such mountains are round about the city of our God! Besides these, there were shoals of flecks that rayed out like fans, or lay stretching away like long unrolled scarfs. It was as if some air-fish were shooting forth, clothed with brilliant scales. In some places the clouds lay in long lines, compact and broad like a mighty highway, cast up for heavenly chariots to run upon. Through the occasional spaces the sun cast forth his fierce light, sometimes straight downward, with unquenched heat, and at other times his beams fell, with long side-way stroke, upon some distant hill, or carried down an atmosphere of light into some stream-fed valley.

Thus we sped on from station to station, the hills growing larger all the way, until, at three o'clock, we reached Lenox. But the rain was there before us, and merrily it played, beating each leaf with its musical drops, like a tiny drum. But what is a summer rain to a Berkshire farmer? especially when white rolling clouds from the west, and clear, bright spots shining through, tell us that fair weather is working its way through all the tumult? Bright bay Charley was waiting for his master; and our farm-horses and wagon (think of that!) were waiting for the baggage, and soon we were trotting away, and greeting, as we went, each field, each stately elm, and round maple, and the number of greetings required were not few. As we rose along the ascending road, the hills began to emerge on every side, and as we drew near our dwelling, up rose, far in the north, old Grey-Lock, the patriarch of a wide family of hills, happily settled down about him. As far to the south, dim and blue, the dome of Mount Washington stood, and still stands, the head and glory of innumerable and unnamed hills. Between these two great northern and southern landmarks, a distance of more than sixty miles, lies the Berkshire valley. Not such a valley as you think of along the Connecticut,—wide meadows, flat and fat; but such a valley as the ocean would be, if, when its waves were running tumultuous and high, it were suddenly transfixed and solidified. The most level portion of this region, if removed to Illinois, would be an eminent hill. The region is a valley only because the mountains on the east and on the west are so much higher than the hills in the intermediate space. The endless variety of such a country never ceases to astonish and please. At every ten steps the aspect changes; every variation of atmosphere, and therefore every hour of the day, produces new effects. It is everlasting company to you. It is, indeed, just like some choice companion, of rich heart and genial imagination, never twice alike, in mood, in conversation, in radiant sobriety, or half-bright sadness; bold, tender, deep, various!

Not yet having had leisure to build our farm-house, that is to be, (for we have resolved that it should be a *farm-house*, and not a mansion,) we have rented the very comfortable house of our neighbor Clark, next adjoining our grounds. We mention this confidentially, to save further inquiries. It was to this that we drove. The rain continued diligent. All that trooping of white clouds in the west; all that opening and shutting of bright spaces, which pretended a clearing off—was, after all, but some private arrangement among the clouds for their own comfort. Here is to be no fair weather, and no venturing out to-night! But there were domestic reasons for remaining in-doors, in the shape of eight trunks, four carpet-bags, and sundry other items, to be opened and disposed of. Besides, the boys, who had been here some weeks before-hand, came tearing in to see us, and the brother's family were all astir on the same errand. There was at least an hour in which words rained down as copiously in the house as did the cloud-drops without. Then came the first tea, made the more piquant by all those little shifts which precede a full settling down; the odd things; the queer uses of strange things. Every body was hunting for every thing, and each zealous to bring something, so that we liked to have had the whole contents of the house on the tea-table. There is something very pleasant in the first meal which a family takes in a new house. It should always be an evening meal. The later hours of the day have a softening influence upon us. Of course, the parents take the end seats, then the children are to be appointed to their posts; then all join with an unusual heartiness in the blessing which is asked of God upon the food, and that heart were strangely remiss that did not ask a blessing upon the house, upon the household, and upon the whole summer's hoped-for joy.

The meal proceeds. This butter is from *our* cows. This is cheese which grandmother made. The bread is so white, the currants are so red, the shaved-beef so country like, the tea just as good as city tea. The boys are bursting to narrate the wonders of their experience. The woodchucks, the squirrels, the hawks, were all chronicled; the rides, the accidents, the hen's nests found, and a world of eager news, were duly set forth. Each boy was eager to go forth and show us all the wonders of the new place; the barn, the woodhouse, the well, the great elm tree, the cellar, the garret, the orchard, and the garden.

The evening grows darker. The trees wave their clammy leaves, dripping with wet, to each sighing of the moist and fitful wind. Now it swells and beats the window-frames with a slashing sound; then it dies away, and leaves only the drowsy murmur of incessant drops pattering upon innumerable leaves, filling the air with somnolence. At nine o'clock every yawning mortal wends to bed. No crickets chirped, no dogs, near or distant, barked; no cows lowed, no wagons rolled past, no foot-fall came from the road. It was all dark out of doors, and nothing was heard but the droning rain that hummed among the leaves, all night long, and the modest clock that hardly dared to tick out loud.

This morning came up in clouds, the clouds grew to mist, and the mist rolled out of the valley, and hung ragged and wild upon the mountain side. All the trees do clap their hands in the merry wind that now, unburdened of its moisture, runs nimbly through the sunny air. We open the front door, and sit upon its threshold. We look out under the maple trees that shade the yard, over fields, across to the mountain sides, that now stand in the freshest, deepest green. We take our book, and holding it with folded hands behind us, we walk, with uncovered head, up and down the road before the house, beneath the trembling shadows which the maples cast westward—shadows that play upon the ground in gold and dark, as the small wind opens and shuts the spaces of the tree to the sunlight! This is perfect rest. The ear is full of birds' notes, of insects' hum, of the barn-yard clack of hens and peeping chickens; the eye is full of noble outlined hills, of meadow-growing trees, of grass glancing with light shot from a million dew-drops, and of the great heavenly arch, unstained with cloud, from side to side without a mote or film: filled with silent, golden ether, which surely descends on such a morning as this from the very hills of heaven. Angels have flown through it, and exhaled their joys, as flowers leave their perfumes in the evening air. Thus to walk, to read now and then some noble passage of some great heart, to fall off again to musing, to read again half aloud or in a murmuring whisper some holy poetry, this it is to be transcendently happy. I say holy poetry, for when men speak of truth with their earthly thoughts, it is but prose; but when they speak truths from their spiritual, and with such efflorescent words as shall be to the thinking what dew-beads are to grass and flowers, that is poetry. It is after long labor that such periods of rest become doubly sweet. For unwearied hours one drifts about among gentle, joyous sensations or thoughts, as gossamers or downy seeds float about in the air, moved only by the impulses of the coquetting wind. Most happily planted here, we shall await September. And if, in the spheres whence the months issue, or along that airy way by which they travel, there is such a thing as breaking down, or detention, may September experience it, and be held back long after her time!

XXIII.

DREAM-CULTURE.

LENOX, *August*, 10, 1854.

THERE is something in *the owning* of a piece of ground, which affects me as did the old ruins of England. I am free to confess that the value of a farm is not chiefly in its crops of cereal grain, its orchards of fruit, and in its herds; but in those larger and more easily reapt harvests of associations, fancies, and dreamy broodings which it begets. From boyhood I have associated classical civic virtues and old heroic integrity with the soil. No one who has peopled his young brain with the fancies of Grecian mythology, but comes to feel a certain magical sanctity for the earth. The very smell of fresh-turned earth brings up as many dreams and visions of the country as sandal-wood does of oriental scenes. At any rate, I feel, in walking under these trees and about these slopes, something of that enchantment of the vague and mysterious glimpses of the past, which I once felt about the ruins of Kenilworth Castle. For thousands of years this piece of ground hath wrought its tasks. Old slumberous forests used to darken it; innumerable deer have trampled across it; foxes have blinked through its bushes, and wolves have howled and growled as they pattered along its rustling leaves with empty maws. How many birds; how many flocks of pigeons, thousands of years ago; how many hawks dashing wildly among them;

how many insects, nocturnal and diurnal; how many mailed bugs, and limber serpents, gliding among mossy stones, have had possession here, before my day! It will not be long before I too shall be as wasted and recordless as they.

Doubtless the Indians made this a favorite resort. Their sense of beauty in natural scenery is proverbial. Where else, in all this region, could they find a more glorious amphitheater? But thick-studded forests may have hidden from them this scenic glory, and left it to solace another race. I walk over the ground wondering what lore of wild history I should read if all that ever lived upon this round and sloping hill had left an invisible record, unreadable except by such eyes as mine, that seeing, see not, and not seeing, do plainly see.

Then, while I stand upon the crowning point of the hill, from which I can behold every foot of the hundred acres, and think what is going on, what gigantic powers are silently working, I feel as if all the workmanship that was stored in the Crystal Palace was not to be compared with the subtle machinery all over this round. What chemists could find solvents to liquefy these rocks? But soft rains and roots small as threads dissolve them and re-compose them into stems and leaves. What an uproar, as if a hundred stone quarries were being wrought, if one should attempt to crush with hammers all the flint and quartz which the stroke of the dew powders noiselessly! All this turf is but a camp of soldier-roots, that wage their battle upon the elements with endless victory. There is a greater marvel in this defiant thistle, which wearies the farmer's wits, taxed for its extermination, than in all the repositories of New York or London. And these mighty trees, how easily do they pump up and sustain supplies of moisture that it would require scores of rattling engines to lift! This farm, it is a vast laboratory, full of expert chemists. It is a vast shop, full of noiseless machinists. And all this is mine! These rocks, that lie in bulk under the pasture-trees, and all this moss that loves to nestle in its crevices, and clasp the invisible projections with its little clinging hands, and all these ferns and sumach, these springs and trickling issues, are mine!

Let me not be puffed up with sudden wealth! Let me rule discreetly among my tenants. Let me see what tribes are mine. There are the black and glossy crickets, the gray crickets, the grasshoppers of every shape and hue, the silent, prudent toad, type of conservative wisdom, wise-looking, but slow-hopping; the butterflies by day, and the moth and millers by night; all birds — wrens, sparrows, king-birds, bluebirds, robins, and those unnamed warblers that make the forests sad with their melancholy whistle. Besides these, who can register the sappers and miners that are always at work in the soil: angle-worms, white grubs, and bugs that carry pick and shovel in the head? Who can muster all the mice that nest in the barn or nibble in the stubble-field, and all the beetles that sing base in the wood's edge to the shrill treble of gnats and myriad musquitoes? These all are mine!

Are they mine? Is it my eye and my hand that mark their paths and circuits? Do they hold their life from me, or do I give them their food in due season? Vastly as my bulk is greater than theirs, am I so much superior that I can despise, or even not admire? Where is the strength of muscle by which I can spring fifty times the length of my body? That grasshopper's thigh lords it over mine. Spring up now in the evening air, and fly toward the lights that wink from yonder hill-side! Ten million wings of despised flies and useless insects are mightier than hand or foot of mine. Each mortal thing carries some quality of distinguishing excellence by which it may glory, and say, "In this, I am first in all the world!"

Since the same hand made me that made them, and the same care feeds them that spreads my board, let there be fellowship between us. There is. I have signed articles of peace even with the abdominal spiders, who carry their fleece in their belly, and not on their back. It is agreed that they shall not cross the Danube of my doors, and I, on the other hand, will let them camp down, without wanton disturbance, in my whole domain beside! I, too, am but an insect on a larger scale. Are there not those who tread with unsounding feet through the invisible air, of being so vast, that I seem to them but a mite, a flitting insect? And of capacities so noble and eminent, that all the stores which I could bring of thought and feeling to them would be but as the communing of a grasshopper with me, or the chirp of a sparrow?

No. It is not in the nature of true greatness to be exclusive and arrogant. If such noble shadows fill the realm, it is their nature to condescend and to spread their power abroad for the loving protection of those whose childhood is little, but whose immortal manhood shall yet, through their kind teaching, stand unabashed, and not ashamed, in the very royalty of heaven. Only vulgar natures employ their superiority to task and burden weaker natures. He whose genius and wisdom are but instruments of oppression, however covered and softened with lying names, is the beginning of a monster. The line that divides between the animal and the divine is the line of suffering. The animal, for its own pleasure, inflicts suffering. The divine endures suffering for another's pleasure. Not then when he went up to the proportions of original glory was Christ the greatest; but when he descended, and wore our form, and bore our sins and sorrows, that by his stripes we might be healed!

I have no vicarious mission for these populous insects. But I will at least not despise their littleness nor trample upon their lives. Yet, how may I spare them? At every step I must needs crush scores, and leave the wounded in my path! Already I have lost my patience with that intolerable fly, and slapped him out of being, and breathed out fiery vengeance against those mean conspirators that, night and day, suck my blood, hypocritically singing a grace before their meal!

The chief use of a farm, if it be well selected, and of a proper soil, is, to lie down upon. Mine is an excellent farm for such uses, and I thus cultivate it every day. Large crops are the consequence, of great delight and fancies more than the brain can hold. My industry is exemplary. Though but a week here, I have lain down more hours and in more places than that hard-working brother of mine in the whole year that he has dwelt here. Strange that industrious lying down should come so naturally to me, and standing up and lazing about after the plow or behind his scythe, so naturally to him! My eyes against his feet! It takes me but a second to run down that eastern slope, across the meadow, over the road, up to that long hill-side, (which the benevolent Mr. Dorr is so beautifully planting with shrubbery for my sake—blessings on him!) but his feet could not perform the task in less than ten minutes. I can spring from Grey Lock in the north, through the hazy air, over the wide sixty miles to the dome of the Taconic mountains in the south, by a simple roll of the eye-ball, a mere contraction of a few muscles. Now let any one try it with their feet, and two days would scant suffice! With my head I can sow the ground with glorious harvests; I can build barns, fill them with silky cows and nimble horses; I can pasture a thousand sheep, run innumerable furrows, sow every sort of seed, rear up forests just wherever the eye longs for them, build my house, like Solomon's Temple, without the sound of a hammer. Ah! mighty worker is the head! These farmers that use the foot and the hand, are much to be pitied. I can change my structures every day, without expense. I can enlarge that gem of a lake that lies yonder, twinkling and rippling in the sunlight. I can pile up rocks where they ought to have been found, for landscape effect, and clothe them with the very vines that ought to grow over them. I can transplant every tree that I meet in my rides, and put it near my house without the drooping of a leaf.

But of what use is all this fanciful using of the head? It is a mere waste of precious time!

But, if it gives great delight, if it keeps the soul awake, sweet thoughts alive and sordid thoughts dead, if it brings one a little out of conceit with hard economies, and penurious reality, and stingy self-conceit; if it be like a bath to the soul, in which it washes away the grime of human contacts, and the sweat and dust of life among selfish, sordid men; if it makes the thoughts more supple to climb along the ways where spiritual fruits do grow; and especially, if it introduces the soul to a fuller conviction of the Great Unseen, and teaches it to esteem the visible as less real than things which no eye can see, or hands handle, it will have answered a purpose which is in vain sought among stupid conventionalities.

At any rate, such a discourse of the thoughts with things that are beautiful, and such an opening of the soul to things which are sweet-breathed, will make one joyful at the time and tranquil thereafter. And if one fully believes that the earth is the Lord's, and that God yet walks among leaves, and trees, in the cool of the day, he will not easily be persuaded to cast away the belief that all these vagaries and wild communings are but those of a child in his father's house, and that the secret springs of joy which they open are touched of God!

XXIV.

A WALK AMONG TREES.

AUGUST 17, 1854.

EVERY one who has read the life of Sir Walter Scott well remembers his love of trees. He used to say that, of all his compositions, he was the most proud of his compositions—for making trees grow. There is yet at East-Hampton, on Long Island, flourishing in a hearty age, an orchard set out by the hands of my father And he used often to say; that, after an absence from home, the first impulse, after greeting his own family, was to go out and examine each tree in his orchard, from root to top. No man that ever planted a tree or loved one but knows how to sympathize with this feeling. A tree that you have planted is born to you. It becomes a member of your family, and looks to you as a child for care and love. Oliver Wendell Holmes spends his summer months upon a beautiful farm near Pittsfield, on which are half a hundred acres of the *original* forest-trees, some of them doubtless five hundred years old; trees that heard the Revolutionary cannon, (or heard of them,) that heard before that, the crack of the rifle in early colonial Indian wars, when Miahcomo, with his fugitive Pequots, took refuge in the Berkshire hills. It is said that Dr. Holmes has measured with a tape-line every tree on his place, and knows each one of them with intimate personal acquaintance. If he has not, he ought to do it.

To the great tree-loving fraternity we belong. We love trees with universal and unfeigned love, and all things that do grow under them, or around them—the whole leaf and root tribe! Not alone when they are in their glory, but in whatever state they are—in leaf, or rimed with frost, or powdered with snow, or crystal-sheathed in ice, or in severe outline stripped and bare against a November sky—we love them. Our heart warms at the sight of even a board or a log. A lumber-yard is better than nothing. The *smell* of wood, at least, is there; the savory fragrance of resin, as sweet as myrrh and frankincense ever was to a Jew. If we can get nothing better, we love to read over the names of trees in a catalogue. Many an hour have we sat at night, when, after exciting work, we needed to be quieted, and read nurserymen's catalogues, and Loudon's Encyclopedias, and Arboretum, until the smell of the woods exhaled from the page, and the sound of leaves was in our ears, and sylvan glades opened to our eyes that would have made old Chaucer laugh and indite a rapturous rush of lines.

But how much more do we love trees in all their summer pomp and plenitude. Not for their names and affinities, not for their secret physiology and as material for science; not for any reason that we can give, except that when with them we are happy. The eye is full, the ear is full, the whole sense and all the tastes solaced, and our whole nature rejoices with that various and full happiness which one has when the soul is suspended in the midst of Beethoven's symphonies, and is lifted hither and thither, as if blown by sweet sounds through the airy passages of a full heavenly dream.

Our first excursion in Lenox was one of salutation to our notable trees. We had a nervous anxiety to see that the ax had not hewn, nor the lightning struck them; that no worm had gnawed at the root, or cattle at the trunk; that their branches were not broken, nor their leaves failing from drought. We found them all standing in their uprightness. They lifted up their heads toward heaven, and sent down to us from all their boughs a leafy whisper of recognition and affection. Blessed be the dew that cools their evening leaves, and the rains that quench their daily thirst! May the storm be as merciful to them when, in winter, it roars through their branches, as is a harper to his harp! Let the snow lie lightly on their boughs, and long hence be the summer that shall find no leaves to clothe these nobles of the pasture!

First in our regard, as it is first in the whole nobility of trees, stands the white elm, no less esteemed because it is an American tree; known abroad only by importation, and never seen in all its magnificence, except in our own valleys. The old oaks of England are very excellent in their way, gnarled and rugged. The elm has strength as significant as they, and a grace, a royalty, which leaves the oak like a boor in comparison. Had the elm been an English tree, and had Chaucer seen and loved and sung it; had Shakspeare, and every English poet, hung some garlands upon it, it would have lifted up its head now, not only the noblest of all growing things, but enshrined in a thousand rich associations of history and literature.

Who ever sees a hawthorn or a sweet-brier (the eglantine) that his thoughts do not, like a bolt of light, burst through ranks of poets, and ranges of sparkling conceits which have been born since England had a written language, and of which the rose, the willow, the eglantine, the hawthorn, and other scores of vines or trees, have been the cause, as they are now and for evermore the suggestions and remembrancers? Who ever looks upon an oak, and does not think of navies; of storms; of battles on the ocean; of the noble lyrics of the sea; of English glades; of the fugitive Charles, the tree-mounted monarch; of the Herne oak; of parks and forests; of Robin Hood and his merry men, Friar Tuck not excepted; of old baronial halls with mellow light streaming through diamond-shaped panes upon oaken floors, and of carved oaken wainscotings? And who that has ever traveled in English second-class cushionless cars has not other and less genial remembrances of the enduring solidity of the impervious, unelastic oak?

One stalwart oak I have, and only one, yet discovered. On my west line is a fringe of forest, through which rushes in spring, trickles in early summer, and dies out entirely in August, the issues of a noble spring from the near hill-side. On the eastern edge of this belt of trees stands the monarchical oak, wide-branching on the east toward the open pasture and the free light, but on its western side lean and branchless, from the pressure of neighboring trees; for trees, like men, can not grow to the real nature that is in them when crowded by too much society. Both need to be touched on every side by sun and air, and by nothing else, if they are to be rounded out into full symmetry. Growing right up by its side, and through its branches, is a long wifely elm—beauty and grace imbosomed by strength. Their leaves come and go together, and all the summer long they mingle their rustling harmonies. Their roots pasture in the same soil; nor could either of them be hewn down without tearing away the branches and marring the beauty of the other. And a tree, when thoroughly disbranched, may, by time and care, regain its health again, but never its beauty.

Under this oak I love to sit and hear all the things which its leaves have to tell. No printed leaves have more treasures of history or of literature to those who know how to listen. But, if clouds kindly shield us from the sun, we love as well to couch down on the grass some thirty yards off, and amidst the fragrant smell of crushed herbs, to watch the fancies of the trees and clouds. The roguish winds will never be done teasing the leaves, that run away and come back, with nimble playfulness. Now and then, a stronger puff dashes up the leaves, showing the downy under-surfaces that flash white all along the up-blown and tremulous forest-edge. Now the wind draws back his breath, and all the woods are still. Then, some single leaf is tickled, and quivers all alone. I am sure there is no wind. The other leaves about it are still. Where it gets its motion I can not tell, but there it goes fanning itself, and restless among its sober fellows. By and by one or two others catch the impulse. The rest hold out a moment, but soon catching the contagious merriment, away goes the whole tree and all its neighbors, the leaves running in ripples all down the forest-side. I expect almost to hear them laugh out loud.

A stroke of wind upon the forest, indolently swelling and subsiding, is like a stroke upon a hive of bees, for sound; and like stirring a fire full of sparks, for upspringing thoughts and ideal suggestions. The melodious whirl draws out a flitting swarm of sweet images that play before the eye like those evening troops of gauzy insects that hang in the air between you and the sun, and pipe their own music, and flit in airy rounds of mingled dance as if the whole errand of their lives was to swing in mazes of sweet music.

Different species of trees move their leaves very differently, so that one may sometimes tell by the motion of shadows on the ground, if he be too indolent to look up, under what kind of tree he is dozing. On the tulip-tree—(which has the finest name that ever tree had, making the very pronouncing of its name almost like the utterance of a strain of music—*liriodendron tulipifera*)—on the tulip tree, the aspen, and on all native poplars, the leaves are apparently Anglo-Saxon, or Germanic, having an intense individualism. Each one moves to suit itself. Under the same wind one is trilling up and down, another is whirling, another slowly vibrating right and left, and others still, quieting themselves to sleep, as a mother gently pats her slumbering child; and each one intent upon a motion of its own. Sometimes other trees have single frisky leaves, but, usually, the oaks, maples, beeches, have community of motion. They are all acting together, or all are alike still.

What is sweeter than a murmur of leaves, unless it be the musical gurgling of water that runs secretly, and cuts under the roots of these trees, and makes little bubbling pools that laugh to see the drops stumble over the root and plump down into its bosom! In such nooks could trout lie. Unless ye would become mermaids, keep far from such places, all innocent grasshoppers, and all ebony crickets! Do not believe in appearances. You peer over and know that there is no danger. You can see the radiant gravel. You know that no enemy lurks in that fairy pool. You can see every nook and corner of it, and it is as sweet a bathing pool as ever was swum by long-legged grasshoppers. Over the root comes a butterfly with both sails a little drabbled, and quicker than light he is plucked down, leaving three or four bubbles behind him, fit emblems of a butterfly's life. There! did I not tell you? Now go away all maiden crickets and grasshoppers! These fair surfaces, so pure, so crystalline, so surely safe, have a trout somewhere in them lying in wait for you!

But what if one sits between both kinds of music, leaves above and water below? What if birds are among the leaves, sending out random calls, far-piercing and sweet, as if they were lovers, saying, "My dear, are you there?" If you are half reclining upon a cushion of fresh new moss, that swells up between the many-plied and twisted roots of a huge beech tree, and if you have been there half an hour without moving, and if you will still keep motionless, you may see what they who only walk through forests never see.

Yonder is a red squirrel on the ground, utterly without fear, and prying about in that pert and nimble way that always makes me laugh. They are so proud of their tails too! They always hold them up, and coquette with them as a lady twirls and flourishes her fan. And though when running on the ground, or peeping about for seeds, they trail them at full length, yet they never sit down for a moment without closing up this important member as if they feared that something would step on it. If you lie down, you may now and then see gray squirrels in the tops of trees, playing with great glee, and quite as supple as their smaller kindred. They travel along a forest top, springing from branch to branch almost as easily as a man walks across a meadow.

But we must enjoy the sight of birds that come down on to the ground, inquiring after their dinner. A bird is the perfection of grace, of motion, of symmetry of form, and of personal neatness. Their walk is so comical when they do walk, and their hop, if hopping is their preference, is so agile and pretty, their habit of prying under leaves, of looking into crevices, of searching the axils of leaves for a chance morsel that may have been put away there, keeps one that watches in a perpetual smile.

But, to return to the leaves, our settled conviction is, that it is best for every leaf to use its own stem in its own way; and for every tree to follow its own inward impulse, upward, outward, in form and motion of leaf, twig, bough, and trunk. Where trees can not help themselves, we should advise them to grow in forests, long-drawn and lean, with no side-branches, but only a top, spread to the sun, far up. Thus growing, they will hold each other up; and, being shallow-rooted, resist the storm by their common strength. Thus do men in cities, and it will not injure trees any more than it doth men. They will be good for timber, for fuel, and for solitude of shades. But if it be given to a tree to stand out where the east and the west, the north and the south, do all look at it at once, each one giving it gifts of beauty, rounding it up into a mighty tower of strength, so let it stand to tell the world what God thought of when he first thought of a tree!

Thus do you stand, noble elms! Lifted up so high are your topmost boughs, that no indolent birds care to seek you; and only those of nimble-wings, and they with unwonted beat, that love exertion, and aspire to sing where none sing higher.—Aspiration! so Heaven gives it pure as flames to the noble bosom. But debased with passion and selfishness it comes to be only Ambition!

It was in the presence of this pasture-elm, which we name the Queen, that we first felt to our very marrow, that we had indeed become owners of the soil! It was with a feeling of awe that we looked up into its face, and when I whispered to myself, This is mine, there was a shrinking as if there were sacrilege in the very thought of *property* in such a creature of God as this cathedral-topped tree! Does a man bare his head in some old church? So did I, standing in the shadow of this regal tree, and looking up into that completed glory, at which three hundred years have been at work with noiseless fingers! What was I in its presence but a grasshopper? My heart said, "I may not call thee property, and that property mine! Thou belongest to the air. Thou art the child of summer. Thou art the mighty temple where birds praise God. Thou belongest to no man's hand, but to all men's eyes that do love beauty, and that have learned through beauty to behold God! Stand, then, in thine own beauty and grandeur! I shall be a lover and a protector, to keep drought from thy roots, and the ax from thy trunk."

For, remorseless men there are crawling yet upon the face of the earth, smitten blind and inwardly dead, whose only thought of a tree of ages is, that it is food for the ax and the saw! These are the wretches of whom the Scripture speaks: "*A man was famous according as he had lifted up axes upon the thick trees.*"

Thus famous, or rather infamous, was the last owner but one, before me, of this farm. Upon the crown of the hill, just where an artist would have planted them, had he wished to have them exactly in the right place, grew some two hundred stalworth and ancient maples, beeches, ashes, and oaks, a narrow belt-like forest, forming a screen from the northern and western winds in winter, and a harp of endless music for the summer. The wretched owner of this farm, tempted of the Devil, cut down the whole blessed band and brotherhood of trees, that he might fill his pocket with two pitiful dollars a cord for the wood! Well, his pocket was the best part of him. The iron furnaces have devoured my grove, and their huge stumps, that stood like gravestones, have been cleared away, that a grove may be planted in the same spot, for the next hundred years to nourish into the stature and glory of that which is gone.

In other places, I find the memorials of many noble trees slain; here, a hemlock that carried up its eternal green a hundred feet into the winter air; there, a huge double-trunked chestnut, dear old grandfather of hundreds of children that have for generations clubbed its boughs, or shook its nut-laden top, and laughed and shouted as bushels of chestnuts rattled down. Now, the tree exists only in the form of loop-holed posts and weather-browned rails. I do hope the fellow got a sliver in his finger every time he touched the hemlock plank, or let down the bars made of those chestnut rails!

What then, it will be said, must no one touch a tree? must there be no fuel, no timber? Go to the *forest* for both. There are no individual trees there, only a forest. One trunk here, and one there, leaves the *forest* just as perfect as before, and gives room for young aspiring trees to come up in the world. But for a man to cut down a large, well-formed, healthy tree from the roadside, or from pastures or fields, is a piece of unpardonable Vandalism. It is worse than Puritan hammers upon painted windows and idolatrous statues. Money can buy houses, build walls, dig and drain the soil, cover the hills with grass, and the grass with herds and flocks. But no money can buy the growth of trees. They are born of Time. Years are the only coin in which they can be paid for. Beside, so noble a thing is a well-grown tree, that it is a treasure to the community, just as is a work of art. If a monarch were to blot out Ruben's Descent from the Cross, or Angelo's Last Judgment, or batter to pieces the marbles of Greece, the whole world would curse him, and for ever. Trees are the only art-treasures which belong to our villages. They should be precious as gold.

But let not the glory and grace of single trees lead us to neglect the peculiar excellences of the forest. We go from one to the other, needing both; as in music we wander from melody to harmony, and from many-voiced and intertwined harmonies back to simple melody again.

To most people a grove is a grove, and all groves are alike. But no two groves are alike. There is as marked a difference between different forests as between different communities. A grove of pines without underbrush, carpeted with the fine-fingered russet leaves of the pine, and odorous of resinous gums, has scarcely a trace of likeness to a maple woods, either in the insects, the birds, the shrubs, the light and shade, or the sound of its leaves. If we lived in olden times among young mythologies, we should say that pines held the imprisoned spirits of naiads and water-nymphs, and that their sounds were of the waters for whose lucid depths they always sighed. At any rate, the first pines must have grown on the sea-shore, and learned their first accents from the surf and the waves; and all their posterity have inherited the sound, and borne it inland to the mountains.

I like best a forest of mingled trees, ash, maple, oak, beech, hickory, and evergreens, with birches growing along the edges of the brook that carries itself through the roots and stones, toward the willows that grow in yonder meadow. It should be deep and somber in some directions, running off into shadowy recesses and coverts beyond all footsteps. In such a wood there is endless variety. It will breathe as many voices to your fancy as might be brought from any organ beneath the pressure of some Handel's hands. By the way, Handel and Beethoven always remind me of forests. So do some poets, whose numbers are various as the infinity of vegetation, fine as the choicest cut leaves, strong and rugged in places as the unbarked trunk and gnarled roots at the ground's surface. Is there any other place, except the sea-side, where hours are so short and moments so swift as in a forest? Where else, except in the rare communion of those friends much loved, do we awake from pleasure, whose calm flow is without a ripple, into surprise that whole hours are gone which we thought but just begun—blossomed and dropped, which we thought but just budding! It is no place for busy men. Let not those resort thither who have vocations of labor and care. Nay, rather, let those who, too busy, need to be more away from strife and overtasking labor, seek the forest. Let it sing to them, and in its twilights let oblivious quiet steal over their cares, as the tides, rising silently from the ocean, creep upon rude-visaged rocks and cover them down beneath their placid depths.

XXV.

BUILDING A HOUSE.

A HOUSE is the shape which a man's thoughts take when he imagines how he should like to live. Its interior is the measure of his social and domestic nature; its exterior, of his esthetic and artistic nature. It interprets, in material forms, his ideas of home, of friendship, and of comfort.

Every man is, in a small way, a creator. We seek to embody our fancies and thoughts in some material shape—to give them an incarnation. Born in our spirit—invisible and intangible—we are always seeking to thrust them forth, so that they shall return to us through some of the physical senses. Thus speech brings back our imaginings to the ear; writing brings them back to the eye; painting brings out the thoughts and feelings, in forms and colors, addressed, through the eye, to several inward tastes; and building presents to our senses our thought of home-life.

But one's dwelling is not always to be taken as the fair index of his mind, any more than the richness of one's mind is judged by one's fluency in speech or skill in writing. The conceiving power may be greater in us than the creative or expressing power. But there are other considerations which usually have more to do with building, especially in America, than a man's inward fancies. In fact, in the greatest number of instances, a man's house may be regarded as simply the measure of his purse. It is a compromise between his heart and his pocket. It is a memorial of his ingenuity in procuring the utmost possible convenience and room from the least possible means; for our young men—ninety-nine in a hundred—are happily born; that is, born poor, but determined to be rich. This gives birth to industry, frugality, ingenuity, perseverance, and success, inward and outward; for, while making his fortune, the man is making himself. He is extracting manly qualities out of those very labors or endurances by which he achieves material wealth. In the career of every such young man, his little accumulations have to perform three functions—to carry on his business, to meet the annual expenses of his little but growing family, and to build and beautify their home. Thus, his property, slender at best, even if it all rose in one channel, must move in a threefold channel, to carry three mills. The portion set apart for building, therefore, must be very little. Indeed, it is to be doubted whether one in a hundred knows how he shall pay for more than half his house, when he begins to build, and he is seldom much wiser when he ends. He draws upon hope, and when, in five or ten years, the house is paid for, it would puzzle him to say how he had done it. Now, under such circumstances, it would be absurd to look for what are called architectural effects. There must be, if possible, a kitchen and a bed-room. In pioneer life, even these must come together, and one room serve every purpose. But, usually, a man can afford a kitchen, a dining-room, (which is also a parlor,) and a bed-room. These three rooms are the seed and type of all other rooms which can be built; for all apartments must serve our bodily wants, our social domestic wants, and our social public wants. The kitchen and dining-room, and all appurtenances thereof, are for the animal nature; our bed-room and sitting-room and library are for our home social wants; and our parlors, halls, etc., for our more public social necessities. While one is yet poor, one room must serve several uses. In the old-fashioned country houses the kitchen was also the dining-room; and never will saloon, how admirable soever, be so pleasant as our remembered hours in the great, broad, hospitable kitchen. The door opened into the well-room, on one side, whence came the pitcher, all dripping and bedewed; another door opened into the cheese-room, rich with rows of yellow cheeses; while the front door, wide open in summer, attracted clucking hens and peeping chickens, who cocked an eye at you, or even ventured across the threshold after a stray crumb.

The sitting-room and parlor, too, must often be one and the same, and in the same space must be the library, if such a thing is known in the dwelling. Bed-rooms are more independent and aristocratic than anything else, cultivating very exclusive habits. Yet, even bed-rooms must contrive to be ingenious. Curtained corners, cloth partitions, trundle-beds and sofa-beds, that disappear by day, like some flowers, unfold only at night.

But, in proportion as one's means increase, the

rooms, like branches in a plant, grow out of each other, kitchen and dining-room must separate and live by themselves. The sitting-room withdraws from the parlor, taking all the ease and comfort with it, and leaving all the stateliness and frigid dignity. All the books walk off into a little black-walnut room by themselves, where they stand in patient splendor and silent wisdom behind their glass doors. The flowers abandon the windows, and inhabit a formal conservatory. Bed-rooms multiply, each one standing in single blessedness. The house is full grown. Alas! too often all its comfort goes, just when it should stand full blossomed! How many persons, from out of their two-story frame dwellings, have sighed across the way for the log cabin! How many persons have moved from a home into a *house;* from low ceilings, narrow halls, rooms of multifarious uses, into splendid apartments, whose chief effect was to make them homesick. But this is because pride or vanity was the new architect. For a *large* house is a grand and almost indispensable element to our fullest idea of comfort. But it must be social largeness. The broad halls must seem to those that enter like open arms holding out a welcome, not like the aisles of a church, lifted up out of reach of human sympathy. The staircase should be so broad and gentle in inclination, that its very looks invite you to try it. But, then, a large house ought to have great diversity; some rooms should have a ceiling higher than others; doors should come upon you in unexpected places; little cosy rooms should surprise you in every direction. Where you expected a cupboard, there should be a little confidential entry-way. Where the door seems to open into the yard, you should discover a sweet little nest that happened into the plan as bright thoughts now and then shine in the soul. All sorts of closets and queer cupboards should by degrees be found out.

Now, such a house never sprang full-grown from an architect's brain, as did the fabled deity from Jupiter's head. It must grow. Each room must have been needed for a long time, and come into being with a decided character impressed upon them. They will have been aimed at some real want, and, meeting it, will take their subtile air and character from it. Thus, one by one, the rooms will be born into the house as children are into the family. And, as our affections have undoubtedly a certain relation to form, color, and space, so our rooms will in their forms, dimensions, and hues, indicate the faculties which most wrought in their production.

We all know what is meant, in painting, in music, and in writing, by *conventionalism.* Men write or fashion, not to give ease to an impulse in them that struggles for a birth, but because they have an outside knowledge that such and such things would be proper and customary. So do men build conventional houses. They put all the customary rooms in the customary manner. They express themselves in this room as kitchens are usually expressed; they fashion parlors as they remember that parlors have been made; they go to their books, their plans, and portfolios of what has been done, and, selecting here a thing and there a thing, they put a house together as girls do patchwork bed-spreads, a piece out of every dress in the family for the last year or two. These are conventional houses. Such are almost all city houses—the original type of which was a *ladder;* from each round, rooms issue, in ascending order, and the perpendicular stairs still retain the peculiar properties of the type. Such, too, are almost all ambitious country houses, built in conspicuous places, in the most intrusive and come-and-look-at-me manner; painted as brilliantly as flash peddlers wagons, or parrots' wings.

Until men are educated, and good taste is far more common than it is, this method of building houses, by the architect's plans, and not by the owner's disposition, must prevail; and it is not the worst of earth's imperfections. But a genuine house, an original house, a house that expresses the builder's inward idea of life in its social and domestic aspect, can not be *planned* for him; nor can he, all at once, sit down and plan it. It must be a result of his own growth. It must first be wanted—each room and each nook. But, as we come to ourselves little by little and gradually, so a house should either be built by successive additions, or it should be built when we are old enough to put together the accumulated ideas of our life. Alas! when we are old enough for that, we are ready to die; or Time hath dealt so rudely with our hearts, that, like trees at whose boughs tempests have wrought, we are not anxious to give expression to ourselves. The best way to build, therefore, is to build, as trees grow, season by season; all after-branches should grow with a symmetrical sympathy with older ones. In this way, too, one may secure that mazy diversity, that most unlooked-for intricacy in a dwelling, and that utter variation of lines in the exterior, which pleases the eye, or ought to please it, if it be trained in the absolute school of Nature, and which few could ever invent at once, and on purpose!

We abhor Grecian architecture for private dwellings, and especially for country homes. It is cheerless, pretentious, frigid. Those cold long-legged columns, holding up a useless pediment that shelters nothing and shades nothing, reminds one of certain useless men in society, for ever occupied with maintaining their dignity, which means their perpendicularity. In spite of Mr. Ruskin, we *do* like Grecian architecture in well-placed public buildings. But it gives us a shiver to see dwellings so stiff and stately.

We have, too, a special doctrine of windows. They are designed to let the light in, and equally to let the sight out; and this last function is, in the country, of prime importance. For, a window is but another name for a stately picture. There are no such landscapes on canvas as those which you see through glass. There are no painted windows like those which trees and lawns paint standing in upon them, with all the glory of God resting on them! Our common, small, frequent windows in country dwellings are contemptible. We love rather the generous old English windows, large as the whole side of a room, many-angled, or circular; but, of whatever shape, they should be recessed—glorious nooks of light, the very antitheses of those shady coverts which we search out in forests, in hot summer days. These little chambers of light, into which a group may gather, and be both in doors and out of doors at the same time; where, in storms or in winter, we may have full access to the elements without chill, wet, or exposure,—these are the glory of a dwelling. The great treasures of a dwelling are, the child's cradle, the grandmother's chair, the hearth and old-fashioned fire-place, the table, and the window.

Bed-rooms should face the east, and let in the full flush of morning light. There is a positive pleasure in a golden bath of early morning light. Your room is filled and glorified. You awake in the very spirit of light. It creeps upon you, and suffuses your soul, pierces your sensibility, irradiates the thoughts, and warms and cheers the whole day. It is sweet to awake and find your thoughts moving to the gentle measures of soft music; but we think it full as sweet to float into morning consciousness upon a flood of golden light, silent though it be! What can be more delicious than a summer morning, dawning through your open windows, to the sound of innumerable birds, while the shadows of branches and leaves sway to and fro along the wall, or spread new patterns on the floor, wavering with perpetual change!

XXVI.

CHRISTIAN LIBERTY IN THE USE OF THE BEAUTIFUL.

In an age when men more and more feel the duty of employing their strength and their wealth for the education of their fellows, it becomes a question of supreme moment, to what extent a Christian man may surround himself with embellishments and luxuries of beauty.

There be many who would walk through a noble gallery of paintings with an accusing conscience, repeating to themselves, with poignant sincerity, the hollow words of the old traitor, when the alabaster box of precious ointment was poured upon His head, "To what purpose is this *waste?* . . . . Why was it not sold for three hundred pence, and given to the poor?"

Nor is the self-accusation lessened when one perceives that elegance and luxury are most often employed as a shining barrier, built up between the cultured and the vulgar—the barrier around a *class* more impenetrable than the conventional distinctions of artificial nobility. For no customs of law or usage have such force as those which spring from the soul's own living consciousness of *difference* and *superiority.*

Many earnest men, therefore, have associated embellishments with selfishness, and forswear them as a part of their fealty to Benevolence.

It seems to me that God has ordained a usefulness of the beautiful, as much as of knowledge, of skill, of labor, and of benevolence. It was meant to be not alone a cause of enjoyment, but a positive means of education. Is wealth allowable, if one will employ it benevolently? Is philosophy allowable, if one will apply it to the uses of men? Is scholarship virtuous, if it be a treasure held in trust for all kinds of ignorance? Is skill praiseworthy, if employed to promote the human weal? And why is not the possession of architectural beauty, of art-treasures, of landscape beauty, the beauty of grounds and gardens, of homes and furniture, if they are held conscientiously amenable to the law of usefulness?

Society grows, as trees do, by rings. There are innumerable circles formed, with mutual attractions. The lowest section feels and emulates that which is next above; *that* circle is aspiring to the level next above *it*. This one, in its turn, is attracted by one yet higher; and that by another.

There are some influences, to be sure, that are general, and that strike right through from top to bottom of life. And there are many special influences which, like comets, come unexpectedly blazing along their orbits, with streaming influences, long trailed. But there are certain organic conditions of life, founded upon gradations of mind-power, or of development.

The ditcher aspires to the position of a husbandman; the apprentice emulates the prosperous master-mechanic; the mechanic looks up to those whose wealth is allied to education; the plainly-bred citizen aspires to the mental activity of professional men and scholars; and these, in turn, acknowledge gradations among themselves to the very top of genius; and all men are reaching after some ideal, or some example that hangs above them. So that, when a man has no longer any conception of excellence above his own, his voyage is done, he is dead—dead in trespasses and sins of blear-eyed vanity!

We can not always tell the exact gradations, nor mark off the sections like inches on a rule. Society is so vast a thing, that its growths are like the luxurious up-sproutings of a tropical forest, choked with abundance, forcing up its vines and plants and trees, in sinuous interlacings that quite bewilder the eye that would trace the outward form, or the research that would follow the flow of sap from rootlet to topmost leaf. Yet, we know that it is in society as it is in vegetation. It is not the sun upon the *root* that begins growth in a tree, but the sun upon its *top*. The outermost wood awakes and draws upon that below it, and sends progressing activity down to its root. Then begins a double circulation. The root sends up its crude sap, the leaf prepares it with all vegetative treasures, and back it goes on a mission of distribution to every part, to the outmost root. And thus, with striking analogy, is it in society. The great mass are producing gross material that rises up to refinement and power, that, in turn, send back the influence of refinement and power upon all the successive degrees, to the bottom!

It is in this point of view that the very highest forms of literary and scientific institutions are to be judged and justified.

An astronomical observatory may seem to have no relation to the welfare of a community. What have eclipses and planetary transits to do with human life? When the invisible paths of all stars are traced by mathematical faith, what have parallaxes and multitudinous calculations to do with men's ordinary business? But experience will, in a generation, show, that those who first feel the fruits and elevation of such pursuits will be few; but they will become broader, deeper, and better. Through them, but diluted and not recognized, the next class below will be influenced—not by *astronomy*, but by the moral power of men who have been elevated by astronomy. Every part of society is affected when *men* are built up. They impart their own growth to whatever they touch. Enlarge men, and you enlarge everything.

There be some who rail at universities as too remote from practical life and living wants, and who propose colleges to teach men their very trades and professions. But these subordinate colleges will depend upon the superior influences of institutions above them, that are the standards—the Chronometers of LEARNING.

There never can be too many libraries, too many cabinets, too many galleries of art, too many literary men, too much culture. The power of mind at *the top of society* will determine the ease and rapidity of the ascent of the bottom—just as the power of the engine at the top of the inclined plane will determine the length of the train that can be drawn up, and the rapidity of its ascent.

This marks the distinction between natural and artificial nobility. All societies have nobles. We have a nobility as really as do monarchies. But in England it is an order *separated from those below;* and there is no free circulation. No one can rise into it by force of moral excellence and culture, though he may be really equal to its members. Artificial aristocracy stands looking down upon the mass of men, as did Father Abraham, saying: "*Between us and you there is a great gulf fixed, so that they which would pass hence to you can not; neither can they pass to us that would come from thence.*"

Natural aristocracy is the eminence of men over their fellows, in real mind and soul. They are above men because they are wiser and better; and any one may join them whenever he is as wise and as good. They are above society, not to spread their roots in the great democracy and sustain the glory of the field by filching out its strength, but rather, as clouds are above the earth, to open their bosoms, and cast down fertilizing rains, that all the earth, and every living thing, may rejoice.

It is upon this great principle that men may become the benefactors of their race by the indulgence of beauty, and embellishments, if they be employed generously and public-spiritedly. Every mansion that enlarges men's conceptions of convenience, of comfort, of substantialness and permanence, or of beauty, *is an institution.*

It may have been selfishness that built it; extravagance may have been the ruling spirit. The owner may have been some imbecile for whose vanity some noble architect wrought; the completed work may leave the luckless owner bankrupt; and all men may deride the folly of costly buildings and expensive grounds. Every reproach may fall upon his empty head most righteously; yet his folly may have done more for the village than the wisdom of all the rest!

The work is done. What that stately mansion is, it is in itself. It stands through generations a form of beauty lifted up. When its owner's history is a legend, its lines will stand unbroken, its shadows will be as fresh as on the day when they first fell trembling from the glances of the sun. The old trees will outlive generations of men. They will proclaim the glory of God to the eye by day, and awake at midnight, in the summer winds, to sing their solemn song of praise!

But how much more will all this be, if such a structure is in due proportion to its builder's means; if it be no creature of his vanity, but born legitimately of his sense of grandeur and beauty; if it be the magazine, too, of his beneficence, so that out of it shall issue all gentleness, all due humility, all neighborly love, all grace and purity of life, and, effluent as the golden airs of summer days, charities and public bounties, enriching the wide circle about, and making angels stoop to kiss with reverent love the noble brow that lived in such joy of beauty as this!

It is wealth selfishly kept or spent that is mean.

It is architecture that shuts a man's heart in from his fellows that is mean ; that stands with effrontery, saying to all who pass, "*Come and worship me.*"

It is *selfishness*, in short, under what form of knowledge, refinement, power, wealth, or beauty, that curses man, and is itself accursed.

The question is not what proportion of his wealth a Christian man may divert from benevolent channels for personal enjoyment through the element of the beautiful. For, if rightly viewed, and rightly used, his very elegances and luxuries will be a contribution to the public good. One may well say, "How can I indulge in such embellishments in my dwelling, when so many thousands are perishing for lack of knowledge about me." This is conclusive against a selfish use of the beautiful. But rightly employed, it becomes itself a contribution to the education of society. It acts upon the lower classes by acting first upon the higher. It is an education of the educators. And the question becomes only this: How much of my wealth given to the public good shall be employed *directly* for the elevation of the ignorant, and how much *indirectly?* How much shall I bring to bear directly upon the masses, and how much indirectly through institutions and remote instrumentalities?

I can not but think that Christian men have not only a right of enjoyment in the beautiful, but a duty, in some measure, of producing it, or propagating it, or diffusing it abroad through the community.

Some may build their work in words, and live in

literature. Some may shape their sense into sound, and live in the world's song. Some may insphere themselves in art, and transmit the statue, the canvas, or the stately pile.

Some may contribute to this realm of beauty in that only department in which America has an original architecture with native lines of beauty, expressed in those storm-driven Temples of the Deep.

And if there are aspiring natures that wistfully ask, with empty hands, What may we with our poverty do to embellish the earth, to them I say, When all the works of man are ended, he has not approached the inexpressible beauty of God's architecture.

Those stately elms, that teach us every winter how meekly to lay our glories by, and receive the reverses of inevitable misfortune, and that soon will teach us to look forth out of all misfortunes, and clothe ourselves afresh after every winter, what have ye that may compare with *them?* The cathedrals of the world are not traced as these, nor so adorned, nor so full of communion, nor have they pliant boughs on which with humble might they swing the peaceful singing-bird, and from whose swaying, night or day, there is music in the air for them that know the sound! Of all man's works of art, a cathedral is greatest. A tree is greater than that! Of all man's instruments of sound, an organ uttering its mazy harmonies through the somber arches of the reverend pile, is the grandest; but the sound of summer in the forest, is grander than that!

And, if we wander out from the arid city till we

come to these crowned monarchs of the fields, we need not be ashamed to stand with lifted hands and bless our God for a gift of beauty greater than any man may build!

It is, then, here, that every one may yield to life some embellishment. To the home of your youth you may return with gathered wealth to replant it with flowers. Your native village you may imbosom in well-selected forests. The traveler may, in another generation, journey along our roads, overarched with elms or shaded with stately oaks.

Your villages may grow lovely in a thousand features now unknown. Every yard and garden may be a paradise.

The church, no longer gaunt, shattered, and decaying, may, by the loving hands of those whose boyhood was nurtured there, rise in renewed beauty. Or, if its hereditary ailments or proportions defy remedy, from your zeal may spring another structure, harmonious in every proportion, a joy to the eye, signaling the distant traveler with its spire, its solemn bell, through all the hours of day and night, ringing out the sound of our footsteps toward eternity!

The old graveyard, that shame of many villages, where death and weeds reign triumphant over the forgotten graves of parents and dear hearts, hath thy hand no bounty wherewith to yield to it a reverend beauty?

Shall the old school-house stand longer mounted in the eye of the summer sun, the very target of the winter wind, treeless, bare, filthy? By thy bounteous hand let it be cleansed by fire, and from its ashes bid arise a phenix that shall be just what for the most part school-houses are *not.*

But in all your labors for the Beautiful, remember that its mission is not of corruption, nor of pride, nor of selfishness, but of *benevolence!* And as God hath created beauty, not for a few, but hath furnished it for the whole earth, multiplying it until, like drops of water and particles of air, it abounds for every living thing, and in measure far transcending human want, until the world is a running-over cup, so let thine heart understand both the glory of God's beauty and the generosity of its distribution. So living, life shall be a glory, and death a passing from glory to glory!

XXVII.

NATURE A MINISTER OF HAPPINESS.

LENOX, *August* 27, 1854.

IT was not meant that the enjoyments of life should be few and intense, but many and gentle; and great happiness is the sum of a multitude of drops. Those days which are the channels of mighty joys are, perhaps, the most memorable. But they exhaust. They unfit us for common duties. We regard them as we do mountain-tops. We go up occasionally, not to dwell there, but to see at a glance the whole of that which, upon the plains, we see only in succession and in detail. But the staple of pleasure must be found in small measures, and in common things. They who are seeking enjoyment in remote ways, abandoning familiar things and common experience for wild and outstretched flights, will find more and more, as life advances, that they have taken the road to yearnings, but not to enjoyment. The secret of happiness lies in the health of the whole mind, and in giving to each faculty due occupation, and in the natural order of their superiorities, the Divine first, the human second, the material last. And every one can find, but in different degrees, the food for all their faculties in that sphere into which God has cast their lot. Instead of seeking happiness by going out of our place, our skill should be to find it where we are. Our pleasures, like honey, should be extracted not from a few stately flowers, named and classic, but from the whole multitude, great and small, which God has sown with profuse hand to smile in every nook, and to make the darkest corners warm with their glowing presence. Every thing which is made has an errand to us, if we will hear. No difference among men is more noticeable than the facility of happiness. No gift of God should be more gratefully recognized than a nature easily tending toward enjoyment. So that of its own accord, it avoids sources of annoyance, and discerns in every thing some ray of brightness.

On such a glorious morning of a perfect day as this, when all the smoky haze has gone from the horizon, when the sun comes up fresh and clear, and will go down unreddened by vapor, the mountains come back from their hiding, and I wander forth, wondering how there should be sorrow in the world. It seems as if it were a thing that I had read about in fictions, but had half-forgotten, like a fading dream. Every sense is calmly alive, and every faculty that lies back of sense is quietly exultant. My soul is like a hive, and it swarms with thoughts and feelings going nimbly out, and returning with golden thighs to the growing comb. Each hour is a perfect hour, clear, full, and unsated. It is the joy of being alive. It is the experience of that living joy which God meant to exhale from each faculty, just as odors do from flowers. Such days are let down from heaven. On such days the gate that looks toward the earth has surely been set wide open, and hours are but the spaces which lie between the angels that God sends to bear to us immortal joys.

From the grand tranquillity that reigns on every side I turn my thoughts, with dreamy surprise, to those whirlpools of excitement where men strive for honor, and know not what is honorable; for wealth, and do not know true riches; for pleasure, and are ignorant of the first elements of pleasure. There comes to me a sad sense of the turmoil of men fiercely bent upon happiness, who will never know it. They are starving amidst unexampled abundance. In their Father's house is bread enough and to spare, and a divine wine that inspires ardor, without intoxication, within the soul. Why should they be furrowed with care, and my unwrinkled heart be purpled over with blossoming joy? Are we not made alike? Have they not every one of the faculties that I have? Every sense that rings to the strokes of joy they have even as I have. And they have, too, the very things that make me supremely joyful, a hope of immortality, a present and paternal God, the sun, the face of the world, the clouds, the trees and the birds which keep house in them, the air, the innumerable grass! It is not any thing that I own, it is no stroke of grand fortune, no special success, that rejoices me. It is nothing but the influence of those things in which every man has common possession—days, nights, forests, mountains, atmosphere, universal and unmonopolized nature! But having eyes they will not see, and ears they will not hear, and a heart they will not understand. As the old prophet touched his servant's eyes, and he beheld the mountains filled with the angels and chariots of God, and feared no more; so, methinks, if I could but bring the eager thousands forth who pant and strive for joy, only for joy, and unseal their eyes, they should behold and know assuredly that happiness was not in all the places where they delve and vex themselves. In the presence of these heavenly hours, riches, touched with the finger of God, would say, "Joy is not in me." Fame would say, "It is not in me." Passion, hoarse from toils of grossness, would say, "It is not in me." And amidst their confessions a voice should come down through the clear air from heaven and the very bosom of Christ, saying, "Come unto Me, all ye that labor and are heavy laden, and I will give you rest." In that rest, which Christ gives every created thing, lies an atmosphere of enchanted beauty!

Yea, Lord! that promise is a highway without a chasm. Ten thousand feet have trod it, and found it true. My own soul knoweth it right well. And this out-spread crystal vault is full of the light of thy countenance. This earth, which the sun unrolls and reads daily, is thy written parchment! It were a dead and mute thing but for the presence of the living God. As upon mountain-tops, the noise of the valley dies away and is not heard, and men's dwellings are no bigger than leaves, and all the mightiest uproars are whispers, and the silent spectator looks down upon life unharassed by its currents, so, in such hours as this, the soul stands with God, and moves somewhat in the eternal course of the Divine soul; while the eddies, the dark dangers of the deep pools in life's rocky stream, the hoarse, rushing, and impetuous outburst of the furious currents of human passions are so far below, that we either see them not or see them as a silent vapor! Thus, Lord, wilt thou hide whom thou choosest in thy pavilion, and the storm shall thunder unheard beneath them, the darkness shall be light around about them, and perfect peace shall abide upon their hearts for ever!

Is it Nature that has the power of conferring such religious joy, or is it Religion that inspires Nature to such celestial functions? To a Christian heart it is both. The soul seeks and sees God through nature, and nature changes its voice, speaking no longer of mere material grandeur and beauty, but declares through all its parts the glory of God. Then when Christ is most with us, do we find nature the most loving, the most inspired; and it evolves a deeper significance, in all its phases, and chants, with its innumerable voices, solemn but jubilant hymns of praise to God!

But let no one go forth to declare what nature shall do for him. Let no one sound the key-note of his own desire first, and ask nature to take up the harmony and evolve it. Let one go as a little child, opening his heart, and waiting to see what God shall do unto him. Let him accept just what is sent—clouds when clouds are sent, sunlight when sunlight comes; little things, rude things—all things.

The fullest enjoyment of the country does not arise

from stray excitements acting in straight lines; not from august mountains, wide panoramas, awful gorges, nor from any thing that runs in upon you with strong stimulations. All these things have their place. But they are occasional. They are the sub-base, and come in as the mighty undertone upon which soft and various melodies float. A thousand daily little things make their offering of pleasure to those who know how to be pleased.

We have said that there is no difference between one person and another more characteristic and noticeable than the facility of being happy. Some seem pierced with half a hundred windows, through which stream warmth, light, and sounds of delight. Others have but one or two stately doors, and they are mostly shut. Some persons are always breaking out into happiness, because every thing is bringing them pleasure. It comes in at the eye, and at the ear, at the portals of smell, taste, and touch, in things little and great, in shapes and colors, in contrasts and analogies, in exactitudes, and in fanciful associations; in homely life, and in wild and grand life. But others there are that go for enjoyment to nature just as they dress for company, and receive pleasure formally, and in the stiffness of ceremony. They march out to behold noble aspects, as if they felt bound to keep up a respectable show before nature. The full enjoyment of nature requires that we should be as many-sided as nature herself. It is to be considered that God found a reason of pleasure in every individual thing which he has made, and that an education on our part, toward God in nature, consists in developing in ourselves a pleasure in every single object which exists about us. So sadly are we brought up in this respect, that it must be a very serious education to most persons.

As things go in our utilitarian age, men look upon the natural world in one of three ways: the first, as a foundation for industry, and all objects are regarded in their relations to industry. Grass is for hay, flowers are for medicine, springs are for dairies, rocks are for quarries, trees are for timber, streams are for navigation or for milling, clouds are for rain, and rain is foi harvests. The relation of an object to some commercial or domestic economy, is the end of observation. Beyond that there is no interest to it.

The second aspect in which men behold nature, is the purely scientific. We admire a man of science who is so all-sided that he can play with fancy or literality, with exactitudes or associations, just as he will. But a mere man of accuracy, one of those conscientious-eyed men, that will never see any thing but just what is there, and who insist upon bringing every thing to terms; who are for ever dissecting nature, and coming to the physical truths in their most literal forms, these men are our horror. We should as soon take an analytic chemist to dine with us, that he might explain the constituent elements of every morsel that we ate; or an anatomist into a social company, to describe the bones, and muscles, and nerves that were in full play in the forms of dear friends. Such men think that nature is perfectly understood when her mechanism is known; when her gross and physical facts are registered, and when all her details are catalogued and described. These are nature's dictionary-makers. These are the men who think that the highest enjoyment of a dinner would be to be present in the kitchen and that they might see how the food is compounded and cooked.

A third use of nature is that which poets and artists make, who look only for beauty.

All of these are partialists. They all misinterpret, because they all proceed as if nature were constructed upon so meager a schedule as that which they peruse; as if it were a mere matter of science, or of commercial use, or of beauty; whereas these are but single developments among hundreds.

The earth has its physical structure and machinery, well worth laborious study; it has its relations to man's bodily wants, from which spring the vast activities of industrial life; it has its relations to the social faculties, and the finer sense of the beautiful in the soul; but far above all these are its declared uses, as an interpreter of God, a symbol of invisible spiritual truths, the ritual of a higher life, the highway upon which our thoughts are to travel toward immortality, and toward the realm of just men made perfect that do inherit it.

No one who has made himself conversant with the representations given of the natural world by the old Hebrew mind, but will feel the infidelity of our modern occidental mind. When the old prophet felt his sense kindled by the divine touch, and read the face of the heavens and of the earth, as God meant them to be read, how full of meaning and of majesty were the clouds, the mountains, the morning and the evening, the storms, the birds and beasts, the insects, and the grass through which they creep!

When clouds begin to gather, and, growing dark and blacker, travel up from the horizon full of solemn intent, their folds moving upon themselves, and their whole aspect full of an unspeakable majesty, as if they did not see the earth, nor know so small a thing in their headlong march toward some distant goal, the Anglo-Saxon remarks that it is a fine thunder gust, and speculates upon the probability of rain! The old Hebrew would chant, in low and reverent tone, "He bowed the heavens also, and came down, and darkness was under his feet, and he rode upon a cherub, and did fly, yea he did fly upon the wings of the wind. He made darkness his secret place; his pavilion round about him were dark waters and thick clouds of the sky." Thus gazing upon the grandeur of the gathering storm, beholding in it the robes which hid the majesty of Jehovah, the clouds are rent with lightnings, and the heaven roars with awful thunders which fly in terrible echoes from cloudy cliff to cliff, bellowing and rolling away in sullen sounds into interior depths of the heaven. It is the voice of God. It is the glance of the eye of Him upon whom no man can look and live: "The Lord also thundered in the heavens, and the

Highest gave his voice, hail-stones and coals of fire."

As the burden of the storm passes, and we see its fiery forks plunging upon the mountain with silent vehemence, *we* say, the lightning struck something; and we reflect upon electricity and lightning-rods, upon Dr. Franklin and his kite. The old Hebrew would have thought: These be the arrows which God shooteth forth. He searcheth out his enemies. The Lord sitteth upon the flood. The Lord sitteth King for ever! All the aspects of the earth ministered sublime conceptions of God. Mountains were his highway. The clear, open sky, declared his glory. The light was his raiment of joy; the darkness of storms his terrible apparel of judgment. Flowers and sparrows taught his providence and care.

Our modern method of instructing ourselves in the attributes of God is the philosophical method, or the method of ideas, as distinguished from the natural, or the method of feeling and imagination. Seeking to evolve a more symmetrical and thorough view of God, we have relied almost wholly upon the reasoning faculties. Our Deity is a system of attributes. To the Hebrews, God was a Living Presence; to us he is a remote category of abstractions.

The Hebrew found God in nature, we in the catechism. We do not say that there are no advantages in a psychological method; but only, that whatever we gain in that direction, we can never come to a sense of *a living and present God*, until we also include in our methods the old Hebrew way of beholding God in living activity, moving in the heavens and along the earth, guiding the day and the night, and as variously active as all the flowers, the trees, the birds, the beasts, and the nations of men, whom he creates, and leads forth with daily care and love.

XXVIII.

SPRINGS AND SOLITUDES.

LENOX, *October*, 1854.

I HAVE always wished that there might be a rock-spring upon my place. I could wish to have, back of the house some two hundred yards, a steep and tree-covered height of broad, cold, and mossy rocks; rocks that have seen trouble, and been upheaved by deep inward forces, and that are lying in every way of noble confusion, full of clefts, and dark and mysterious passages, without echoes in them, upholstered with mosses and pendulous vines. Upon all this silent tumult of wild and shattered rocks, struck through with stillness and rest, the thick forests should shed down a perpetual twilight. The only glow that ever chased away its solemn shadows should be the red rose-light of sunsets, shot beneath the branches and through the trunks, lighting up the gray rocks with strange golden glory. What light is so impressive as this last light of the day streaming into a forest so dark that even insects leave it silent.

In such a rock-forest as I have spoken of, far up in one of its silent aisles, a spring should burst forth, making haste from the seams of the rock, as if just touched with the prophet's rod, cold, clear, copious, and musical from its birth. All the way to the outer edge of the forest it should find its own channels, and live its own life, unshaped by human hands. But, before the sun touched it, we would have a rock-reservoir, into which it should gather its congregation of drops, now about to go forth into useful life. Thence it should have liberty of will to flow through strong pipes into every chamber of the house. And it should be to every room copious as the atmosphere, so that one might bathe in molten ice every hour of the day, if he chose, without fear of exhausting the fountain, and in the joy of abundance beyond all squandering.

Just such a spring I have *not*, and can not have. One just as different as possible I have, at the bottom of the hill, in the open field. There are no vines or bushes to cover it in summer; no trees send down their fiery leaves to be quenched in its autumnal stream. It bubbles up from a soft soil, and flows away through rank grasses. Coming up from a bed of gravel, it is every day shifting its mouth, and if stopped up in one place, it breaks out in another, like the heart's instincts, whose channels you may appoint, but whose flowing is beyond your control. I have often scooped away the soil trodden by cattle all about this cold-boiling spring. For a moment the little pool will be full of sand and mud; and I have never watched it clearing itself and coming back to transparency without thinking that just so human life cleanses itself. A stagnant heart, when deeply disturbed, is long in settling; but a living, outflowing heart, carries away its sorrows down its own stream, and deposits them speedily far from the fount.

It is all that my poor little spring can do, in summer, to maintain a respectable drink for the cattle which pasture about it. But these are the days of its humiliation. It has periods of greatness. In the spring and in late autumn, it is the happy parent of an illustrious stream of water, that, even at a hundred paces distant, is ankle deep. It is possessed by the pretty vanity of all rivers, and flowing down a little ways, it turns back to see what it has been doing, thus twining and looping itself, like a bit of white ribbon carelessly thrown down. It lifts up its voice over roots, and gurgles around stones; it excavates little pools, and institutes in them all the bubbles, the pet eddies, and diminutive currents, upper and under, which big rivers are known to practice on a larger scale. Indeed, it has also its pin-fish, and when, some acres further down, it has earned the title of *brook*, it is the belief of all the boys in this neighborhood that there are trout in it. But these mythical personages, like ancient ghosts, are never seen by any who go on purpose to see them. But you will find much else well worth seeing if you walk, on a right cool day, down all the brook-side to the edge of Laurel Lake, not a long though a circuitous walk. For there is a peculiar charm in a perfectly transparent brook, flowing gently over a pebbly bottom, in and out of bushes, across the road, through the meadows, zig-zag, up and down, winding about as if it were, like ourselves, sauntering for mere pleasure, and searching for all the beautiful places. What can be more delightful than a clear-eyed brook by the road-side, traveling for miles with you, sometimes hid but heard, then flashing out with impetuous joy of return, eyeing you from around a rock, or spreading itself a little that it may mimic your face in its dazzling mirror, then running away again, under green bushes with a coy and sedate look, as if mischief were far from its thoughts; and then dashing down a little descent, laughing all the way at its own musical tricks? Now it plashes right across your path, to cool your horse's feet, if you ride—your own, if you walk; then you hear it running away through the leaves of the wood, into which it has turned apparently to cut up some extreme antics, not grave enough for the open road.

But our little spring-begotten brook, after a mile's circuit, gives up its individuality, and is spread abroad through the pet lake. A beautiful sheet of water it is, but more beautiful by far it was before rapacious hands cleared away the fine forests that girded it round. But no violence can destroy its morning brightness, nor the delicate evening lights that glance from its tranquil surface. I never pass it at evening, in the twilight, the faint glow of the skies just dying out of its surface, and the darkness settling down upon those edges which are yet forest-shaded, without pausing to be stirred with its mysterious influences.

But there is something besides poetry about the lake. There is a "Water-Lily" larger than the largest *Victoria Regia* that was ever exhibited at a horticultural show. It is yellow within, white without, and green at the bottom. It is so large that it will hold several persons, and serves to enliven the lake, and bear us to the fishing-grounds. But there is no use to which the boat is ever put productive of more pleasure than mere sauntering. We gently pull along the shores, with strokes so quiet that hardly a bubble springs from the oar, or a wake follows the keel.

Are there degrees in the sense of solitariness? One is alone in a deep woods, but so much life is found even there, and such nearness of objects that have life by association, that we do not think of forests as lonely places. Indeed, we used to feel, after long prairie rides, a most refreshing joy when we struck the "timber." We had company as soon as we had trees. Next in loneliness is a hill-top, lifted up so high in the air that you are above all houses, all objects, all near heights, until you feel that you are inhabiting the very air. There is a certain wild sense of solitariness in that, such as one might be supposed to feel who should sail in a balloon, in a quiet moonlight night, over forests, over mountains, over cities, that lay so far down that their lights were like pale glow-worms by the road side. As I walk in the silent evenings over the hill-top, and the mountain winds come playing about my hair, it seems as if I should certainly soon hear a voice of spirits;—and there is no loneliness greater than in a place where one might meet with spirits of the air.

And yet, upon thinking again, we believe one to be yet more solitary who sits alone in his little boat, upon a wide piece of water, sees the sun go down, hears the last noises of distant farms die away, sees the trees growing dark and indistinct, sees the shadows creeping upon the water and effacing all shore lines, sees the stars coming one by one, hears every drop of water dripping from his oar, hears all those sounds which daylight never hears, which are unaccountable because unfamiliar. As one thus lingers far into evening, separated from life not by distance alone, but by the untrodden waters, that will not endure a footstep, he almost loses his own identity, so do fancies work upon him.

But there is a wide difference between solitudes. Some are very empty, and some very populous; some are dreary, and others most cheerful; some oppress and suffocate the soul, while others refresh it, and tempt it forth into that freedom from which it shrinks among the hard ways of life;—just as birds, in the deep solitude of the woods will sing and disport themselves as they never dare to do in the open air where hawks are flying.

One ought to love society if he wishes to enjoy solitude. It is a social nature that solitude works upon with the most various power. If one is misanthropic, and betakes himself to loneliness that he may get away from hateful things, solitude is a silent emptiness to him. But as, after a bell has tolled or rung, we hear its sounds dying away in vibrations fainter and fainter, and when they have wholly ceased, feel that the very silence is musical too, so is it with solitude, which is but a few bars of rest between strains of life, and would not be what it is if we did not go from activity to it, and into activity from it.

Silence is thus a novelty; and a sympathy with forms of nature, and with phenomena of light or twilight, is heightened by its contrast with ordinary experience. Besides, one likes to stand out alone before himself. In life he is acting and acted upon. A throng of excitements are spurring him through various rapid races. Self-consideration is almost lost. He scarcely knows what of himself is himself, and what is but the working of others upon him. It is good, now and then, to sit by one's self, as if all the world were dead, and see what is left of that which glowed and raged along the arena. What are we out of temptation, out of excitement? In the loom we are the shuttle, beaten back and forth, carrying the thread of affairs out of which grows the fabric of life. Slip the band; stop the loom. What is the thread? What is the fabric?

Then there are some thoughts that will no more come upon the soul among rude sounds and harsh labors than dews will fall at mid-day. There are message-thoughts which come to us from God; there are soul-certainties of God himself; there are convictions of immortality far deeper than reasonings ever bring—intuitions, eye-sight, rather than deductions.

That longing which the soul feels that there should be some *voice* of God, actual, audible, is never so great as in solitudes of beautiful scenery. Why will He not speak to us? What need of an everlasting silence? We speak to Him, and none answers. We pour out our heart's confession; it dies away into the air, and none answers. We yearn and beseech for the food of life, on which the soul of man must feed. Whatever we get, we get it silently. Minds speak, trees speak, waters speak, human life, with mingled myriad voices, speaks; but God never! He is the Eternal Silence. It was not always so. In olden days men heard the voice of God. It shall not always be so. That voice will be heard again. I have a firm faith of the future. I shall behold him face to face. I shall hear him and be satisfied. But oh! in the struggle, in the task of duty, and the strife of battle, *one word* of God would be worth all the voices of that angelic choir which sang the coming of Christ! But wait, O my soul! Thou art a seed just sprouted. Ask not for blossoms before thy leaves are grown; ask not for fruit before thy blossoms open.

There are times in the seclusion of the forest, or upon a sequestered lake, or upon a leafy hill-top, that one can bear to unbury their dead, behold again their pale faces, unlock old joys of love, and let the specters forth. There are some things which one can think of only once in a great while.

Our solitudes act upon affections and friendships just as death does. For, death draws into the grave not alone the dishonored body, but also all those weaknesses of the soul and imperfections which sprang from its alliance with the body, and we then see our friends purged from their faults, dressed in the rarest excellencies, and touched with golden glory. Thus, too, is it in the separation and solitude of the wilderness. They whom we love rise up in a mellowed remembrance, as a tree stands charmed in a midsummer's moonlight, its broken branches hidden, its unequal boughs all rounded out and softened into symmetry, and the whole glowing with silver light, as if transfigured. Then we entertain thoughts of affection such as might beseem a God. We enter into its royalties, and conceive its function, and know that it is the life of the world, the breath of every holy soul, the atmosphere of the Divine Heart, and the substance of heaven. When the tranquil eye of God, looking around, traces that circle within which love wholly prevails, so that all things spring from it, and it lives in them always and perfectly, then that circle is heaven, and such are the bounds thereof.

But it is not yet so dark that we can not see those dashes of wind upon the lake's surface. See the dim flash of distant lightnings upon the horizon! At every flash what piles of clouds, like mountainous rocks and gloomy precipices, start forth in the heavens! Like the dropping of a curtain the darkness hides them again. They come and go, spring forth and drop back, palpitate again in light, and die suddenly into darkness. The wind moans in the woods. You can hear the uplifted boughs, which you can not see, creaking and groaning through the forest. As you wend your way along the road, whirls of dust beset you. The air grows darker. The stars are hidden. It is the coming of the long-sought rain. For weeks there has been drought. A heaven without the blessing of rain has well-nigh devoured the earth. The shepherd of the air has long since driven his fleecy flocks of cloud to pasture in other realms, and none have wandered in the clear, hot wilderness above us. So we shall have rain! Bring forth every vessel! Let the eaves be watched!

The night is spent, the sun comes up without a drop of rain! The clouds are all gone, and the Drought yet rules in the heavens and oppresses the earth! Will not God hear the universal prayer for rain? A million flowers pray for it; innumerable forests reach forth their hands for it; every blade of the much-enduring grass beseeches it; men and beasts long for it. How long, O God! how long?

XXIX.

MID-OCTOBER DAYS.

LENOX, *October*, 1854.

AT this season of the year it requires but a few weeks, and often but a few days, to work great changes upon the face of Nature. Lenox in the middle of September stood in untarnished green. Grass and flowers were plump and succulent with copious juices. Here and there a coquetting maple leaf displayed gay colors among its yet sober fellow leaves. A shade of yellow, a bright streak of red, might be seen in single trees, as if Nature, like an artist, was trying its colors, to make sure of the right shades before laying them upon the gorgeous canvas. Yet all these made no impression upon the vast front of the mountains around us, that still lay patiently, like mighty dromedaries, camped down against the horizon—a caravan that shall never rise up to the voice of a driver, nor move, until He who formed them shall scatter them!

It is now mid-October. All things are changed. Of all the railroads near New York none can compare for beauty of scenery with the Housatonic from Newtown up to Pittsfield, but especially from New Milford to Lenox.

That scenery which a few weeks ago stood in summer green now seemed enchanted. The Housatonic was the same. The skies were the same. The mountain forms were unchanged. But they had blossomed into resplendent colors from top to base. It was strange to see such huge mountains, that are images of firmness and majesty, now tricked out with fairy pomp, as if all the spirits of the air had reveled there, and hung their glowing scarfs on every leaf and bough. We were almost sorry to reach our destination and leave the cars. But the first step on our own ground brought content.

Once more I am upon this serene hill-top! The air is very clear, very still, and very solemn, or, rather, tenderly sad, in its serene brightness. It is not that moist spring air, full of the smell of wood, of the soil, and of the odor of vegetation, which warm winds bring to us from the south. It is not that summer atmosphere, full of alternations of haze and fervent clearness, as if Nature were brewing every day some influence for its myriad children; sometimes in showers, and sometimes with coercive heat upon root and leaf; and, like a universal taskmaster, was driving up the hours to accomplish the labors of the year. No! In these autumn days there is a sense of leisure and of meditation. The sun seems to look down upon the labors of its fiery hands with complacency. Be satisfied, O seasonable Sun! Thou hast shaped an ample year, and art garnering up harvests which well may swell thy rejoicing heart with gracious gladness.

One who breaks off in the summer, and returns in autumn to the hills, needs almost to come to a new acquaintance with the most familiar things. It is another world; or it is the old world a-masquerading;

and you halt, like one scrutinizing a disguised friend, between the obvious dissemblance and the subtile likeness.

Southward of our front door there stood two elms, leaning their branches toward each other, forming a glorious arch of green. Now, in faint yellow they grow attenuated and seem as if departing; they are losing their leaves and fading out of sight, as trees do in twilight. Yonder, over against that young growth of birch and evergreen, stood, all summer long, a perfect maple tree, rounded out on every side, thick with luxuriant foliage, and dark with greenness, save when the morning sun, streaming through it, sent transparency to its very heart. Now it is a tower of gorgeous red. So sober and solemn did it seem all summer that I should think as soon to see a prophet dancing at a peasants' holiday, as *it* transfigured to such intense gayety! Its fellows, too, the birches and the walnuts, burn from head to foot with fires that glow but never consume.

But these holiday hills! Have the evening clouds, suffused with sunset, dropped down and become fixed into solid forms? Have the rainbows that followed autumn storms faded upon the mountains and left their mantles there? Yet, with all their brilliancy, how modest do they seem; how patient when bare, or burdened with winter; how cheerful when flushed with summer-green; and how modest when they lift up their wreathed and crowned heads in the resplendent days of autumn!

I stand alone upon the peaceful summit of this hill, and turn in every direction. The east is all a-glow;

the blue north flushes all her hills with radiance; the west stands in burnished armor; the southern hills buckle the zone of the horizon together with emeralds and rubies, such as were never set in the fabled girdle of the gods! Of gazing there can not be enough. The hunger of the eye grows by feeding.

Only the brotherhood of evergreens—the pine, the cedar, the spruce, and the hemlock—refuse to join this universal revel. They wear their sober green straight through autumn and winter, as if they were set to keep open the path of summer through the whole year, and girdle all seasons together with a clasp of endless green. But in vain do they give solemn examples to the merry leaves which frolic with every breeze that runs sweet riot in the glowing shades. Gay leaves will not be counseled, but will die bright and laughing. But both together—the transfigured leaves of deciduous trees and the calm unchangeableness of evergreens—how more beautiful are they than either alone! The solemn pine brings color to the cheek of the beeches, and the scarlet and golden maples rest gracefully upon the dark foliage of the million-fingered pine.

All summer long these leaves have wrought their tasks. They have plied their laboratory, and there that old chemist, the Sun, hath prepared all the juices of the trees. Now hath come their play-spell. Nature gives them a jubilee. It is a concert of colors for the eye. What a mighty chorus of colors do the trees roll down the valleys, up the hill-sides, and over the mountains!

Before October we sought and found colors in single tones, in flowers, in iris-winking dew-drops, in westward-trooping clouds. But when the Year, having wrought and finished her solid structures, unbends and consecrates the glad October month to fancy, then all hues that were before scattered in lurking flowers, in clouds, upon plumed birds, and burnished insects, are let loose like a flood and poured abroad in the wild magnificence of Divine bounty. The earth lifts up its head crowned as no monarch was ever crowned, and the seasons go forth toward winter, chanting to God a hymn of praise that may fitly carry with it the hearts of all men, and bring forth in kindred joy the sympathetic spirits of the dead.

These are the days that one fain would be loose from the earth and wander forth as a spirit, or lie bedded in some buoyant cloud, to float above the vast expanse, in the silence of the upper air. How we would feign be voyagers, pursuing the seasons through all their latitudes, and no longer stand to wait their coming and going about our fixed habitations.

When we were here in August, the odorous barns were full of new-mown hay, and the hay was full of buried crickets and locusts, that chirped away as merrily from the smothered mow as if it were no prison. The barns now are still. The field-crickets are gone, the locust is gone, and the hay has lost its clover-smell. In August we loved to throw wide open the doors, upon the threshing-floor, and let the wind through. But now only the sunny door looking south stands open. No lithe swallow twitters in and out, or in his swift flight marks dark circles in the sky, gone as soon as made.

There are two barns. The floor of the one is covered with shocks of corn, whose golden ears, split through the husk, are showing their burnished rows of grain. The other floor is heaped with unwinnowed buckwheat. O! what cakes shall yet rise out of that dusky pile! But now the buckwheat lies in heaps of chaff that swell the bulk, but diminish the value. If we could sell grain in the chaff as we can books, farming would be very profitable.

I love to sit just within the sunny edge of the south door, whose prospect is large and beautiful, with an unread book for company. For a book is set to sharpen, not to feed the appetite. It whets the drowsy thought, and puts observation into the eye. The best books do not think for us, but stir us to think. They are lenses through which we look—not mere sacks stuffed with knowledge.

A wagon rolls past, rattling over the stones. From under the unthreshed straw mice squeak and quarrel; lonesome spiders are repairing their webs in the windows that catch nothing but dust and chaff. Yet these bum-bailiffs have grown plump on something. I wonder what a spider is thinking about for hours together, down in the dark throat of his web, where he lies as still as if he were dead.

Our old Shanghai steps up with a pert how-do-ye-do-sir, cocking his eye one-sidedly at you, and uttering certain nondescript guttural sounds. He walks off crooning to himself and his dames. It is all still again. There are no flies now to buzz in the air. There is not wind enough to quiver a hanging straw, or to pipe a leaf-dance along the fence. You fall into some sweet fancy that inhabits silence, when all at once, with a tremendous vociferation, out flies a hen from over your head, with an outrageous noise, clattering away as if you had been throwing stones at her, or abusing her beyond endurance. The old Shanghai takes up the case, and the whole mob of hens join the outcry. The whole neighborhood is raised, and distant roosters from far-off farms echo the shrill complaints. An egg is all very well in its way, but we never could see any justification for such vociferous cackling. Every hen in the crowd is as much excited as if she had performed the deed herself. And the cock informs the whole region round about that there never was so smart a crowd of hens as he leads.

Nothing seems so aimless and simple as a hen. She usually goes about in a vague and straggling manner, articulating to herself cacophonous remarks upon various topics. The greatest event in a hen's life is compound, being made up of an egg and a cackle. Then only she shows enthusiasm when she descends from the nest of duty and proclaims her achievement. If you chase her, she runs cackling; if you pelt her with stones, she streams through the air cackling all abroad till the impulse has run out, when she subsides quietly into a silly, gadding hen. Now and then an eccentric hen may be found stepping quite beyond the limits of hen-propriety. One such has persisted in laying her daily egg in the house. She would steal noiselessly in at the open door, walk up stairs, and leave a plump egg upon the children's bed. The next day she would honor the sofa. On one occasion she selected my writing-table, and scratching my papers about, left her card, that I might not blame the children or servants for scattering my manuscripts. Her persistent determination was amusing. One Sabbath morning we drove her out of the second-story window, then again from the front hall. In a few moments she was heard behind the house, and on looking out the window, she was just disappearing into the bed-room window on the ground floor! Word was given, but before any one could reach the place, she had bolted out of the window with victorious cackle, and her white, warm egg lay upon the lounge. I proposed to open the pantry-window, set the egg-dish within her reach, and let her put them up herself; but those in authority would not permit such a deviation from propriety. Such a breed of hens could never be popular with the boys. It would spoil that glorious sport of hunting hen's nests.

How utterly different are birds from their gross congeners. Already the snow-sparrows have come down from the north, and are hopping in our hedges, sure precursors of winter. Robins are gathering in flocks in the orchards, and preparing for their southern flight. May his gun for ever miss fire that would thin the ranks of singing-birds!

Lifted far above all harm of fowler or impediment of mountain, wild fowl are steadily flying southward. The simple sight of them fills the imagination with pictures. They have all summer long called to each other from the reedy fens and wild oat-fields of the far north. Summer is already extinguished there. Winter is following their track, and marching steadily toward us The spent flowers, the seared leaves, the thinning treetops, the morning rime of frost, have borne witness of the change on earth; and these caravans of the upper air confirm the tidings. Summer *is* gone; winter *is* coming!

The wind has risen to-day. It is not one of those gusty, playful winds, that frolic with the trees. It is a wind high up in the air, that moves steadily with a solemn sound, as if it were the spirit of summer journeying past us; and, impatient of delay, it doth not stoop to the earth, but touches the tops of the trees, with a murmuring sound, sighing a sad farewell, and passing on.

Such days fill one with pleasant sadness. How sweet a pleasure is there in sadness! It is not sorrow; it is not despondency; it is not gloom! It is one of the moods of joy. At any rate I am very happy, and yet it is sober, and very sad happiness. It is the shadow of joy upon the soul! I can reason about these changes. I can cover over the dying leaves with imaginations as bright as their own hues; and, by christian faith, transfigure the whole scene with a blessed vision of joyous dying and glorious resurrection. But what then? Such thoughts glow like evening clouds, and not far beneath them are the evening twilights, into whose dusk they will soon melt away. And all communions, and all admirations, and all associations, celestial or terrene, come alike into a pensive sadness, that is even sweeter than our joy. It is the minor key of the thoughts. A right sadness will sometimes cure a sorrow.

The asters, which are the floral rear-guards of the year, are saying to me, that no more flowers shall come after them. The very brightness of their faces makes me sad to think that the next blossoms shall be frost-blooms. I know that seeds and roots do not die; that the winter is but a vacation, in which the year rests from its works; that all things shall come again. What then? It is sad nevertheless to see summer dying out. There is some influence in this hush of the heavens, in the helplessness of vegetation, that by leaves and root striving against the cold nights, can only gather strength to die in glorious colors, which makes one glad and sad together. Your smiles end in tears, and tears exhale to smiles again.

Among all the grateful gifts of summer, none, I think, has been deeper and more various than the sight of the enjoyment of the children. I do pity children in a city. There is no place for them. The streets are full of bad boys that they must not play with, and the house is rich in furniture that they must not touch. They are always in somebody's way, or making a noise out of proper time—for the twenty-fifth hour of the day is the only time when people are willing that children should be noisy. There is no grass in the fieldless, parkless city for their feet, no trees for climbing, no orchards or nut-laden trees for their enterprise.

But here has been a troop of children, of three families, nine that may be called children, (without offense to any sweet fifteen,) that have had the summer before them to disport themselves as they chose. There are no ugly boys to be watched, no dangerous places to fall from, no bulls or wicked hippogriffs to chase them. They are up and fledged by breakfast, and then they are off in uncircumscribed liberty till dinner. They may go to the barn, or to either of three orchards, or to either of two woods, or to either of two springs, or to grandma's, who is the very genius of comfort and gingerbread to children! They can build all manner of structures in wet sand, or paddle in the water, and even get their feet wet, their clothes dirty, or their pantaloons torn, without being aught reckoned against them. They scuffle along the road to make a dust in the world, they chase the hens, hunt sly nests, build fires on the rocks in the pastures, and fire off Chinese crackers, until they are surfeited with noise; they can run, wade, halloo, stub their toes, lie down, climb, tumble down, with or without hurting themselves, just as much as they please. They may climb in and out of wagons, sail chips in the water-trough at the barn, fire apples from the sharpened end of a limber stick, pick up baskets full of brilliant apples in competition with the hired men, proud of being "almost men." Their hands, thank fortune, are never clean, their faces are tanned, their hair is tangled within five minutes after combing, and a button is always off somewhere.

The dog is a creation especially made for children. Our Noble has been at least equal to one hand and one foot extra for frolic and mischief, to each of the urchins. But grandest of all joy, highest in the scale of rapture, the last thing talked of before sleep, and the first thing remembered in the morning, is the going out *a-nutting.* O! the hunting of little baskets, the irrepressible glee, as bags and big baskets, into which little ones are to disembogue, come forth! Then the departure, the father or uncle climbing the tree—"O! how high!"—the shaking of limbs, the rattle of hundreds of chestnuts, which squirrels shall never see again, the eager picking up, the merry ohs! and ouches! as nuts come plump down on their bare heads, the growing heap, the approaching dinner by the brook, on leaves yellow as gold, and in sunlight yellower still, the mysterious baskets to be opened, the cold chicken, the bread slices—ah me! one would love to be twenty boys, or a boy twenty times over, just to experience the simple, genuine, full, unalloyed pleasure of children going with father and mother to the woods "a-nutting!"

XXX.

A MOIST LETTER.

ANDOVER, MASS., *November*, 1854.

THE rain is doing at last its long delayed duty. It has for two days poured forth abundantly, and still pours; sometimes with steady downward plash, but with every gust of wind that goes fitfully about the air, it dashes against the windows, as if it were determined to take refuge within. There is much going on up in the clouds. There is a great racing and chasing of scuds, as if conveying orders on a field of battle, while the more distant and solid masses move slowly and solemnly. Now and then, along the horizon, the skirt is lifted for a moment, and fair weather looks through to assure us that it is there, and will by and by come back in triumph. Every one feels that storms are specialities, and fair weather the settled order of nature. Clear heavens, transparent air, and shining suns, are for common and daily use; good robust storms, for variety. But if it will rain, we do love decision and earnestness of purpose. We love to see Nature really in earnest, and black-faced storms out as if they had a worthy errand. Great rugged clouds, and the whole heaven full of them, winds that are wide awake, rain that comes as if it was not afraid of exhausting the supply, and general commotion of all sorts—these make one glad. We always wish life and energy in storms. Anything but a dull, foggy drizzle, either in storms or men.

But all this copious rain comes too late for roots and flowers. They are dead, or sleeping past all autumn waking. The frost, like a fierce sheriff, has been in and taken possession or sealed up all the effects of the year. The trees are stripped to their very outline. The grass is seared. Gardens are utterly put out. Where is all this goodly garniture which a few weeks ago reveled in such luxuriant abundance? It is always a graveyard business to me to walk in a yard or garden just after the killing frosts have been at it. The dahlias, that hold up their heads with such unconscious state, and that are so full of sap that their stems look like solidified liquid, or juice with a skin on, now hang so utterly desolate, collapsed, decaying, even slimy and filthy!

We come to see the changes of trees with composure. We know that life is in them yet. Their leaves change gradually. They thin out and blow away, and frosts, when they come, have but the gleanings. And all ligneous plants die clean. It is different with herbaceous plants. In one night, by one stroke, gorgeous flower, plump leaf, hearty stem, are turned black, and hang down with funereal gloom.

We feel the irremediable destruction of flowers more than we do the stripping of trees and shrubs, because these appeal more than they to our protection and to our fondness.

We look up to trees as superiors, in whom reside guardianship and protection. They teach us patience, endurance, and unwearied hope. We see them beaten bare by autumn-storms, and perfectly content to stand bare. The moment the winter relents, they spring forth again, and all summer long you hear them singing, but never do you hear a tree rehearse its wrongs. It forgets the past. It lives outwardly so long as it can, and then retreats within itself, patient to wait for better times. And we feel also, in the case of trees, something of the veneration which antiquity always inspires. They are old chronologers. They are older than the oldest living men. That old oak was an old oak when that crippled old man yonder was a little boy, and it was an old tree in the days of his fathers. These faces that grimly hang upon our walls—the portraits of shadowy ancestors that long since have ceased to make a noise in the world—these very old faces, in generations gone by, used to look up into these fresh and hearty trees that carry themselves so youthfully, and marvel how high they were, and wonder that little birds were not afraid of falling down off from their perilously high branches. The annual changes of trees are therefore devoid of the sense of death. Leaves die. We pity them. But trees do not die. They undress. They sleep in naked majesty. What time they will, when the south wind blows its horn among the hills, they rouse themselves and put on again their robes and go forth as at other times.

It is not so with flowers. They are like little infant children. They look up to *us* for protection. They have no life that lasts. When they are stricken they make no resistance. They utterly die. And it is a real pain that we do not choose to encounter, to go out after the final frost-stroke, and see all the plants which we have nursed and fondled, not gone, but lying there in colors so disgraceful to their former beauty. All these fine-edged leaves, these delicate lineations, these exquisite hues and shades of color, these matchless forms and symmetries, whatever is superlative in fineness, delicacy, variety, profusion, gorgeous richness, now lying a heap of undistinguishable decay and loathsomeness. The dank smell of decomposing vegetation drives you from your garden as from a graveyard. The brilliant generous verbenas, the pensile and graceful fuchsias, the geraniums, the maurandyas, the tufted ageratum, and the other scores which blossom all the summer long, from which you had gathered hundreds of bunches of flowers to cheer your parlor, to inspire your pen while writing, to furnish you silent loving company as you walked about among frigid men or barren things, they have all gone to corruption before your eyes.

As I looked out of the window this morning, I could not help thinking how sweet this rain would have been if the flowers could only have contrived to live until now. It will clear up, and warm suns will shine. We shall have a week of shadowy summer weather, but without leaves or flowers. I always think of these summer days that are wont to come in November, as if they were sent back to see if they could do anything for the poor flowers which they had left in their retreat. They come as birds do, singing and chirping after some one of their young that may have been left in the tree behind when the other young flew away with the old ones.

All summer long the rain has been frugal. It has carried economy to stinginess. Now it has begun to exhibit generosity. It is full time. It would be a disastrous year if, after such summer drought, the winter should come on with springs feeble, rivers shallow, ponds half full, wells almost dry, and a general stint of water. But, thanks to a benignant Providence, we shall now have water enough. The shrunk veins of the earth will fill out again. Cranberry swamps will have their much-needed liquid coverlet. Boys shall have skating, and cattle shall have drink!

Rain away, then, full-breasted clouds! Drench the forests, make new channels down the hill-sides, fill up the ditches, drive out the margins of the ponds, and make the well meet the bucket half-way down, not half the coil run out! We wipe off the mud from our shoes with great satisfaction. We hear the gurgling moisture oozing out about our shoes at every step we tread upon the saturated sod without a sense of annoyance, and we look up at the surliest clouds and say, You are handsome, and quite welcome!

I had almost forgotten an experience which must not be forgotten—a midnight ride. Traveling by night, in boat or car, is so common as to fall among the ordinary experiences. Not so a buggy-ride. We lectured at Lynn on Saturday evening. It was our wish to spend the Sabbath at Andover. Now Andover and Lynn are about twenty miles apart, and unfrequented miles; for I could find no one who exactly knew the way from one to the other. The stable-keeper was doubtful; *he* did not know the route, none of his men knew it, the night was very dark, it was raining in torrents. But go I must and would. Those who had faith in the almanac said the moon would rise at ten o'clock. I agreed to wait till then. The lecture was given, and I must say, to the praise of old Lynn, to the bravest audience of about a thousand that I ever saw gathered, in spite of such a remorseless rain. We returned to our friend Shackford's, to wait for the moon, and whiled away the time in discourse of pears, illustrated by some most juicy specimens. The moon came, and the driver with it, and his light-covered buggy. Packed up with robe, coat, and shawl, we pushed out into darkness. The rain rattled and sung on the back and top of the cover, the roads ran streams of water, the horse splashed merrily along, lights gleamed out of dwellings, flashed across the path, sunk behind, and went out to us. First came Danvers, a town fast asleep, silent, motionless. We passed through like shadows in a dream. We took a wrong road; it grew rough and cart-like, full of thumping stones; soon the wheels rolled smotheringly in grass, then bushes began to whip the spokes, and finally we brought up against a stone wall—full in the pastures! Back we went, roused up the good sleeping woman of the first house, inquired the way, were in doubt after leaving her about the direction which she had given, whether it was left hand or right hand, that we were to turn at a given corner. We solved it by waking up another sleeper. At length we got safely on to a smooth road to Middleton. Then we began to doze without knowing it. Trees, which in the clouded light of the moon had a spectral look, faded out entirely. We were aroused by the driver, prying into the directions of a guide-board, where the road forked. I got out on the wheel and gazed piercingly. "Danvers--Point." "No," said he, "Danvers Plains." "Tariffville," said I. "No, Tappleyville," said he. That is not the road; the other *was*, and we took it. Again at the next guide-post we stopped. The driver climbed up and got hold of the board, and drawing himself up to his chin, read its direction. We met a solitary man walking between twelve and one at night. It seemed very strange to see anything human moving in the darkness and solitude of midnight. We hailed him, and inquired the way. Then we speculated what errand took him out. Not a thief, surely. Perhaps he has been for a doctor, said the driver; or to watch with some sick neighbor, said I; or, maybe, a-courting, said the driver. But, said I, he was a middle-aged man, and not a young, spruce lover. No matter, says the driver, it's about one thing with old or young when they go a-courting.

Another dreamy, voiceless town! Our wheels echoed from the sides of the houses. We came to a little cluster of dwellings, in the front door of one of which stood a man, as quietly as if it were noonday, and he waiting for a friend. We exacted further information. Finally, by dint of guide-boards and chance stragglers, and waking up people in their houses, at two o'clock we reached Andover. A venerable father and mother, two sisters, three brothers, and uncounted children—was it not worth such a ride to spend a Sabbath with them?

XXXI.

FROST IN THE WINDOW.

BOOKS have been written of painted windows, and journeys long and expensive have been made to see them. And without a doubt they are both curious and more than curious; they are admirable. One such work of art, standing through generations of men, and making countless hearts glad with its beauty, is a treasure for which any community may be grateful.

But are we so destitute of decorated windows as, at first, one might suppose? Last night the thermometer sank nearly to zero, and see what business Nature has had on hand! Every pane of glass is etched and figured as never Moorish artist decorated Alhambra. Will you pass it unexamined, simply because it cost you nothing—because it is so common—because it is, this morning, the property of so many people—because it was wrought by Nature and not by man? Do not do so. Learn rather to enjoy it for its own elegance, and for God's sake, who gave to frosts such wondrous artist tendencies.

The children are wiser than their elders. They are already at the window interpreting these mysterious pictures. One has discovered a silent, solitary lake, extremely beautiful, among stately white cliffs. Another points out a forest of white fir trees and pines, growing in rugged grandeur. There are in succession discovered mountains, valleys, cities of glorious structures, a little confused in their outline by distance. There are various beasts too;—here a bear coming down to the water; birds in flocks, or sitting voiceless and solitary. There are rivers flowing through plains; and elephants, and buffaloes, and herds of cattle. There are dogs and serpents, trees and horses, ships and men. Beside all these phantom creatures, there are shadowy ornaments of every degree of beauty, simple or complex, running through the whole scale, from a mere dash of the artist's tool to the most studied and elaborate compositions.

Neither does Night repeat itself. Every window has its separate design. Every pane of glass is individual and peculiar. You see only one appearance of anxiety in the artist, and that is, lest time and room should fail for the expression of the endless imaginations which throng his fertile soul.

There is a generous disregard of all fictitious or natural distinctions of society in this beautiful working. The designs upon the Poor House windows are just as exquisite as any upon the rich man's mansion. The little child's bed-room window is just as carefully handled as the proudest window in any room of state. The church can boast of nothing better than the emblazonings on the window of the poor seamstress who lives just by. For a few hours everybody is rich. Every man owns pictures and galleries of pictures!

But then comes the Iconoclast—the Sun! Ah, remorseless eyes! why will you gaze out all these exquisite figures and lines? Art thou jealous lest Night shall make sweeter flowers in Winter time than thou canst in all the Summer time? For shame, envious Father of Flowers! There is no end of thy abundance. Around the Equator the Summer never dies; flowers perfume the whole Ecliptic. And spreading out thence, the Summer shall travel northward, and for full eight months thou hast the temperate zones for thy gardens. Will not all the flowers of the tropics and of eight-month zones suffice? Will not all the myriads that hide under leaves, that climb up for air to tree-tops, that nestle in rock-crevices, or sheet the open plains with wide effulgence, that ruffle the rocks and cover out of sight all rude and homely things—suffice thy heart, that thou must come and rob from our Winter canvas all the fine things, the rootless trees, the flowers that blossom without growing, the wilderness of pale shrubberies that grow by night to die by day? Rapacious Sun! thou shouldst set us a better example.

But the indefatigable Night repairs the desolation. New pictures supply the waste ones. New cathedrals there are, new forests, fringed and blossoming, new sceneries, and new races of extinct animals. We are rich every morning, and poor every noon. One day with us measures the space of two hundred years in kingdoms —a hundred years to build up, and a hundred years to decay and destroy; twelve hours to overspread the evanescent pane with glorious beauty, and twelve to extract and dissipate the pictures!

How is the frost-picturing like fancy painting! Thus we fill the vagrant hours with innumerable designs, and paint visions upon the visionless sphere of Time, which, with every revolution, destroys our work, restoring it back to the realm of waste fantasies!

But is not this a type of finer things than arrant fictions? Is it not a mournful vision of many a virtuous youth, overlaid with every device of virtue which parental care could lay on, dissolved before the hot breath of love, blurred, and quite rubbed out!

Or shall we read a lesson for a too unpractical mind, full of airy theories and dainty plans of exquisite good, that lie upon the surface of the mind, fair indeed, till touched? The first attempt at realization is as when an artist tries to tool these frosted sketches; the most exquisite touch of ripest skill would mar and destroy them!

Or, rather, shall we not reverently and rejoicingly behold in these morning pictures wrought without color, and kissed upon the window by the cold lips of Winter, another instance of that Divine Beneficence of beauty, which suffuses the heavens, clothes the earth, and royally decorates the months, and sends them forth through all hours, all seasons, all latitudes, to fill the earth with joy, pure as the Great Heart from which it had its birth?

XXXII.

SNOW-STORM TRAVELING.

The sensations with which we are affected by a fall of snow depend much upon our position and prospective enterprises. If one is journeying across a prairie, no more terrible thing can befall him than the coming on of a driving snow. All landmarks are shut in, all paths are covered; the air is darkened; the wind pierces the very heart with chills, and if he had not the good luck to bring with him a compass, he will soon grow bewildered, and travel about in useless circuits, till he grows numb, slumberous, and dies, with the storm going on above him, and heaping him up with snowy burial. Snow is worse than fire. Against fire you can set fire, and escape in the track of the flame which you yourself have kindled. You can not set snow against snow.

Falling snow is beautiful in a forest. It comes wavering down among the trees, without a whisper, and takes to the ground without the sound of a footfall. Evergreen trees grow intense in contrasts of dark green ruffled with radiant white. Bush and tree are powdered and banked up. Not the slightest sound is made in all the work which fills the woods with winter soil many feet deep. But, nowhere else is snow so beautiful as when one sojourns in a good old-fashioned mansion in the country, bright and warm, full of home-joy and quiet. You look out through large windows and see one of those flights of snow in a still calm day, that make the air seem as if it were full of white millers, or butterflies, fluttering down from heaven. There is something extremely beautiful in the motion of these large flakes of snow. They do not make haste, nor plump straight down with a dead fall like a whistling raindrop. They seem to be at leisure, and descend with that quiet, wavering, sideway motion, which birds sometimes use when about to alight. You think that you are reading; and so you are, but it is not in the book that lies open before you. The silent, dreamy hour passes away, and you have not felt it pass. The trees are dressed with snow. The long arms of evergreens bend with its weight; the rails are doubled, and every post wears a virgin crown. The well-sweep, the bucket, the well-curb are fleeced over. And still the silent quivering air is full of trooping flakes, thousands following to take the place of all that fall. The ground is heaped, the paths are gone, the road is hidden, the fields are leveled, the eaves of buildings jut over, and, as the day moves on, the fences grow shorter and gradually sink from sight. All night the heavens rain crystal flakes. Yet, that roof, on which the smallest rain pattered audible music, gives no sound. There is no echo in the stroke of snow, until it waxes to an avalanche and slips from the mountains. Then it fills the air like thunderbolts.

When the morning comes, then comes the sun also. The storm has gone back to its northern nests to shed its feathers there. The air is still, cold, bright. But what a glory rests upon the too brilliant earth! Are these the January leaves, is this the winter efflorescence of shrub and tree? You can scarcely look for the exceeding brightness. Trees stand up against the clear, gray sky, brown and white in contrast, as if each trunk, and bough, and branch, and twig, had been coated with ermine, or with white moss. There is an exquisite airiness and lightness in the masses of snow on trees and fences when seen just as the storm left them. The wind or sun soon disenchants the magic scene.

Already snow-birds are fluttering for a foothold, and showering down the frosty dust from the twigs. The hens and their uplifted lords are beginning to wade with dainty steps through the chilly wool. Boys are aglee with sleds; men are out with shovels, and dames with brooms. Bells begin to ring along the highway, and heavy oxen with craunching sleds are wending toward the woods for the winter's supply of fuel. The school-house is open, and a roasting hot fire rages in the box stove. Little boys are crying with chilblains, and little girls are comforting them with the assurance that it will "stop aching pretty soon," and the boys seem unwilling to stop crying till then. Big boys are shaking their coats, and stamping off the snow, which peels easily from sleek blackballed boots, or shoes burnished with tallow. Out of doors the snow-balls are flying, and everybody laughs but the one that's hit. Down go the wrestlers. The big ones "rub" the little ones; the little ones in turn "rub" the smaller ones. The passers-by are pelted; and many a lazy horse has motives of speed applied to his lank barrel. Even the school master is but mortal, and must take his lot; for many an "accidental" snow-ball plumps into his breast and upon his back before the rogues will believe that it *is* the schoolmaster!

But days go by. The snow drifts. Fences are banked up ten feet high. Hills are broken into a "coast" for boys' sleds. They slide and pull up again, and toil on in their slippery pleasure. They tumble over, and turn over; they break down, or smash up; they run into each other, or run races, in all the moods and experiences of rugged frolic. Then comes the digging of chambers in the deep drifts, room upon room, the water dashed on over night freezing the snow walls into solid ice. Forts also are built, and huge balls of snow rolled up, till the little hands can roll the mass no longer.

But do not think that the steady fall of snow brought any such pleasing visions to our mind. It suggested rather visions of blocked up railways, disarranged trains, discontented passengers, appointments missed;—for we were to start the next day for Utica and Watertown upon a lecturing tour.

Our trip thither was not impeded; but, as the storm continued, we were sadly delayed in returning, and obliged to spend a Sabbath at Albany. To have a sudden and unexpected day of absolute rest and unresponsibility intercalated in the week was a strange and blessed luxury.

A RIDE BEHIND THE SNOW-PLOW.—Among the

things which I have always longed to see, is the snow-plow, driven along the covered track, and through heaped and drifted snows. This I have at length seen. The train came to Watertown from Cape Vincent, New York, with two engines and a snow-plow. When we reached Pierpont Manor, the conductor kindly acceded to my wish to go forward and take a berth with the engineer. I was soon in position. For two days it had been storming. The air was murky and cross. The snow was descending, not peacefully and dreamily, but whirled and made wild by fierce winds. The forests were laden with snow, and their interior looked murky and dreadful as a witch's den. Through such scenes I began my ride upon the plow-shoving engine. The engineers and firemen were coated with snow from head to foot, and looked like millers who had never brushed their coats for ten years. The floor on which we stood was ice and snow half melted. The wood was coated with snow. The locomotive was frosted all over with snow —wheels, connecting-rods, axles, and everything but the boiler and smoke-stack. The side and front windows were glazed with crusts of ice, and only through one little spot in the window over the boiler could I peer out to get a sight of the plow. The track was indistinguishable. There was nothing to the eye to guide the engine in one way more than another. It seemed as if we were going across fields and plunging through forests at random. And this gave no mean excitement to the scene, when two ponderous engines were apparently driving us in such an outlandish excursion. But their feet were sure, and unerringly felt their way along the iron road, so that we were held in our courses.

Nothing can exceed the beauty of snow in its own organization, in the gracefulness with which it falls, in the molding of its drift-lines, and in the curves which it makes when streaming off on either side from the plow. It was never long the same. If the snow was thin and light, the plow seemed to play tenderly with it, like an artist doing curious things for sport, throwing it in exquisite curves that rose and fell, quivered and trembled as they ran. Then suddenly striking a rift that had piled across the track, the snow sprang out, as if driven by an explosion, twenty and thirty feet, in jets and bolts; or like long-stemmed sheaves of snow—outspread fan-like. Instantly, when the drift was past, the snow seemed by an instinct of its own to retract, and played again in exquisite curves, that rose and fell about our prow. "Now you'll get it," says the engineer, "in that deep cut." We only saw the first dash, as if the plow had struck the banks of snow before it could put on its graces, and shot it distracted and headlong up and down on either side, like spray or flying ashes. It was but a second. For the fine snow rose up around the engine, and covered it in like a mist, and sucking round, poured in upon us in sheets and clouds, mingled with the vapor of steam, and the smoke which, from impeded draft, poured out, filled the engine-room and darkened it so that we could not see each other a foot distant except as very filmy specters glowering at each other. Our engineers had on buffalo coats, whose natural hirsuteness was made more shaggy by tags of snow melted into icicles. To see such substantial forms changing back and forth every few moments from a clearly earthly form into a spectral lightness, as if they went back and forth between body and spirit, was not a little exciting to the imagination.

When we struck deep bodies of snow, the engine plowed through them laboriously, quivering and groaning with the load, but shot forth again nimble as a bird the moment the snow grew light and thin.

Nothing seemed wilder than to be in one of these whirling storms of smoke, vapor and snow, you on one ponderous monster, and another roaring close behind, both engines like fiery dragons harnessed and fastened together and looming up when the snow and mists opened a little, black and terrible. It seemed as if you were in a battle. There was such energetic action, such irresistible power, such darkness and light alternating, and such fitful half-lights, which are more exciting to the imagination than light or darkness. Thus, whirled on in the bosom of a storm, you sped across the open fields, full of wild, driving snow; you ran up to the opening of the black pine and hemlock woods, and plunged into their somber mouth as if into a cave of darkness, and wrestled your way along through their dreary recesses, emerging to the cleared field again, with whistles screaming and answering each other back and forth from engine to engine. For, in the bewildering obscurity, we have run past the station, and must choke down the excited steeds and rein them back to the depot.

We think that Mazeppa's ride, lashed to a wild horse, and rushing through the forests wolf-driven, was rather exciting. If a man in a buffalo hunt, by some strange mishap, should find himself thrown from his horse and mounted on the shaggy back of an old, fierce buffalo bull, and go off with a rush, in cloud and dust, among ten thousand tramping fellows, pursued by yelling Indians—that, too, would be an exciting ride. But neither of these would know the highest exhilaration of the chase, until in a wild storm, upon a scowling day in January, he rides upon a double engine team behind a snow-plow, to clear the track of banks and burdens of snow.

Waiting for the Cars.—At about twelve of the day we reached Rome. All the trains on the Central Road were behind time, but they were just about to arrive, and they were just a-going to arrive for five hours. The room in the station-house was soon filled. Ladies there were, but in no proportion to the gentlemen. They were more patient, at least, outwardly; staying in the house was more natural to them. But the men were full of calculations—how long before the train must arrive? and how long *now?* When would it reach Syracuse going east, and when Buffalo going west? What were the chances of reaching New York? Every one took his turn in the calculation, and reckoned the matter over and over, and consulted with each new comer, as if some effect would be produced upon the tardy trains. There were seats in the gentlemen's room for eight, and there were from thirty to fifty persons present. Some heaped up the indolent mail-bags and sat on them. A roll of buffalo robes behind the door was a special luxury. Some mounted on trunks that had accumulated in one corner. Apparently they were not soft, as they seemed willing to exchange for the buffalo robe whenever it was vacated. Others stood about the outrageously hot stove. Everybody seemed to be seized with a desire to put in a stick, and when it could hold no more, they would occasionally open the door, look in, poke and kick with their feet to crowd the wood closer, and so it roared red-hot and terrible as a red dragon. But stout, full-blooded men sat about it with great-coats and mufflers on, drinking in heat as if they had a salamander enjoyment of it. The only relief was in the frequent opening of the door to let in new-comers. They came pushing in with red faces and white coats, powdered with snow like a confectioner's cake. The first business of every one, on entering, was to ask after the train, to which some gave quizzical answers, some peevish and querulous answers, some downright truth; a few were always hopeful, and not a few sat silent and even sullen.

The next resource of every one seemed to be in an attack upon the pop-corn and apple baskets. It was a great day for the apple-boys. When the sale seemed to flag, they would fill up with fresh specimens, and one of them would come rushing in from the telegraph office—"Train only got to Little Falls." "Little Falls!" exclaim a score of westward-going passengers, "it won't be here for an hour." At that they turned disconsolately to the apples again. By and by, in plumps another boy. "Express train only just reached Syracuse; just come from telegraph." This was a clap upon us eastward-going passengers—going, but not gone; and we sighed, and remarked, and comforted ourselves with—apples!

Men gathered into groups and talked, at first of produce, then of politics; next they told stories as long as their memory held out; and then each would saunter up and down the room, with hands in his pockets, or behind his back. Newspapers, of which a few were present, were read through—advertisements and all. One great comfort was found in going to the ticket-office window and peering in—for questions were out of the question—the ticket-master lying in a corner snoozing. At length he got up and shut his window. This was a great misfortune. Men now would walk up and look very solemnly at it, as if to be sure that it *was* shut, and then they would go disconsolately to the door or window as if determined to look out of something. At last, some one pulled a sliver from the wood and began to whittle. In a few moments another followed suit, and before long half a dozen were contentedly whittling. I envied them. At last they seemed consoled. I envied that fat man in the corner, who sat without winking, certainly without a single motion that I could notice, for a full hour. He seemed entirely occupied in breathing. I envied that old farmer that fell asleep sitting bolt upright, but gradually, like an apple roasting before a good old-fashioned fire, slept himself down to a heap. I envied the imperturbable content of that plump country-girl who stood before the glass combing her hair with a fine-toothed comb, and dividing, and smoothing, and placing it as if she were in a summer afternoon chamber all alone, fixing for a visit from her "intended." The boys were the only utterly cheerful and happy set. Their sales over, they amused themselves with all manner of boyish tricks, giving each other a sly nip, or a choking pull at each other's tippet, knocking off each other's caps, or crushing them down over the eyes, snapping apple-seeds, or throwing cores, and performing besides these all manner of monkey-tricks such as boys only and boys always know.

We read all the show-bills, all railroad placards, all the time-tables, all the advertisements, and studied all the veracious railroad maps, on which rams-horn railroads were made to flow on in straight lines or very gradual curves, while competing roads were laid down in all their vicious sinuosities.

When I say that the boys were the only happy ones, I must except the happy old lady in the corner with her knitting. She has two younger women by her, and the three are talking and working just as placidly and contentedly as if in the great kitchen at home. Ah! blessed be knitting! Who ever saw a person other than quiet and peaceful that knits? If anger breaks out, the knitting is laid aside. When the needles begin again, you may be sure that it is all right within.

At length the five hours were accomplished; the train came thundering up with a double team of engines. The crowd poured forth eagerly, and in a few moments we were dashing off toward Albany, which we reached at ten o'clock Saturday evening; too late for any train to New York that night.

THE END.